GCSE

GEOGRAPHY

Clifford Lines
Laurie Bolwell
Melanie Norman

EDUCATIONAL

Every effort has been made to trace copyright holders and to obtain their permission for the use of copyright material. The author and publishers will gladly receive information enabling them to rectify any error or omission in subsequent editions.

First Published 1979
Revised 1981, 1983, 1989, 1992, 1994, 1997
Reprinted 1995 (twice), 1996, 1997, 1998

Letts Educational
Aldine House,
Aldine Place,
London W12 8AW
0181 740 2266

Text: © C.J. Lines and L.H. Bolwell 1979, 1981, 1983, 1987, 1989, 1992, 1994,
© C.J. Lines, L.H. Bolwell and M. Norman 1997
Design and illustrations: © BPP (Letts Educational) Ltd., 1979, 1981, 1983, 1987,
1989, 1992, 1994, 1997

British Library Cataloguing in Publication Data
A CIP record for this book is available from the British Library
ISBN 1 85758 581 X

Acknowledgements
The authors and publishers are grateful to the following organisations for permission to reprint material to which they hold copyright:

Text and Artwork:
Examining Groups: Northern Examining and Assessment Board; Midland Examining Group; London Examinations; Welsh Joint Education Committee; Northern Ireland Schools Council for Curriculum Examinations and Assessment.

Photographs
Aerofilms, pp. 35, 38; Felixstowe Dock and Railway Co, p. 133; Hull Daily Mail, p. 131; Oxfam p.77; Popperfoto, p. 46; Spectrum, p. 90; Toyota Motor Manufacturing (UK) Ltd, p 145; USDA Soil Conservation Service, p. 161.

Printed and bound in Great Britain by WM Print Ltd, Walsall, West Midlands WS2 9NE
Letts Educational is the trading name of BPP (Letts Educational) Ltd

Contents

Introduction

This revision guide will help you to prepare for a GCSE or for the Scottish Certificate of Education Standard Grade exam in geography. The main purpose of the book is to help you reinforce your geographical knowledge, understanding and skills, so that you give your best performance in the geography exam. This book contains:
- core material central to the syllabuses
- self-test questions at the end of each section
- advice on the skills used in geography
- an analysis of exam questions with guidelines as to how they should be answered
- exam questions and answers for both Foundation and Higher Tier
- advice on carrying out your coursework and fieldwork components of the examination
- a glossary of geographical terms

To get the best from this book you should follow the advice below.

How to use this book

In order to make the most of this revision guide the first step is to find out which syllabus you are studying at school or college. Your teacher will be the best person to give you this information. Make sure you know the correct number or code letter for the syllabus you are studying, as all Exam Boards offer more than one GCSE exam for geography. Once you are sure of the syllabus, look at the Syllabus Checklists on pages 3 to 20. These checklists will help you to identify the topics in your syllabus and which Units of the book to read and revise.

If you are a private candidate not attending a school or college, you should contact the Exam Board whose exam you intend to take and obtain a syllabus and entry form from them.

The GCSE Syllabuses

New GCSE geography syllabuses were introduced in September 1996 and the first exams for these syllabuses will be held in 1998.

   All the new syllabuses:
- build on knowledge, understanding and skills established by the national curriculum
- have a coursework element with a weighting of between 20% and 25%
- include a final exam which involves question papers targeted at two Tiers which are graded as follows:
        – Foundation Tier, Grades C–G
        – Higher Tier, Grades A★–D

Your school or college will decide whether to enter you for the Foundation Tier or the Higher Tier according to your level of performance in geography during the time you are studying for the GCSE.

All geography syllabuses have a balanced coverage of physical, human and environmental aspects of geography as well as drawing on examples of different scales, from the local to the global. In other words you need to be familiar with geographical examples in your local or regional area, in Britain as a whole, as well as using locations on an international scale, for example from Europe, Asia or Africa.

Assessment Objectives

A proportion of the marks in the GCSE exam will be allocated for factual information or knowledge which you should have learned. However, you cannot get by on facts alone. You will also be marked on your understanding of the facts and your ability to apply this knowledge to different situations. Geographical *skills* are also very important and form the basis of many GCSE questions. Marks are therefore awarded for knowledge, understanding and skills in roughly equal proportions. Each Exam Board produces a set of assessment objectives which outlines what each candidate will be expected to demonstrate in terms of knowledge, understanding and skills in the GCSE exam. The assessment objectives vary between syllabuses, so the following list gives you a general idea of expectations.

Knowledge
- Having a recall of specific facts
- Knowing a variety of locations
- Giving examples at local, regional, national and international scales
- Using geographical terms correctly.

Understanding
- Applying knowledge to a variety of situations, e.g. social, environmental and economic circumstances
- Understanding patterns and processes in geography
- Appreciating how decisions are made and the values and attitudes of different groups of people
- Knowing how various environments are managed

Skills
- Being able to use maps
- Interpreting satellite images, photographs, graphs and charts
- Drawing maps, sketches and sections
- Recording and presenting information.

The Exam Boards recognise that no one aspect of geographical study is considered more important than another; they are all important and contribute equally to the whole study of geography.

Syllabus analysis

MIDLAND EXAMINING GROUP (MEG)

Address: 1 Hills Road, Cambridge CB1 2EU Tel: 01223 553311

Syllabus A 1586

Syllabus topics	Covered in Unit No	✓
Unit 1 People and the Physical World		
Plate Tectonics		
(a) Distribution of earthquakes	1.8	
(b) Causes and effects of earthquakes	1.8	
(c) Why people live in tectonic areas	1.8	
Rivers		
(a) Hydrological cycle	1.4	
(b) Erosion and deposition	1.4	
(c) Flooding	1.4, 1.8	
Coasts		
(a) Coastal erosion	1.6	
(b) Causes and effects of coastal erosion	1.6	
Unit 2 People and Places to Live		
Population		
(a) Density and distribution of population	2.1, 2.3	
(b) Variations in population density	2.1	
(c) Variations in population structure	2.2	
(d) Population growth	2.1	
(e) International migration	2.4	
Settlement		
(a) Rural to urban migration	3.3	
(b) Urban land use zones	3.4	
(c) Traffic in urban areas		
(d) Services in urban and rural areas	3.2	
(e) Urban to rural migration	2.4, 3.3	
Unit 3 People and their Needs		
The Quality of Life		
(a) Imbalances in quality of life between countries	2.2, 5.7, 5.10	
(b) Employment structure	5.4	
(c) Reasons for rapid economic growth	5.8	
Economic Activities		
(a) Contrasts between commercial and subsistence farming	4.2, 4.6, 4.7, 4.8	
(b) How farming is changing	4.4, 4.6, 4.8	
(c) Location of manufacturing activity	5.1, 5.6	
(d) Effects of tourism	6.9, 6.10	
(e) Effects of changing activity on communities	5.6, 5.8, 5.9	

Syllabus topics	Covered in Unit No	✓
Energy		
(a) Rising demand for energy	6.3	
(b) Changing importance of energy sources	6.3, 6.8	
(c) Consequences of energy budget changes	6.3, 6.8	
Unit 4 People and the Environment		
Resource development and the Local Environment		
(a) Extraction of raw materials	6.3	
(b) Environmental costs of energy provision	6.3, 6.8	
Management of Environments		
(a) Tropical rain forest	4.6, 6.1	
(b) National Parks	6.9	
(c) Pollution of a river, lake or sea	1.9, 1.10	
The Global Environment		
(a) Acid rain	1.10	
(b) Environmental effects on world temperatures	1.3	

Paper Analysis

Candidates answer two written papers and submit Coursework.

Paper 1	*2 hours*	Eight short questions, two from each unit
	Foundation Tier	of syllabus. All eight questions to be answered
Paper 2	*2 Hours*	Eight longer questions, two from each unit
	Higher Tier	of syllabus, four to be answered, one from each unit
		45% of total marks
Paper 3	*1 1/4 hours*	Understanding and skills
	Foundation Tier	Two questions set, both to be answered
		30% of total marks
Paper 4	*Higher Tier*	As for paper 3
Coursework		Either one longer or two shorter investigations
		25% of total marks

Syllabus B 1587 (Avery Hill) and WJEC

Syllabus topics	Covered in Unit No	✓
Unit 1 Climate, the Environment and People		
Weather and Climate		
1 Measurement of weather	1.1	
2 Different atmospheric systems	1.1, 1.2	
3 Weather and people	1.1	
Natural Environments		
4 Environmental systems	1.4	
5 Ecosystems	1.9, 4.6	
6 Changes in ecosystems	1.9, 4.5	
7 Impact of people on ecosystems	1.10, 4.6, 6.1, 6.4	
An Issue of International/Global Concern		
8 Changes in weather and climate of international concern	1.10	
Unit 2 Water, Landforms and People		
The Hydrosphere		
1 Systems in the hydrosphere	1.4	
2 Hydrological cycle	1.4	
3 Flooding and drought hazards	1.8, 4.5, 6.4	
4 Distinctive landforms	1.5, 1.6, 1.7	
5 Interaction between landforms and people	1.5, 1.6, 1.7	
6 Interaction between people and landforms	6.9, 6.10	
A Study of a Distinctive Landform		
7 Influence of water on a landform	1.7, 6.2	

Syllabus topics	Covered in Unit No	✓
Unit 3 People and Place		
Inequalities in Urban Areas		
1 Quality of life	2.2, 4.3, 5.7	
2 Inequalities in housing	3.3	
3 Inequalities in service provision	3.4	
Improving the Urban Environment		
4 Changes in housing and service provision	3.3, 3.4	
5 Influencing urban decisions	3.4, 3.8	
Urban–Rural Interaction		
6 Population changes	2.2, 2.4	
7 Urbanisation and counter-urbanisation	2.4, 3.3	
8 Reasons for migration	2.4	
9 Impact of migration	2.4	
Unit 4 People, Work and Development		
Patterns Of Work And Development		
1 Employment structures vary spatially	5.3	
2 Employment structures vary over time	5.2	
3 Employment opportunities	5.3, 5.4, 5.6, 5.8, 5.9	
4 Measuring economic and social well-being	2.2, 5.7, 5.10	
5 Patterns of economic and social well-being	2.2, 5.7, 5.8, 5.9, 5.10	
Work and Development Process		
6. Variations in processes for economic development	5.6, 5.8, 5.9	
7 Employers and employment opportunities	5.6, 5.8, 5.9	
8 Economic activity and the physical environment	1.3, 1.10, 6.4, 6.10	

Paper Analysis

Candidates answer two written papers and submit coursework.
Units to be assessed in each Paper will be changed from year to year.

1998	Papers 1 and 2	Units 2, 3, 4
	Papers 3 and 4	Unit 1
1999	Papers 1 and 2	Units 1, 2, 4
	Papers 3 and 4	Unit 3
2000	Papers 1 and 2	Units 1, 3, 4
	Papers 3 and 4	Unit 2
2001	Papers 1 and 2	Units 1, 2, 3
	Papers 3 and 4	Unit 4
Paper 1	*1 3/4 hours*	Six questions set, two from each Unit to be tested
	Foundation Tier	One question from each Unit to be answered
Paper 2	*2 hrs*	As for Paper 1
	Higher Tier	45% of total marks
Paper 3	*1 1/2 hrs*	Problem-solving paper
	Foundation Tier	
Paper 4	*1 3/4 hours*	As for Paper 3
	Higher Tier	
		30% of total marks
Coursework		Two pieces of work, A Study; A Cross-Unit Task
		Fieldwork must form base of one piece of work
		25% of total marks

Syllabus C (Bristol Project)

Syllabus topics	Covered in Unit No	✓
Theme 1 Physical Systems and Environments		
(a) Geomorphic processes and landforms	1.4, 1.5	
(b) Atmospheric processes and climate	1.1, 1.2, 1.3	
(c) Physical environments and systems	1.4	
Theme 2 Natural Hazards and People		
(a) The nature and distribution of natural hazards	1.8	
(b) The processes responsible for natural hazards	1.8	
(c) The effects of natural hazards on people	1.8	
Theme 3 Economic Systems and Development		
(a) Economic systems	4.1, 5.1	
(b) Economic activity, growth and change	4.2 to 4.8, 5.3 to 5.8	
(c) International disparities, trade and interdependence	5.9, 5.10	
Theme 4 Population and Settlement		
(a) Population distribution, structure and change	2.1, 2.2, 2.4	
(b) The location and functions of settlements	3.1, 3.2	
(c) Land use within settlements	3.4	
(d) The growth and decline of settlements	3.5, 3.6	
Theme 5 People's Use of the Earth		
(a) The Earth's resources	6.1	
(b) Exploitation and management of natural resources	6.3, 6.4	
(c) Resolving issues	6.6, 6.7	

Paper analysis

Candidates answer one written paper on Themes 1 to 4. Theme 5 forms the basis for a decision making exercise taken in the second half of the Spring Term of the year of the examination.

Paper 1	*2 1/4 hours*	Section A three questions set, two to be answered
	Foundation Tier	25% of total marks
		Section B
		Four questions set, one on each theme
		Two to be answered, one on either Theme One or Two,
		One on either Theme Three or Four.
		25% of total marks
Paper 2	*Higher Tier*	As for Paper 1
Paper 3	*1 1/2 hours*	Decision making exercise
	Foundation Tier	25% of total marks
Paper 4	*Higher Tier*	As for Paper 3
Coursework		Two pieces

- A geographical investigation supported by fieldwork
  15% of total marks
- Either a coursework unit or a portfolio of coursework pieces
  10% of total marks

Syllabus 3580 (Short Course)

Syllabus topics	Covered in Unit No	✓
Unit 1 Hydrological Themes		
Hydrological cycle	1.4	
River processes	1.4	
Flooding	1.8	
Water supply	1.4, 6.2	
Unit 2 Environmental Themes		
Water pollution	1.10	
Managing environments	6.1, 6.6	
Global climate change	1.3, 1.10	
Changing ecosystems	6.7, 6.10	
Unit 3 Economic Themes		
Employment structure	2.2	
Economic decline and growth	4.2 to 4.8, 5.2 to 5.8	
Development strategies	5.10, 6.8	
International trade	5.9	
Unit 4 Urban Themes		
Urbanisation	3.3	
Urban land use	3.4	
Urban problems	3.7	
Solutions to urban problems	3.7	

Paper Analysis

Candidates answer one paper and submit coursework.

Paper 1	*2 hrs*	One question on map skills
	Foundation Tier	Four other questions, one on each Unit, all to
	Higher Tier	be answered
		75% of total marks
Coursework		One large piece or two shorter pieces
		25% of total marks

Northern Examinations and Assessment Board (NEAB)

Address: 12 Harter Street, Manchester M1 6HL Tel: 0161 953 1180

Syllabus A 2153 (Short Course)

Syllabus topics	Covered in Unit No	✓
Theme 1 Living in Cities		
C Dynamism in urban areas; Migration	2.4	
D The Challenge of urban environments	3.3, 3,4, 3.6	
Theme 2 Living In the Natural World		
A Environmental systems		
(i) Landscape systems	1.5, 1.7, 6.1	
B Managing the living world		
(i) People and ecosystems	1.9, 4.6	
(ii) Hazardous natural events	1.8	
(iii) Leisure and the environment	6.9, 6.10	
(iv) Industry and the environment	6.3	
Theme 3 Living with Economic Change		
C Economic growth and decline	5.1, 5.3, 5.6, 5.7, 5.8	

Paper analysis

Candidates answer one written paper, Foundation Tier, Paper F, Higher Tier, Paper H. Coursework to be submitted.

Paper 1   *1hr 25mins*   Section A
Multiple choice and/or short answer questions
Section B
Structured questions
75% of total marks

Coursework   Fieldwork-based Geographical Investigation
25% of total marks

Syllabus A 1153

Syllabus topics	Covered in Unit No	✓
Theme 1 The Challenge of Urban Environments		
A Patterns and processes of urban growth	3.3, 3.5	
B Patterns of land use	3.4	
C Dynamism an urban areas; Migration	3.4, 3.7	
D Challenge of change in urban environments	3.7	
Theme 2 Managing Natural Environments		
A Environmental systems		
(i) Landscape systems	1.4, 1.5, 1.6, 1.7	
(ii) Drainage basin systems	1.4, 5.2	
B Managing the living world		
(i) People and ecosystems	4.1, 4.2, 4.5, 4.6, 4.7, 4.8	
(ii) Natural hazards	1.8	
(iii) Leisure and the environment	1.5, 5.9,	
(iv) Industry and the environment	6.3, 6.5, 6.7	
Theme 3 The Impact of Economic Change		
A What is economic change?	5.3, 5.8	
B Changes in the location of economic activity	5.1, 5.8	
C Economic growth and decline	5.1, 5.6, 5.7, 5.8, 5.9, 5.10, 6.10	

Paper analysis

Candidates answer two written papers, Foundation Tier Papers F1, F2. Higher Tier Papers H1, H2. Coursework to be submitted.

Paper 1	*1hr*	Multiple choice questions
		25% of total marks
Paper 2	*2hrs*	Structured questions including OS map.
		50% of total marks
Coursework		Geographical investigation
		25% of total marks

Syllabus B 1154

Syllabus topics	Covered in Unit No	✓
The United Kingdom		
Urban growth and change	3.3	
The farm as a system	4.1	
Electricity generation	6.3	
Water resources	6.2	
Factors affecting the location of industry	5.1	
Tourism	6.9, 6.10	
Ports	5.5	
Road transport	–	
The European Union		
Farming in Southern Italy	4.8	
The Ruhr conurbation and its changing industrial development	5.2	
Tourism in Mediterranean Spain	6.4, 6.10	
The Rhine Waterway	5.2	
The growth of Rotterdam/Europort	5.5	
The Wider World		
Amazonia	4.6, 6.1	
Ganges Delta (India and Bangladesh)	1.8	
Japan	–	

Paper analysis

Candidates answer two written papers, either Paper 1F and 2F, Foundation Tier or Paper 1H and 2H. Higher Tier. Coursework to be submitted.

Papers 1F and 1H	*1 1/2 hrs*	Four structured questions on the UK,
		All questions to be answered
		OS map question
		35% of total marks
Papers 2F and 2H	*2 hrs*	Five structured questions
		All questions to be answered
		40% of total marks
Coursework		A Geographical Investigation
		25% of total marks

Syllabus C 1155

Syllabus topics	Covered in Unit No	✓
A Natural Hazards		
A1 Unstable plate margins	1.8	
A2 Storms	1.8	
A3 River floods	1.8, 6.2	
B Fragile Environments		
B1 Disappearing tropical rain forests	6.1	
B2 Soil damage	6.4	
B3 Threatened natural landscapes in the UK	6.5, 6.9	
C Population Issues		
C1 Famine and starvation	4.3	
C2 Ageing populations	2.2, 2.4	
C3 International migration	2.4	
D Urban Issues		
D1 Pressures at the rural–urban fringe	3.3	
D2 Inner cities	3.4	
D3 Urban transport	–	
E Resource Issues		
E1 Water supply	1.4, 6.2	
E2 Resource depletion	6.1	
E3 Power generation in the UK	6.3	
F Development Issues		
F1 Unequal development	5.7, 5.10	
F2 Swing to services	5.4	
F3 A new agricultural revolution	4.4, 4.8	

Paper Analysis

Candidates answer two written papers, either Papers 1F and 2F, Foundation Tier or Papers 1H and 2H, Higher Tier. Coursework to be submitted.

Paper 1	*1 1/2 hrs*	Issues evaluation exercise based on an Advance Information Booklet. Structured questions, some short–answer 25% of total marks
Paper 2	*1 1/2 hrs* *Foundation* *1 3/4 hrs* *Higher*	Section 1 Key Areas A and B Section 2 Key Areas C and D Section 3 Key Areas E and F Two questions set in each section One question to be answered from each section Two questions set in each section Tier F short–answer and structured questions Tier H structured questions 50% of total marks
Coursework		Either a single item involving fieldwork and decision-making or two items, one of which must involve fieldwork and the other decision-making 25% of total marks

Northern Ireland Council for the Curriculum, Examinations and Assessment (NICCEA)

Address: Clarendon Dock, 29 Clarendon Road, Belfast BT1 3BG Tel: 01232 261200

Syllabus

Syllabus topics	Covered in Unit No	✓
Theme A The Atmosphere		
Weather	1.1, 1.2	
Variations in climate	1.1	
Human responses	1.1, 1.3, 1.10, 6.10	
Theme B Earth Structure and Landscape Development		
Earthquakes and volcanoes	1.8	
Impact on environments	1.8	
Landforms and rock structure	1.7	
Drainage basins	1.4	
Associated management issues	1.4	
Theme C Ecosystems		
Interaction in an ecosystem	4.5, 1.9	
People and ecosystems	1.9	
Soils	1.9	
Soil erosion and conservation	6.4	
Theme D Population		
Distribution of population	2.3	
Population structure and change	2.2, 2.4	
Migration	2.4	
Pressure on resources	6.1	
Overpopulation	2.1	
Theme E Economic Activity and Development		
Location of economic activity	5.1	
Industrial change	5.6, 5.8	
Uneven levels of development	5.7	
Government policies	4.8, 5.1, 5.4 to 5.8	
Aid and trade	5.9, 5.10	
Theme F Settlement		
Location and growth of settlement	3.1	
Spheres of influence	3.2	
Land use zones	3.4	
Urbanisation	3.3	
Counter-urbanisation	2.4, 3.3	
Urban and rural planning	3.5	

Paper Analysis

Candidates answer two papers, either Foundation or Higher Tier and submit coursework.

Paper 1	*1 1/2 hrs*	Three compulsory multi-part questions, one each on Themes A, B and C 40% of total marks
Paper 2	*1 1/2 hrs*	Three compulsory multi-part questions, one each on Themes D, E and F 40% of total marks
Coursework		An investigative study 20% of total marks

Scottish Qualifications Authority (formerly SEB)

Address: Ironmills Road, Dalkeith, Midlothian EH22 1LE Tel: 0131 663 6601

Standard Grade

Syllabus topics	Covered in Unit No	✓
The Physical Environment		
1 Physical landscapes	1.4, 1.5	
2 Weather	1.1, 1.2	
3 Climatic zones	1.9	
4 Human activities in the environment	6.1	
5 Demands on rural landscapes	6.6, 6.7	
6 Physical environment as a resource	6.1	
The Human Environment		
7 Characteristics of settlements	3.1	
8 Urban settlements problems and solutions	3.3, 3.7	
9 Farming systems	4.1	
10 Manufacturing industry	5.8	
11 Economic change and its consequences	5.6, 5.8	
International Issues		
12 Population is unevenly distributed	2.1	
13 Population characteristics can be measured	2.2	
14 Population changes and migration	2.2, 2.4	
15 International relations and trade	5.9	
16 Regions linked through trade	5.9	
17 Self-help and international aid	5.10, 6.8	

Paper Analysis

Candidates answer either one or two papers, Foundation Level only or Foundation and General Levels only or General and Credit Levels only. An Investigating Study to be submitted.

Paper	Grades Assessed	Time Allocation
Foundation Level	6,5	1 hr
General Level	4,3	1 1/4 hrs
Credit Level	2,1	1 3/4 hrs

Each paper will contain questions based on each of the three themes.

Southern Examining Group (SEG)

Address: Stag Hill House, Guildford, Surrey GU2 5XJ   Tel: 01483 506506

Syllabus A (2000)

Syllabus topics	Covered in Unit No	✓
Paper 1: *any three from*		
1 Tectonic activity	1.8	
2 Rocks and landscape	1.7	
3 River landscape processes and features	1.4	
4 Glacial landscape processes and features	1.5	
5 Coastal landscape processes and features	1.6	
6 Weather and climate	1.1, 1.2	
7 Ecosystems	1.9, 4.6	
Paper 2: *one from*		
1 Population	2.1 to 2.4	
2 Settlement	3.1, 3.2	
one from		
3 Agriculture	Section 4	
4 Industry	5.1, 5.4, 5.6 to 5.9	
one from		
5 Managing resources and tourism	1.3, 1.10, 6.1, 6.9, 6.10	
6 Development and interdependence	1.8, 5.7, 5.9, 5.10, 6.8	

Paper Analysis

Candidates answer two papers and submit coursework.

Paper 1	*1 3/4 hrs*	Section A Skills including OS maps Section B Seven resource-based, structured questions set, three to be answered 40% of total marks
Paper 2	*1 1/2 hrs*	Three sections, each with two resource-based questions, three to be answered, one from each section 35% of total marks
Coursework		Option 1 Fieldwork investigation Option 2 Shorter fieldwork investigation and a piece of coursework 25% of total marks

Syllabus B (2050)

Syllabus topics	Covered in Unit No	✓
Topic A People and Urban Change		
Population distribution	2.1	
Towns and cities	3.3 to 3.7	
Migration and urban growth	2.4, 3.3	
Topic B Leisure, Recreation and Tourism		
Tourism and the economy	6.10	
The provision of leisure activities	6.9	
The management of recreation and tourism environments	6.4, 6.9	
Topic C The Physical Environment		
Atmospheric processes and climate	1.1, 1.8	
Tectonic activity	1.8	
Water	1.4, 1.6, 6.2, 6.8	
Topic D Economic Development		
Levels of development	2.2, 5.7	
Changing levels of economic activity	5.8, 6.8	
Economic and environmental pressures	1.3, 1.10, 6.1, 6.4	

Paper analysis

Candidates answer two papers and submit coursework

Paper 1	*1 1/2 hrs*	Skills based paper involving decision making. Structured questions 25% of total marks
Paper 2	*2 hrs*	One structured question set on each of the four topics. All four questions to be answered 50% of total marks
Coursework		Option 1 Fieldwork investigation Option 2 Shorter fieldwork investigation and a piece of coursework 25% of total marks

London Examinations (EDEXCEL)

Address: Stewart House, 32 Russell Square, London WC1B 5DN Tel: 0171 331 4000

Syllabus A (1310)

Syllabus topics	Covered in Unit No	✓
Unit A People and Places		
A1 Population		
1 Rates of population change vary	2.2	
2 Population density and distribution vary	2.1	
3 Population characteristics vary	2.2	
4 Standards of living and quality of life vary★	2.2, 4.3, 5.7	
5 Population movement★	2.4	
A2 Settlement		
1 Each settlement has distinctive characteristics	3.1	
2 Settlements can be classified	3.1	
3 Patterns of land use can be identified in towns	3.4	
4 Relationships between settlements in an area★	3.2	
5 Urban growth creates problems and opportunities★	3.7	
Unit B People and Work		
B3 Agriculture		
1 Farming can be seen as a system	4.1	
2 Farming systems can be classified	4.1, 4.2	
3 Agricultural land use patterns	4.2	
4 Agricultural systems change★	4.2, 4.4, 4.8	
5 Agricultural practices impact on the environment★	4.5	
B4 Industry		
1 An industry can be seen as a system	5.1	
2 Industry can be classified	5.1	
3 Location of industry	5.1	
4 Industries are interdependent★	5.8, 5.9	
5 Industrial activity impacts on the environment★	5.8	
Unit C Landscapes: Challenge and Management		
C5 Coasts		
1 The coastline is a system	1.6	
2 Landforms can be classified	1.6	
3 Base level changes	1.6	
4 Natural and human changes create problems★	6.5	
5 Economic opportunities in coastal zones★	6.5, 6.10	
C6 Valleys		
1 A valley is part of a system	1.4	
2 Landforms can be classified	1.4	
3 Glaciated valleys	1.5	
4 Natural and human processes create problems★	1.8, 1.10	
5 Economic opportunities in valleys★	1.5	
Unit D Environmental Systems		
D7 Climate, Weather and Water★		
1 Elements of the weather can be measured	1.1	
2 Distinctive climates can be recognised	1.9, 4.5, 4.6	
3 The water cycle	1.4	
4 Management of the environment is important	1.10	

Syllabus topics	Covered in Unit No	✓
D 8 Soils, Vegetation and Ecosystems★		
1 Soils can be classified	1.9	
2 Vegetation communities	1.9, 4.5, 4.6	
3 Small-scale ecosystems	1.9, 4.6	
4 Ecosystem balance can be upset	6.1, 6.4, 6.8	

★ Indicates option topics; all others are core.

Paper Analysis

Candidates answer two written papers, Foundation Tier, Papers 1 and 2. Higher Tier, Papers 3 and 4. Coursework to be submitted.

Candidates must choose Key Ideas 4 and 5 from either A1 or A2 and from either B3 or B4 and from either C5 or C6 and either Option D7 or D8.

Papers 1 and 3	*1 hr*	Mainly short answer questions testing the core. Key Ideas 1, 2 and 3 of Units A, B and C 25% of total marks
Papers 2 and 4	*2 hrs*	Two questions set for each of the four units Four questions to be answered one from each unit depending on Options chosen 50% of total marks
Paper 5		Coursework Geographical investigation based on field work 25% of total marks

Syllabus B 1311

Syllabus topics	Covered in Unit No	✓
Theme 1 Issues in Natural Environments		
Unit 1 Drainage basins	1.4, 6.2	
Unit 2 Coastal Management	1.6	
Unit 3 Environmental Hazards	1.2, 1.8, 1.10	
Theme 2 Issues In Rural Environments		
Unit 1 Primary Activities and the Rural Environment	4.1, 4.2, 4.5 to 4.8	
Unit 2 Recreation and the Rural Environment	6.9	
Unit 3 Rural-Urban Links	3.3	
Theme 3 Issues in Economic Development		
1 Spatial variations in levels of economic development	5.7	
2 Environmental constraints	6.1	
Population densities	2.1	
Resource exploitation	6.1	
Neo-colonialism and trans-national corporations	5.9	
3 Regions of economic growth/decline	5.3, 5.6, 5.8	
4 Political and economic factors	5.1, 5.4, 5.6 to 5.8, 6.8	
Theme 4 Issues In Urban Environments		
Unit 1 Internal Structure of Urban Areas	3.4	
Unit 2 Journeys within and between Urban Areas	3.2, 3.8	
Unit 3 Changes in Urban Population	2.4, 3.3, 3.6	

Paper Analysis

Candidates answer two written papers, Foundation Tier, Papers 1 and 2. Higher Tier, Papers 3 and 4. Coursework to be submitted.

Papers 1 and 3   *2 hrs*   Six structured questions set, all to be answered
                                   50% of total marks

Papers 2 and 4   *1 1/4 hrs*   Decision making exercise based on a resource booklet.
                                   25% of total marks

Paper 5   Coursework, two items
                                   Item A based on fieldwork relating to one or more key
                                   ideas in the syllabus
                                   Item B Fieldwork and/or secondary data relating to one or
                                   more key ideas drawn from a different syllabus theme
                                   25% of total marks

Syllabus A (Short Course) (3310)

Syllabus topics	Covered in Unit No	✓
Theme A: People and Places – Settlement		
1 Each settlement has distinctive characteristics	3.1	
2 Settlements can be classified	3.1	
3 Patterns of land use can be identified in towns	3.4	
Theme B: People and work – Agriculture		
1 Farming can be seen as a system	4.1	
2 Farming systems can be classified	4.1, 4.2	
3 Agricultural land use patterns	4.2, 4.8	
Theme C: Coastal Landscapes		
Challenge and Management		
1 The coastline is a system	1.6	
2 Landforms can be classified	1.6	
3 Natural processes and human activities create problems	1.6, 6.5	
Theme D: Environmental Systems		
Either Weather and Climate *or* Ecosystems		
Weather and Climate		
1 Elements of the weather can be measured	1.1	
2 Management of the environment is important	1.10	
Ecosystems		
1 Small-scale ecosystems	1.9, 4.6	
2 Ecosystem balance can be upset	6.1, 6.4, 6.8	

Paper Analysis

Candidates answer two written papers, Foundation Tier, Papers 1 and 2. Higher Tier Papers 3 and 4. Coursework to be submitted.

Papers 1 and 3   *45 mins*   Themes A, B and C examined *not* Theme D
                                 Short answers with opportunities for extended prose
                                 Map question will be set
                                 30% of total marks

Papers 2 and 4   *1 hour*   All Themes will be examined
                                 45% of total marks

Paper 5   Coursework. A geographical investigation based
                                 on fieldwork
                                 25°% of total marks

Syllabus B (Short Course) 3311

Syllabus topics	Covered in Unit No	✓
Theme 1 – Issues in Natural Environments		
Either Unit 1 *or* Unit 2 together with Unit 3		
Unit 1 The Drainage Basin	1.4, 6.2	
Unit 2 Coastal Management	1.6	
Unit 3 Environmental Hazards	1.2, 1.8, 1.10	
Theme 2 – Issues in Economic Development		
1 Spatial variations in levels of economic development	5.7	
2 Environmental constraints	6.1	
Population densities	2.1	
Resource exploitation	6.1	
Neo-colonialism and trans-national corporations	5.9	
3 Regions of economic growth/decline	5.1, 5.3, 5.6, 5.8	
4 Political and economic factors	4.8, 5.1, 5.4 to 5.8, 6.8	
Theme 3 – Issues in Urban Environments		
1 Internal Structure of Urban Areas	3.4	
2 Journeys within and between Urban Areas	3.2, 3.8	

Paper Analysis

Candidates answer one written paper, Foundation Tier, Paper 1, Higher Tier Paper 2. Coursework to be submitted.

Papers 1 and 2   *1 1/2 hrs*   Five structured questions
one question on each
of Units in Themes 1 and 3, one question on
Theme 2. Four compulsory questions, plus one
question based on option chosen in Theme 1
75% of total marks

Paper 3   Coursework. One item based on fieldwork
25% of total marks

Welsh Joint Education Committee (WJEC)

Address: 245 Western Avenue, Cardiff CF5 2YX Tel: 01222 561231

Syllabus A (Mainstream)

Syllabus topics	Covered in Unit No	✓
Unit 1 The Fragile World – Physical Systems and Environmental Issues		
1A Ice, rivers and the sea create landscapes		
1 Weathering in upland glaciated landscapes	1.5	
2 Glaciers – erosion, transport, deposition	1.5	
3 Glacial landforms	1.5	
Rivers *or* the sea		
4 Weathering	1.4, 1.6	
5 Erosion, transport, deposition	1.4, 1.6	
6 Landforms	1.4, 1.6	
1B Distinctive patterns of weather and climate		
1 Weather	1.1	
2 Air masses	1.1	
3 Weather over the British Isles	1.2	
4 Factors affecting climate	1.1	
1C Human activities and the physical environment		
1 River or coastal flooding	1.8	
2 Pollution by energy sources	6.3	
3 Tourism	1.5, 6.9, 6.10	
1D Exploitation of fragile environments		
1 Demand for resources	6.1, 6.7	
2 Desertification	4.5	
3 Acid rain	1.10	
Unit 2 The Interdependent World – Economic activities global inequalities, places		
2A Different areas have different economic activities		
1 Factors affecting location of economic activities	5.7	
2 Upland rural areas	4.2, 5.6	
3 Lowland rural/urban areas	4.2, 5.3, 5.6, 5.8	
4 Urban/industrial areas	5.3	
5 Urban areas shopping habits	3.2, 5.4	
2B Economic and social changes influence urban development		
1 Causes of urban growth	3.3	
2 Urban land use patterns	3.4	
3 Urban change	3.5, 3.6	
4 Difference between MEDC and LEDC urban areas	3.3	
2C Global inter-dependence through trade		
1 Different patterns of trade	5.9	
2 Trade dominated by some MEDCs	5.9	
3 Countries of the Western Pacific rim	5.6, 5.8, 5.9	
4 Trans-national companies	5.9	
2D Global inequalities		
1 Imbalance leading to migration	2.4, 6.1, 6.6	
2 Differences in quality of life	2.2, 4.3, 5.7	
3 Inequalities within countries	5.1, 5.6	
4 Agencies working to reduce inequalities	5.10, 6.8	

Paper Analysis

Candidates answer two papers, Foundation or Higher Tier. Coursework to be submitted.

Paper 1	*1 3/4 hrs*	Four compulsory questions based on Unit 1
		Data response and extended prose questions
		40% of total marks
Paper 2	*1 3/4hrs*	Four compulsory questions based on Unit 2
		Data response and extended prose questions
		40% of total marks
Coursework		One of the following:

l   One larger piece of coursework involving fieldwork and secondary data

ll   Two short pieces of coursework, a fieldwork investigation and a teacher-devised classroom investigation

lll   Two short pieces of coursework, a classroom investigation based on secondary data and a teacher-devised field investigation

20% of total marks

WJEC Avery Hill Syllabus see MEG Syllabus B 1587 (Avery Hill) on pages 4 and 5

Studying and revising

Planning a revision programme

Geography is a subject which deals with an extensive variety of facts and these need to be learned and understood.

There are a number of ways in which this can be done:
- read and reread about something then test yourself on what you can remember
- write notes and draw sketch maps as you read and use the notes to revise from
- write down only key words or sentences to learn by heart.

It is important to choose a method which suits you, do not be concerned if your friends use a different approach. You cannot base your learning solely on your ability to remember facts. Use the range of questions on pages 191–202 to practise your techniques and test your understanding.

There is much to be said for having a systematic revision programme which will allow you to produce your best performance at the time of the examination. The emphasis must be on *planning* the work and *keeping to a timetable*. Geography is only one of a number of subjects you will be taking at GCSE so a *revision schedule* should give sufficient time to each of your GCSE subjects. The following timetable is suggested for an exam in the middle of June. You can adjust it accordingly if your exam falls at a different time of the year.

Last week in March
- review your performance in the mock exam
- identify any weaknesses for particular attention
- plan a weekly programme for April and May.

Remember to use the school holiday as a time for more intensive revision.

April and May
- allow about five hours per week for geography revision, in 1-hour sessions
- complete your revision schedule two weeks before the exam.

The two weeks before the exam
- use this time to look at main revision points
- use the self-test questions in this revision guide
- continue to practise answering the exam questions provided in this guide.

Examination Techniques

- Don't revise on the evening before nor in the hours immediately before the exam
- Spend time before the exam making sure you have the correct equipment e.g. two HB pencils; pen; rubber; ruler; four coloured pencils (brown, green, red, blue); compass; protractor.
- *Read the whole paper carefully* including the rubric to check how many questions you must answer. No marks are given for extra questions answered and you will penalise yourself if you do not answer sufficient questions.

- Where you have a choice of questions spend time deciding which ones you can answer best.
- *Time yourself carefully throughout the exam.*
- Answer first the question you know most about. Leave to last the one you are least happy with.
- Leave sufficient time at the end to read through your answers and make minor corrections if necessary.

REMEMBER! Up to 5% of the total mark can be *added* for accurate spelling, punctuation and grammar; this is true of all components including coursework. This means you can get an *extra* 5 marks on a paper marked out of 100. These marks can be very important in achieving the grade you want.

Chapter 1
Physical Systems and Environments

1.1 Weather and climate

Weather describes the state of the atmosphere at a particular place and time. **Climate** is the average weather conditions over many years for a large area.

Measuring weather

Weather can be measured using automatic electronic instruments or by taking daily readings of instruments and recording the results.

Sometimes an Exam Group will set a question on a weather station rather than on a weather map. The question may include all or some of the following:

- Descriptions of the instruments and how they work.
- Suitable location for a school weather station and the positions of the individual instruments.
- How weather records should be kept and the information displayed. The instruments most commonly found at a school weather station are:

> Stevenson screen, maximum and minimum thermometer, hygrometer (measures humidity [the amount of water vapour in the atmosphere]), rain gauge and measuring cylinder, wind vane, anemometer (measures wind speed), sunshine recorder.

- Questions on modern aids to weather forecasting, e.g. satellites, computers.

You should be able to draw meteorological instruments, know how they work and also know where they should be placed to be most effective. Daily readings of maximum and minimum temperatures can be averaged over a month but remember that the rainfall for each day of the month is added to give the month's total. Line graphs, bar charts and wind roses provide suitable means of displaying the information. Recordings made over a period of time may form part of your coursework for the GCSE exam.

Weather conditions and their causes

Rainfall
There are three types:
- **Cyclonic rain**, caused by warm air being undercut by colder air in a low pressure system.

- **Convectional rainfall**, caused by air warmed by the hot earth rising and cooling as it meets colder layers.
- **Relief or orographic rainfall**, caused by moist air being cooled as it is forced to rise up the sides of hills or mountains.

Snow

Crystals of ice produced when condensation takes place, below freezing point. The crystals combine to form snowflakes.

Hail

Raindrops which pass through a layer of air below freezing point may freeze to form hail. In turbulent air the hail may be tossed about, collecting more rain droplets and becoming larger. Finally, the hail may fall as large stones, damaging crops.

Frost

On a clear calm night in winter the earth's surface cools by **radiation** and the air close to the earth also cools. Any moisture it contains will condense on cold surfaces and freeze to give a white frost. Valleys can become frost pockets, as cold air tends to sink to the valley bottom.

Fog

If air containing water vapour is cooled the point may be reached where the water vapour condenses into tiny drops of water which remain suspended in the air to form a fog. Dust, smoke or other pollutants in the air may cling to the water droplets to form 'smog'. Frost and fog often occur in high pressure conditions.

Apart from the five types of weather described above you should also know what causes such things as thunderstorms, gales, and land and sea breezes.

Air masses

An **air mass** is the air with similar properties of temperature and moisture which covers a large area. These properties are derived from the source region below the air mass. When air masses move they take their characteristics to the areas they cross. Air masses formed over:

- a warm land are called **Tropical continental**   **Tc**
- a warm sea are called **Tropical maritime**   **Tm**
- a cold land are called **Polar continental**   **Pc**
- a cold sea are called **Polar** or **Arctic maritime**   **Pm** or **Am**

The weather over the British Isles and the neighbouring regions of Europe is influenced by these air masses, which give great variations to the weather, Fig. 1 .1.

When air masses meet, fronts are formed. These will be explained in Unit 1.2.

People and weather

Human activity is influenced by weather, and humans can also modify weather conditions. A large number of people and organisations require accurate weather information regularly. The Meteorological Office provides special phone and fax numbers for sailors, aircraft pilots and people travelling to different parts of the world, as well as three-hourly weather updates for motorists and others.

People intentionally modify weather conditions in a number of ways.

- **Seeding** clouds to produce rain. For clouds with below-freezing temperatures the seeding agent used by aircraft is dry ice (solid carbon dioxide). Cumulus clouds may produce rain if sprayed with a fine water spray or seeded with salt particles.
- **Windbreaks** to protect crops and homes.
- Using **greenhouses**, and by using polythene over the soil to protect plants.
- **Irrigation**.

People can also modify weather and climates unintentionally.

- Urban **microclimates** (the climate of a small area). Large cities and **conurbations** (a group of towns that have joined to form an extensive urban area), have different climatic conditions to the surrounding countryside. Buildings and roads store heat during the day and release it slowly at night. Heat is also obtained from car exhausts, heated buildings, factories and power stations.

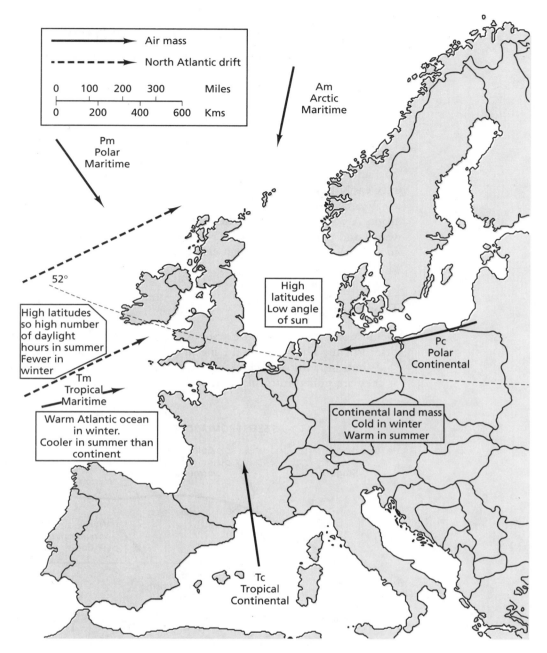

Fig. 1.1 Some factors which influence N.W. European weather

Cities also generate more dust and nuclei, which attract more condensation than country areas. As a result an urban heat island is formed which, at its centre, may be 5° C warmer in summer than the surrounding countryside. **Insolation**, the radiant energy that reaches the surface of the earth from the sun, may be reduced by as much as 5% in summer, when dust and other particles absorb and reflect insolation. Fog is also more common as a result of the concentration of **condensation nuclei**—smoke particles, dust and salt. Clouds are thicker and more frequent than in rural areas and the mean annual precipitation is increased. Although buildings reduce wind velocity, very tall buildings create canyons through which winds blow strongly.

- Acid deposition (see Unit 1.10)
- Global warming (see Unit 1.3)
- Desertification (see Unit 4.5)

1.2   Interpretation of weather maps and meteorological information

Fronts

Day-to-day variations in the weather are caused by the influence of different air masses. Warm maritime air from the tropics and cold air from polar regions have different characteristics and the boundary between them is called a front. These air masses do not mix easily because they have different temperatures and densities. The warmer tropical air is forced up and over the colder polar air to form a bulge on the front called a warm front. A cold front occurs where cold sinking air undercuts the warm air mass. At both warm and cold fronts the rising air is cooled and clouds form, leading to rain (or snow in winter). Fronts can be seen clearly on satellite weather photographs as thick bands of cloud.

Depressions

Depressions, or low pressure systems (lows), occur when moist Tm air meets colder and drier Pm air. The stages in the life of a depression are shown in Fig. 1.2.

Winds blowing anti-clockwise round the centre of the depression can be very strong as they are pulled into the centre where the pressure is lowest. This low pressure results

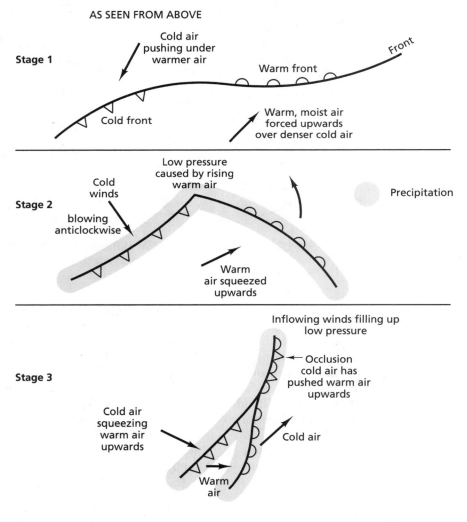

Fig. 1.2 The life of a depression

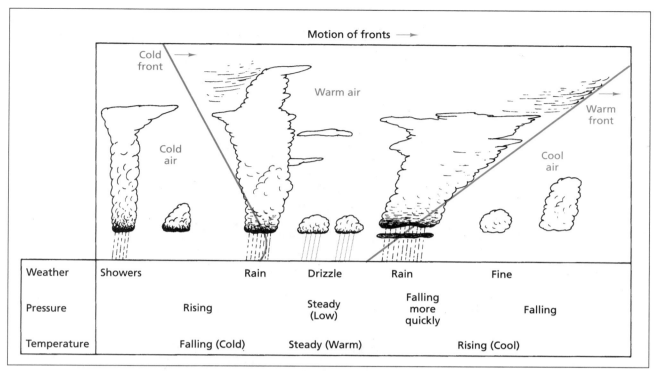

Fig. 1.3 Cross-section through the fronts of a low pressure system

from the warm air being pushed upwards. Most depressions move from west to east across the British Isles, with the cold front moving faster than the warm front. Figure 1.3 shows a cross-section through a depression and the weather conditions that can be expected as it moves across the country.

Anticyclones

Areas of sinking air which result in high pressure are called anticyclones or highs. Winds are light and circulate outwards in a clockwise direction around the high-pressure system.

Anticyclones are much larger than depressions and can give many days or even weeks of settled, calm weather. Anticyclones often block the routes of depressions, slowing them down or forcing them around the high pressure system. They are then called **'blocking highs'**. Weather conditions in an anticyclone vary between summer and winter and can be characterised as follows:

- **Summer**—Hot sunny days with few or no clouds. No rain but cooling of the ground by radiation at night can result in dew or mist forming. This quickly clears the following morning. In time, warm moist air rising from the ground by convection may result in thunderstorms. If the high pressure is centred to the north of Britain light winds blowing across the cooler North Sea may bring cloud cover to eastern England.
- **Winter**—Cloudless skies but less radiation because of the low angle of the sun. Temperatures drop, making the days cold and the nights even colder because of the lack of cloud cover. At night, fog and frost may form. Cold air from central Asia passing across the North Sea may bring snow showers to the east coast.

Weather maps and their symbols

Weather symbols

Make sure you know the weather symbols used on meteorological maps. If you are given a weather map question, the symbols may be given you. You can answer the question faster and with greater confidence if you already know the symbols. Look at the symbols used on Fig.1.4. For each weather station the information shown relates to temperature, cloud cover, wind speed and direction, and precipitation.

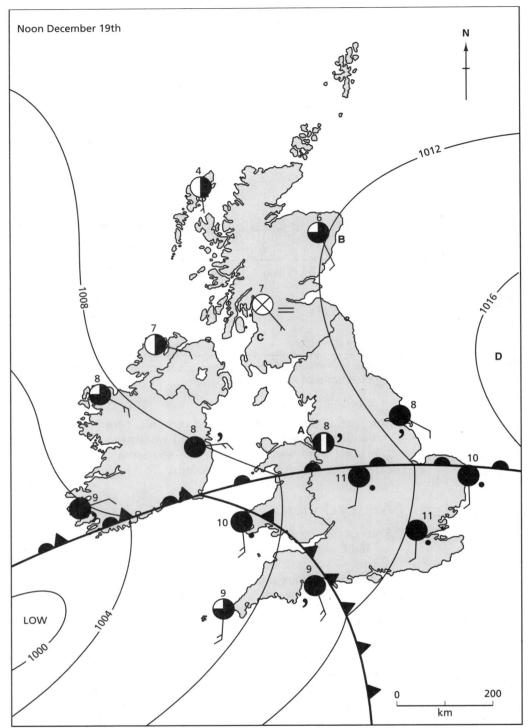

Fig. 1.4 Weather map of Britain

Understanding the weather map

The weather map shows a low pressure system passing over southern England, with higher pressure over the North Sea. Lows, like the one shown, are very common over Britain and can occur at any time of the year. They usually swing from west to east and the weather experienced as the low passes usually follows a distinctive pattern, as shown in Fig. 1.3.

1.3 Global warming

The climate in the 21st century

What will a weather forecast for Britain tell us in thirty years time? Many scientists believe that by then there will be a world-wide increase in temperatures, with a rise of about 1°C in Britain. Less rainfall in southern Britain may give long periods of summer drought, whereas in Scotland, Northern Ireland and northern England rainfall could increase. Temperature increases could be higher in other parts of the world. This gradual increase in the earth's temperature is known as **global warming**, which is caused by changes in the earth's heat balance.

The earth's heat balance

The earth receives its heat from the sun in the form of incoming radiation (short-wave radiation) and outgoing reradiation and reflection from the earth's surface (long-wave or infra-red radiation). There is normally a state of equilibrium between the incoming and outgoing radiation. Some parts of the earth's surface receive more heat than others. For example, the northern hemisphere with large land areas has a positive heat balance whereas the polar regions have a negative heat balance. The heat is transferred away from the tropics by winds and ocean currents to provide an overall balance. Heat is also transferred upwards from the earth's surface into the atmosphere by radiation, conduction and convection.

E xaminer's tip

Do not confuse the hole in the ozone layer, which increases radiation and can lead to skin cancer, with global warming.

The greenhouse effect

The temperature balance on the Earth is partly controlled by much of the outgoing reradiation being absorbed by the water vapour and carbon dioxide in the atmosphere. Therefore the effect is very much like the glass in a greenhouse, holding in heat which would otherwise be lost in the atmosphere. This greenhouse effect helps to explain why clear nights are much cooler than cloudy ones.

Figure 1.5 shows how the greenhouse effect is trapping noxious gases in the lower atmosphere (troposphere).

As more and more fossil fuels, (coal, oil and gas) are burned in power stations, factories and internal combustion engines, the amount of carbon dioxide and nitrous oxide in the atmosphere continues to increase. Other gases come from aerosols, waste heaps and the use of fertilisers. As a result, the troposphere between 6 and 18 kilometres above the earth is being polluted by increasing amounts of **greenhouse gases**.

The oceans absorb carbon dioxide as do plants. Humans and animals breathe out carbon dioxide and produce methane, another greenhouse gas. One reason for concern at the large-scale destruction of the rainforest is because fewer trees means that less carbon dioxide is being absorbed; also, burning the vegetation adds more pollution to the atmosphere.

Possible long-term effects

The high-powered computer used by the Meteorological Office predicts that, on average, world temperatures will rise by 1°C by 2040 and continue to climb. If this estimate is correct the consequences may be devastating for many parts of the world.

- **Higher temperatures** could make Mediterranean resorts unbearably hot in summer and tourists might prefer the warmth and sunshine of resorts in Britain and northern Europe.
- **Sea levels** would rise as the polar ice-caps melt, bringing flooding to low-lying areas around the coast of Britain (Fig. 1.6). Islands just above sea level would disappear and a 1-metre sea level rise would flood 17% of Bangladesh, affecting 70 million people. Countries with low coastlines backed by high population densities, such as Thailand, Indonesia and China, could be devastated by higher sea levels.
- **Natural vegetation** and **wild life** would suffer from climatic changes. Some species might die out completely.

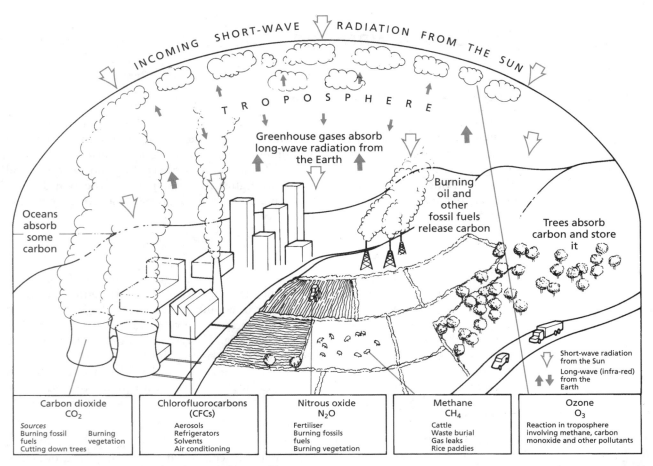

Fig.1.5 The greenhouse effect

Uncertainty about the future

Some scientists believe the threat from the greenhouse effect is not as serious as articles in newspapers and journals suggest. They point to the possibility of counter-balancing effects. For example, when fossil fuels are burned, sulphur dioxide is one of the gases given off. This gas links with specks of dust in the atmosphere to form a haze which reflects sunlight back into space.

The alarming factor, however, is that the concentration of greenhouse gases will carry on rising throughout the 21st century. It is exceedingly important, therefore, to reduce drastically emissions of greenhouse gases as soon as possible.

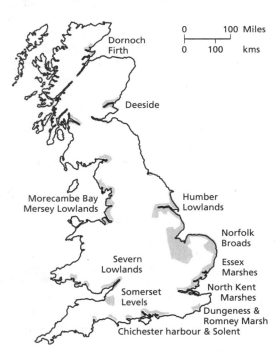

Fig. 1.6 Areas threatened by flooding if sea level rises by 1.5m

1.4 The hydrological cycle : drainage basins

The hydrological cycle

The movement of water between the atmosphere, the land and the sea is known as the **hydrological cycle** (hydrology is the study of water on the earth). It is called a cycle because it is a continuous process. Water circulates from the oceans to the atmosphere and to the land, over and over again. The processes involved are shown in Fig.1.7, and because these processes are linked to one another in a distinct relationship, the hydrological cycle can also be called a **system**. The system requires a supply of energy to keep it going and this energy is provided by the sun.

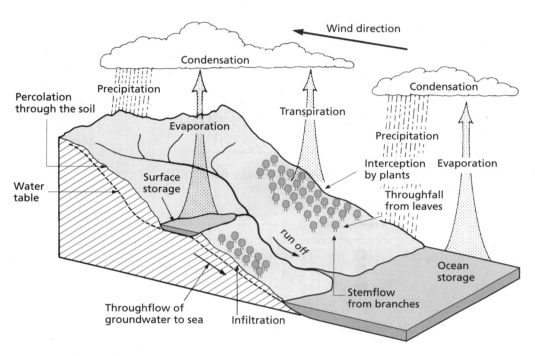

Fig. 1.7 The hydrological cycle

Here are some explanations of the processes and other terms used on Fig.1.7.
- **Evaporation**—Water molecules from the sea, lakes and other sources are transferred into water vapour in the air by the sun's energy (heat). This water vapour rises and cools until it condenses.
- **Condensation**—As the air is cooled, water vapour is transformed into water droplets which form clouds. The droplets increase in size until they fall as precipitation.
- **Precipitation**—Rain, hail or snow falls to the earth and some soaks into the soil, percolates into the underlying rocks and moves slowly downwards through the rocks towards the lower ground and the sea. Some reaches the surface as spring water and then flows as run-off in streams and rivers.
- **Transpiration**—Water from the soil is drawn up into plants by their root systems. Some of this water is released from the plants' leaves into the atmosphere. This process is called transpiration. When the water passes into the air as water vapour, the process is called evapotranspiration.
- **Water table**—The boundary, normally below the ground's surface, which marks the upper limit of water saturation.
- **Infiltration**—The seepage of water into the soil. If the rainfall exceeds the the rate the soil will absorb water (infiltration capacity), the soil becomes saturated and the water flows over the land.

River valleys

Erosion

Erosion occurs where a stream has an excess of energy; this is likely to be the case in the upper course (Fig.1.8). There are three main forms of erosion:

- **hydraulic action**—the dragging effect of the flow of water, which erodes poorly consolidated material
- **corrosion**—the solution of rocks such as chalk and limestone in the flowing water
- **corrasion** (which is the main form of erosion)—the bombardment of the **river bed** and sides by debris carried by the stream. **Vertical corrasion** occurs mainly on the river bed, while **horizontal corrasion** wears away the banks and sides of the channel (Fig.1.9).

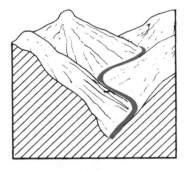

Fig. 1.8 Upper course—stream flowing between interlocking spurs

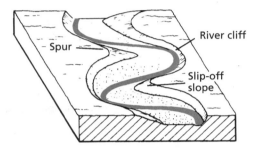

Fig. 1.9 Middle course—meanders eroding the valley sides

Transport

A stream carries material in three ways:
1. the dissolved load of soluble material
2. the suspended load of fine particles
3. the bed load of larger material, which is bounced, pushed and rolled along the channel floor.

Deposition

Deposition occurs when the stream has insufficient energy to transport its load. The material deposited is called **alluvium**, and a number of landforms occur when deposition takes place (Fig.1.10).

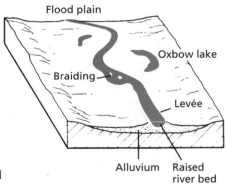

Fig. 1.10 Lower course—wide flood plain and raised river bed

Physical features found in river valleys

You will need to know how the following features are formed and be able to give at least one example of each:

- Gorges and canyons—Grand Canyon, USA.
- Waterfalls—Kaieteur Falls in Guyana.
- Cataracts and rapids—River Nile.

- River terraces—River Thames.
- Deltas—River Mississippi, USA.
- Estuaries—River Mersey.

Drainage basins

Surface run-off in the hydrological cycle takes the form of streams and rivers. The area drained by a single river system is called a drainage basin and is an example of an '**open**' **system**. This means that there are inputs from outside the system, such as precipitation, and outputs from the system, such as the flow of water and the material it carries into the sea or a lake. There are also transfers within the system of such things as the flow of water in the drainage basin and **infiltration** from the surface into the **water table**.

Drainage basin management

The River Adur, West Sussex

The Environment Agency (EA) is responsible for the management of water resources in England and Wales. The River Adur, which flows out to the sea at Shoreham in West Sussex, is managed by the Southern Region of the EA, Fig.1.11.

Examiner's tip

Detailed case studies earn high marks. Add as many as possible to your revision notes and learn them.

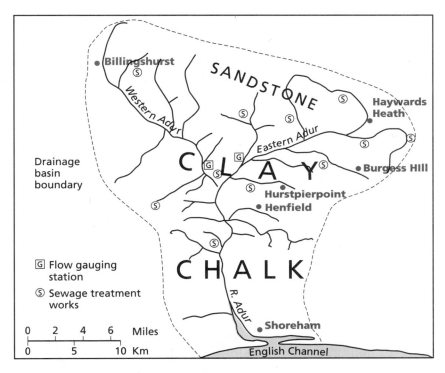

Fig. 1.11 Drainage basin of the River Adur, West Sussex

The problems which concern the EA are water quality and flood defences. The river is not used as a source for reservoirs and only small amounts of water are removed by farmers, mainly for irrigation.

Water Quality

Dormitory towns for London and Brighton, such as Haywards Heath, Burgess Hill and Hurstpierpoint, have grown up in the drainage basin. There are therefore increasing amounts of sewage effluent, in the form of waste water from sewage works, near the headwaters of the drainage basin. The streams in this region flow from clay which does not act as a good reservoir in dry weather.

The streams become very low and up to 7/8ths of the flow in the upper reaches may consist of treated sewage effluent. As a result the water quality is not of Grade 1 quality despite a strict control of the effluent quality entering the drainage basin. Grade 1 water comes from streams rising in the chalk rocks of the South Downs which act as a natural reservoir.

There is also a danger of accidental pollution from farm wastes such as silage liquor, the liquid waste produced when green fodder crops are stored to be used as animal fodder. Water Quality Officers inspect and advise farmers to reduce this danger.

Flood Defence

The EA is responsible for protecting people from tidal and river flooding and this is carried out throughout the drainage basin. Earth banks on either side of the river are maintained and desilting takes place in the tidal section. In the upper reaches weirs (dams) and penstocks (concrete structures with gates to control the water flow) hold back the water in summer and allow flood water to pass in winter. Channels are maintained and obstructions removed to allow flood water to flow freely. The Environment Agency is responsible for a flood warning service. Weather forecasts, weather radar, rainfall, river and tidal levels are continuously monitored and flood warning notices are sent to the police, who are responsible for passing the information to the public and emergency services.

A storm hydrograph

Drainage basin management depends on accurate statistics about water flows. There are two gauging stations (Fig.1.11) on the River Adur, where flow levels are measured. The information can be shown as a graph, known as a hydrograph. It shows water flow over a period of time. The amount of water that comes from the groundwater supply, that is water contained in the soil and underlying rock, is shown as well as any storm flow. This is the increased discharge which follows a period of heavy rainfall, Fig.1.12.

The lag between rainfall and the peak flow depends on such conditions in the drainage basin as soil and rock type, slope, size of the basin and amount of vegetation.

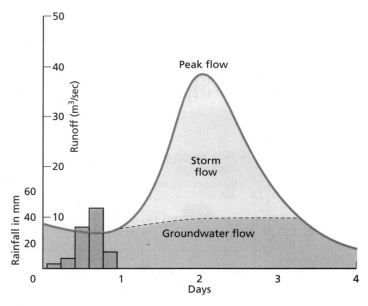

Fig. 1.12 A storm hydrograph

1.5 Glacial environments

In high latitudes or altitudes where there is less heat from the sun the hydrological cycle involves precipitation in the form of snow and rivers of ice instead of water. Glaciers operate within the system like rivers and produce distinctive landforms, which in highland regions are mainly the result of erosion and in lowland regions consist mainly of deposition features.

Fig. 1.13 Grimsel ober unteraargletscher

Highland glaciation

The aerial photograph (Fig.1.13) shows many of the features which are associated with glaciation in a highland region. Erosion by ice has made the valleys U-shaped, while ice erosion and the breaking up of rocks by frost action have carved the landscape into ridges, hollows and peaks. In the photograph, two glaciers can be seen. The larger one which ends in a lake is much darker in colour than the one near E, because it is loaded with rock material, called moraine, which has either fallen on to the glacier or has been torn from the valley sides by the ice. The features marked by letters are:

A   A **ribbon lake** formed from meltwater from the glacier. The lake has filled a part of the valley which was deepened and widened when the glacier was much longer than it is now.

B   A **corrie** (sometimes known as a cirque or cwm), an armchair-like hollow which was formed by ice and frost action.

C   A **waterfall** leading from a hanging valley.

D   The dark stripe is a **medial moraine** formed when two glaciers join. **Lateral moraine** is the name given to the debris on the sides of the glacier, while a **terminal moraine** is formed where the glacier melts.

E   A **glacier snout** with terminal moraine. Streams flow away from the base of the ice sheet.

F   The peaks in the distance are **pyramid-like** in shape with their sides steepened by ice and frost-thaw action.

G   The mountain ridges are steepened in the same way to form **arêtes** or knife-like ridges.

Lowland glaciation

Low-lying areas which have emerged from underneath glaciers contain distinctive features, different from those to be found in glaciated mountain regions. Glaciers passing over lowland regions form an ice sheet which is capable of eroding hollows in the bedrock and reshaping rock outcrops over which it passes. Most features of lowland glaciation are, however, the result of deposition under ice or by meltwater. About ten per cent of the earth's land area is covered by material left behind by Ice Age glaciers and ice sheets. This material is called **glacial drift** and consists of clay (fine rock dust), sand, gravel and boulders. As the ice melts this drift is deposited to form distinctive landforms.

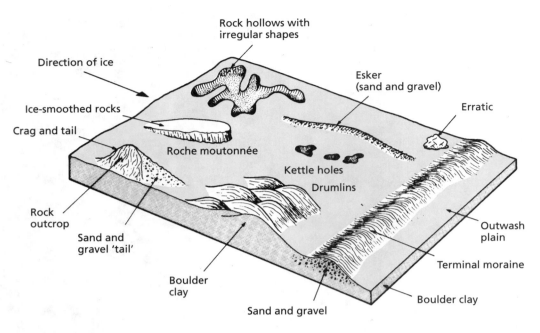

Fig. 1.14 Features of lowland glaciation

The features shown in Fig.1.14 were formed as follows:

Crag and tail—Hard resistant rock with a steep slope on one side and a gentle slope (the tail) of softer rock deposits on the other side.

Roches moutonnées—Outcrops of rock eroded by a glacier to form a steep slope on the downstream side and a gentle slope upstream. They are also a feature of valleys in regions of highland glaciation.

Irregularly shaped lakes—Hollows gouged from the bedrock by glaciers, in which lakes have formed. Northern Canada has many such lakes.

Esker—A snake-like winding ridge of sand and gravel. An esker usually follows the direction of ice flow. Eskers were formed by meltwater streams flowing in or on the ice. Eskers are common in Finland.

Kettle hole—A hollow in the ground, formed by lumps of ice melting within glacial material. There are many in central Ireland.

Drumlin—A smooth mound of boulder clay with a rock core, which is egg-shaped. Drumlins occur in 'swarms', making the landscape look like a 'basket of eggs'. It is not certain how they were formed. The central part of Glasgow is built on drumlins.

Erratic—A boulder carried some distance by a glacier before being deposited when the glacier melted. Erratics in East Anglia originated in Norway.

Terminal moraine—The final melting point of a glacier or ice-sheet. The moraine often forms low hills of sand and gravel. The Holt–Cromer ridge in Norfolk is the remnants of a terminal moraine.

Boulder clay—A clay formed from rock flour which sometimes contains larger pieces of rock. Much of East Anglia is covered by boulder clay.

Outwash plain—A plain covered by material washed away from a glacier or ice sheet. The material consists of sand, gravel and clay which have been sorted into layers by meltwater. Areas of the Midwest in the USA are part of a huge outwash plain.

 **xaminer's tip**

Add local examples to this list where possible.

The human uses of upland glaciated areas

The extensive snowfalls, magnificent mountain scenery and steep-sided valleys are used for a variety of activities. The main uses are: summer cattle and sheep pastures on the uplands, with cultivation on the valley floors; forestry; recreation; tourism; the production of hydroelectric power.

Tourism and skiing in the Scottish Highlands

The Grampian Mountains of Scotland are not as high as the Alps nor do they have pyramidal peaks. They are older mountains than the Alps and are more rounded, but the Ice Age has left its mark with U-shaped valleys, corries and steep slopes. The area has been a popular summer region for tourists for a long time but the development of winter sports has only taken place in the last thirty years. There are now five major ski centres which are busy between November and May and their development has resulted in conflicts of interest, particularly between the conservationists, local people and the promoters of the recreational facilities.

There are costs and benefits to the region as a result of the tourist developments that have taken place.

Costs	Benefits
Soil erosion caused by increase of tourists	Increased employment
More litter attracting lowland crows which rob nests of native birds	Population increasing, not declining as in other parts of Highlands
Increased danger of forest fires	Region meeting increased demand nationally for leisure facilities
Walkers scare deer	All-the-year round tourist resort
Rare birds such as golden eagle disturbed	Other tourist developments attracted to region, e.g. Malt Whisky Trail, Highland Wildlife Park
Rare arctic-alpine ecosystem in danger	

Hydroelectricity

Hydroelectricity has also been developed in the Scottish Highlands but on a much smaller scale than in the European Alps and the mountains of Scandinavia. The lakes and U–shaped valleys have been dammed to provide large quantities of **renewable energy** (energy that can be replaced without reducing the source).

1.6 Coastal environments

Coastal deposition

The aerial photograph of Northam Burrows (Fig.1.15) shows many of the features which are associated with the building up of a section of coastline by deposition of material. Waves are responsible for carrying much sand and shingle along a beach. When winds strike the beach at an angle, waves carry the material along the beach, causing what is known as **longshore drift**. Groynes are built to check this movement and it may also be stopped by a headland or a river mouth. **Currents** are also important carrying agents, particularly in estuaries where tidal currents may clear away deposits, carrying them further along the coast or out to sea.

Figure 1.16 shows a stretch of coastline with the prevailing winds blowing from the south-west. Beach material builds up to the west of the groynes and where there is an opening in the coast a spit develops with marshland behind. Parts of the south coast of England are being shaped in this way with longshore drift up the English Channel from west to east.

Figure 1.17 shows in detail how material such as pebbles moves along a small section of the beach shown in Fig.1.16 as a result of waves breaking at an oblique angle along the shoreline. The **swash** (forward movement) of the waves moves the material diagonally up the beach. The retreating water, or **backwash**, of the waves washes some of the material towards the sea and at right angles to the beach.

Spits

Spits occur where material carried along a coast is deposited as a result of the coast changing direction inwards at a bay or river mouth. The material is piled up on the sea bed and eventually forms a ridge which continues to grow at its tip. New material is added until a spit is formed such as at Orfordness in Suffolk or Spurn Head at the mouth of the Humber.

Material is deposited on the sheltered side during storms and marshes develop linking the spit with the previous coastline.

Fig. 1.15 Aerial view of Northam Burrows

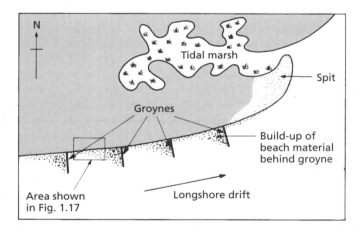

Fig. 1.16 Longshore drift

Waves and cross-currents can form a hook of material at the end of the spit and in time more hooks may be added as the spit grows.

Make a sketch the same size as the photograph, Fig.1.15, marking clearly the following:

1   tip of spit
2   hooked section
3   sand dunes
4   direction of prevailing wind

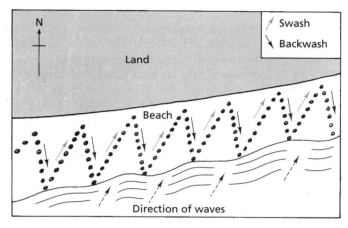

Fig. 1.17 Movement of pebbles along a beach

5 former cliff line
6 marshland
7 reclaimed farmland
8 direction of movement of material.

Bars and tombolos

A spit which grows across a bay, completely sealing it, is called a **bar**, an example is Slapton Sands, Devon. Lagoons and marshes fill the space between the bar and the mainland. Chesil Beach in Dorset has linked the Isle of Portland to the mainland, forming a special kind of connecting bar, called a **tombolo**.

Coastal erosion

The sea erodes in four different ways:
1. By **hydraulic action**, that is the pressure of the waves carrying material crashing against the shore and cliff face.
2. By **corrasion** (abrasion), with waves dragging pieces of rock up and down the beach and acting like a giant piece of glass paper.
3. By **attrition**, when the pieces of rock being carried are themselves worn down.
4. By **corrosion**, especially on coasts made of chalk or limestone where the rock is dissolved in the sea water.

When a stretch of coastline is made up of rocks of differing degrees of hardness, a series of headlands and bays is formed.

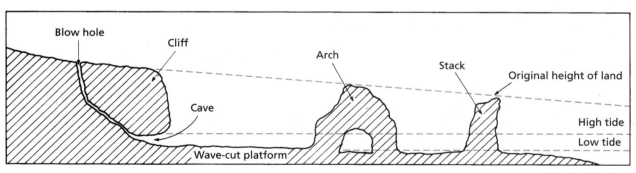

Fig. 1.18 Features of coastal erosion

At Lulworth Cove in Dorset the sea has broken through a layer of hard limestone parallel with the coast and has scooped out the softer rocks behind to form a curved bay.

Erosion of a shoreline by the sea results in the cutting back of the land, which, if it is hilly, will end in a sea cliff. At low tide a **wave–cut platform** marks the area where the cliffs once stood.

Undercutting of the cliffs by wave action may result in **caves**. Where the rocks are strongly jointed, compressed air caused by waves may force a channel up through the joints to the ground above. This results in a **blow hole**, which is most active during storms when waves surge through the cave below.

A **natural arch** is formed when two caves on either side of a headland join. Durdle Door in Dorset and the Needle Eye near Wick in Scotland are arches joined to the mainland. In time the arch is weakened by further erosion and collapses, leaving a stack. The Needles off the Isle of Wight are probably the best known stacks in England.

Sea level changes

Estuaries
An estuary is the tidal mouth of a river which has been widened by tidal currents and a change in base level as a result of sea level rising or the surrounding land sinking. Estuaries make ideal sites for ports and industrial developments. Examples in Britain include Thamesside, Merseyside and Clydeside.

Rias
The increase in sea level at the end of the Ice Age resulted in the submergence of some sections of coastline and the lower parts of the river valleys. In hilly areas the drowned valleys form a **ria**. A ria is funnel shaped and becomes more shallow inland. Surrounding hills rise from the edge of the river as the water has covered the original flood plain. Rias are common in southwest Ireland, Brittany and the south coast of Devon and Cornwall. Plymouth Sound is a ria with deep water, making a suitable anchorage for large ships.

Fjords
These occur in such regions as western Norway, British Columbia, Alaska and New Zealand. They are the result of the drowning of deep glacial valleys which have all the characteristics of glaciation—a U-shape, truncated spurs, hanging valleys and waterfalls.

The Sogne Fjord in Norway is 160 km long. Parallel to the mainland of fjord coasts there is often a series of islands, known in Norway as 'skerries'. They protect shipping from the worst of the storms, but harbours are rare because the fjords are usually too steep-sided for large ports to develop.

Raised beaches
A raised beach is a former beach that has been raised above sea level. The change in sea level is the result of land rising relative to the sea. Raised beaches are found in Scotland, with good examples on the Isle of Arran.

Coastal management

Examiner's tip

Prepare a case study about coastal erosion and management for a section of coast you know well.

Without careful management, sections of the British coastline would disappear under the sea. The Ministry of Agriculture, Fisheries and Food (MAFF) has overall responsibility for flooding and coastal defences. It spends over £350 million each year protecting the coastline. Local councils are responsible for the coastline within their boundaries, and must draw up plans and submit them to MAFF for local sea defence schemes. A percentage of the cost, often 25%, is paid by the MAFF from national funds, the rest must be raised from local taxes. In some areas, such as the coast south of Great Yarmouth in Norfolk, coastal erosion has taken place over hundreds of years and many villages have disappeared into the sea. Some stretches of this coastline are being eroded at a rate of 5 metres a year, and the local council has decided to allow some erosion to go unchecked as the cost of shoring up the cliffs cannot be justified. Elsewhere in Britain strengthening sea defences is essential, in particular the replacing of **groynes**—wooden barriers to check longshore drift.

1.7 Limestone and chalk environments

Landscapes as systems

Landscapes are systems because they are the result of inputs and processes which interact to produce an output in the form of distinctive scenery.

The main *inputs* are:

- the underlying rock and its structure
- climate past and present
- people.

The *processes* involved include:

- weathering and erosion
- deposition of sediment
- human economic activities.

The main *outputs* are:

- scenery, some of which is of great scenic value
- valuable resources including water supply.

Interaction between the natural processes and human activities may give rise to conflicting demands on the environment.

Limestone

Limestone is a form of **calcium carbonate**, which is usually deposited in thick layers. The horizontal divisions are known as **bedding planes**, and **joints** are the vertical divisions that form after deposition.

Rain water, which is slightly acidic, dissolves limestone (**chemical weathering**) and works its way down the joints and along the bedding planes until it reaches an

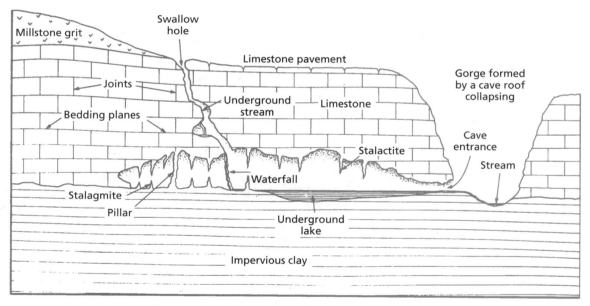

Fig. 1.19 A cross-section of a limestone area

impervious layer. On the surface a '**pavement**' may occur where the bare limestone is exposed in blocks.

Swallow holes are found where the water disappears underground. The scenery of limestone areas is sometimes known as **karst topography**.

Underground features

The dissolving of the limestone results in the development of **underground tunnels and caves**, which are explored by pot-holers. Water rich in calcium drips from the ceilings of these caves to form deposits known as **stalactites** (which hang down), and **stalagmites** (which grow up from the floor). They sometimes join to form pillars and other weird shapes, examples of which may be seen at Kent's Cave near Torquay in Devon, Ingleborough Cave in Yorkshire, and at Cheddar. Underground lakes may occur, with the water reaching the surface many kilometres from the point where it disappears below ground, Fig 1.19.

Natural arches and gorges

Sometimes the roof of a limestone cave collapses, forming a **steep-sided gorge**. If part of the roof survives it forms a natural arch. Gordale Scar near Malham and Trow Ghyll gorge, also in Yorkshire, are both examples formed by the collapse of caves. Cheddar Gorge was most likely formed by river action when the water table was higher.

Chalk scenery

Chalk, a softer rock than limestone, is soluble in rainwater but does not usually produce underground caves. When the rocks are tilted, **scarp and dip slopes** are formed. The dip slope ending in a scarp is called a **cuesta**. Springs appear where the chalk meets clays or similar impervious layers. Water soaks underground so there are no streams, except where rivers cross chalk areas, such as in the Mole valley at Dorking or the river Ouse at Lewes. The scenery produces rolling hills, like Salisbury Plain, with **dry valleys** where streams used to flow when the water table was higher.

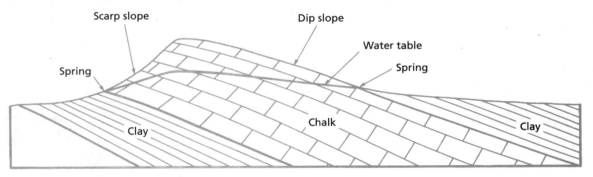

Fig. 1.20 A cross-section of a chalk cuesta

Water held in the chalk saturates the lower layers. The upper surface of this zone of saturated rock is called the **water table**. The water table will come closer to the surface in wet weather and fall during dry spells. Its level is also affected by water being pumped out of the chalk to provide the water supply for neighbouring regions.

Figure 1.21 can be used to demonstrate chalk scenery as a system. Under the headings, Inputs, Processes and Outputs, describe the chalk landscape shown in the sketch.

Human activities in limestone and chalk landscapes

Limestone is an important building stone. Many cathedrals and well-known buildings such as the Houses of Parliament are built of this rock. In some areas it is also used to build dry-stone walls around fields. Both limestone and chalk are sources of lime, which is used in making mortar and cement. It is also used as a fertiliser, particularly on acid soils.

Limestone caves are valuable sources of information about prehistoric people who used them for shelter. For example, early Iron and Bronze Age implements have been found in Kent's Cavern near Torbay in Devon. Early cave paintings have made the limestone caves at Lascaux in France and Altamira in Spain world famous.

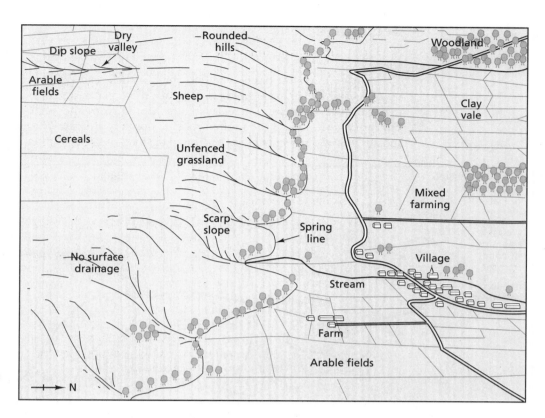

Fig. 1.21 A chalk landscape—the South Downs

Conflicting demands on the landscape

Areas of limestone scenery with underground cave systems and attractive countryside are important tourist regions. Larger underground caves such as Wookey Hole near Cheddar are tourist attractions, while less accessible cave-systems attract pot-holers. There are a number of limestone outcrops in Britain including the Cotswolds, the Mendips, and the Peak District and Yorkshire Dales National Parks. Limestone landscapes are also common in other parts of the world including the Cévennes National Park in France, the Dolomites of northern Italy and the Carlsbad Caverns National Park in New Mexico, USA.

Extensive quarrying of both limestone and chalk produces eyesores which can dominate a scenic area. In the Peak District National Park there are a number of limestone quarries. The best known eyesore, Eldon Hill quarry, near Castleton in Derbyshire, closed in 1997. An attempt to extend its life until 2004 was refused by the Peak District Authority following a public enquiry. New applications to extract limestone are carefully examined but not always rejected. The need to keep the natural landscape relatively undisturbed for tourists is in conflict with the need by industry for limestone and chalk. Employment in the quarries and associated works is available for local people but the hillside eyesores, increase in traffic, noise and dust are environmentally controversial.

1.8 Environmental hazards

Types of hazard

There are two major types of natural hazard which can cause considerable damage and loss of life:

- **Tectonic activity**—forces operating on the earth's crust producing volcanic activity, earthquakes and tsunamis.
- **Extreme weather and climate**—floods, cyclones, hurricanes, tornadoes, drought.

Tectonic activity

Plates

The earth we live on has a very thin shell of rock, called the **crust**. This crust is made up of several pieces, called **plates**. Beneath these plates are partially molten layers which make up the **mantle**. These layers are heated from the earth's core by **convection currents** which cause the molten rock to flow towards the crust, where it is cooled and spreads before sinking back to be heated again.

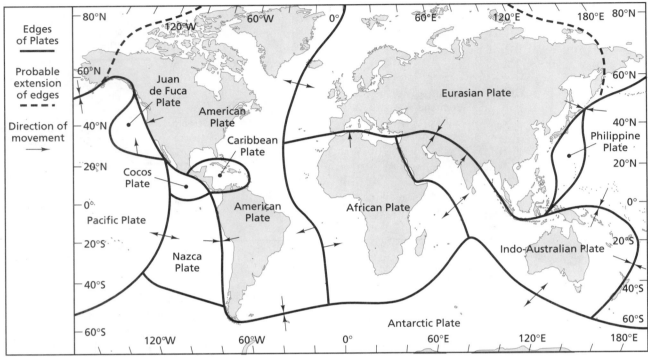

Fig. l.22 Plate boundaries

The plates shown on Fig. 1.22 move slowly over the mantle in the directions shown by the arrows. This means that in some mid–ocean areas the plates are moving apart. Molten rock rises to form a **ridge** where the plates are separating. Elsewhere, as around the edge of the Pacific Ocean, plates move past each other or collide. When two plates collide, one rides over the other, and rocks on or near the earth's surface are **folded** and pushed up to form mountain chains, such as the Alps and Andes. Plates which are moving together are called **converging** plates, while plates moving apart are **diverging**.

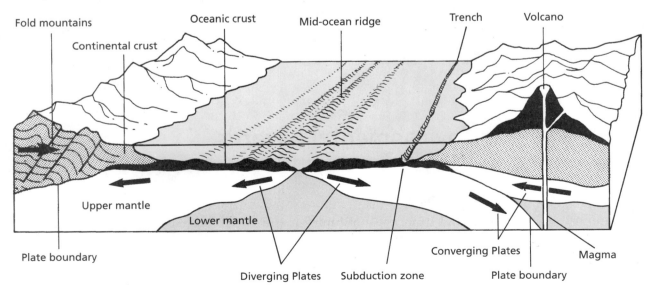

Fig.l .23 Converging and diverging plates

Volcanoes

The boundaries of plates, or **plate margins**, are zones of weakness in the earth's crust and it is here that volcanoes and earthquakes occur.

A volcano erupts when pressure from gases and steam within the earth's crust fractures the crust, allowing the gases and solid and molten magma to escape. Volcanoes may be **active**, **dormant** or **extinct**.

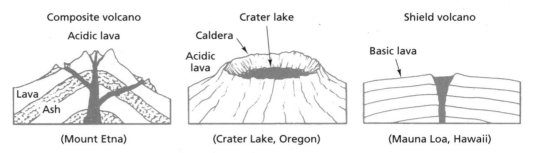

Fig. 1.24 Types of volcanoes

Lava is molten magma which hardens when it has been cooled at the surface. If the lava is **acidic** it contains much silica and it hardens quickly, building steep-sided volcanoes. These are likely to erupt explosively because the vents are sealed by the hardened lava. If it is **basic** lava (rich in iron and other minerals) it cools slowly and may spread out to form a shield volcano. The eruption may be quiet, as the vent is not sealed. Fine powdered lava may also be ejected. This falls as ash and makes an **ash cone.**

Composite cones are made up of layers of ash and lava flows. Some of the lava may flow from **secondary vents**. Mount Etna in Sicily has many such vents.

Some volcanoes have lost the main part of the cone by eruptions or earth movements, leaving a huge rounded basin which is called a **caldera**. Lakes may fill the bottom of the basin with the steep crater sides giving a saucer-like shape. Crater Lake in Oregon, USA fills an ancient caldera.

Although there are no active volcanoes in Britain there are a number of outcrops of volcanic rocks. These include the Giant's Causeway in Northern Ireland, the Campsie Fells in Central Scotland and the central plug or 'neck' of a volcano which forms King Arthur's Seat near Edinburgh.

Eruption of Mount Pinatubo

Mt. Pinatubo in the Philippines is one of the hundreds of volcanoes that form a 'ring of fire' around the Pacific Ocean. It erupted in 1991 and 1992, throwing millions of tonnes of ash into the upper atmosphere and covering the ground with a thick layer. Rainstorms turned the ash into mud and mud slides destroyed many homes, killing more than 500 people. Crops were ruined and over half a million people lost their livelihood. The large United States Air Force base nearby was closed down.

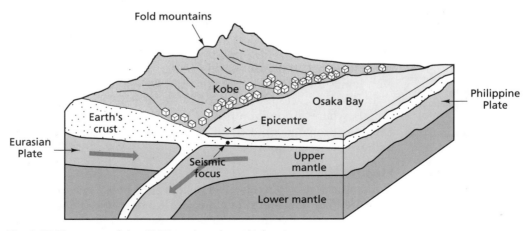

Fig. 1.25 The cause of the 1995 earthquake at Kobe, Japan

Tsunamis

Earthquakes which occur on or under the sea bed can cause waves which increase in magnitude in shallow waters near a coast. In 1983 over 50 people were killed by waves which struck the north-west coast of Japan. The Japanese word *tsunami* is given to this phenomenon.

Earthquake at Kobe

In January 1995 an earthquake severely damaged the port city of Kobe in Japan. It measured 7.2 on the **Richter Scale** and resulted from movement of the Eurasian Plate against the Philippine Plate Fig.1.25.

The tremor lasted less than a minute but over 5500 people were killed, many more were injured and a quarter of a million lost their homes. Buildings, bridges, roads and railway lines were badly damaged. Over a million homes were without gas, water or electricity Fig. 1.26.

Fig 1.26 Photo of Kobe after earthquake, January 17th , 1995

Extreme weather and climate

Examiner's tip

Collect newspaper cuttings about a natural disaster. Prepare a case study on the disaster.

Cyclones

Areas of very low pressure in the tropics are called cyclones. They bring violent storms with winds up to 240 km per hour and torrential rain.

In 1991 a cyclone moved from the Bay of Bengal to the low-lying delta of the Ganges where 110 million people live. The strong winds brought a tidal surge and over 150 000 drowned or died of disease and starvation. The salty flood water ruined millions of hectares of rice.

Floods

Flooding can take place in river valleys after heavy rain or along low-lying coasts when there are high tides and strong onshore winds. Severe flooding of the coast of East Anglia and the Netherlands in 1953 drowned over 2000 people. Heavy rain can also cause mud slides. In the summer of 1996 a mud slide in the Pyrenees killed 23 at a valley campsite.

Hurricanes, Typhoons, Tornadoes

These are violent tropical cyclones with high winds blowing round the low pressure centre called the 'eye'. Hurricanes occur in the Caribbean and along the east coast of the United States and Canada. Typhoons move across the Pacific to the coasts of eastern Asia.

Tornadoes, sometimes called 'twisters' are whirling winds up to a kilometre wide that move over the land as a funnel-shaped cloud. All these cyclones leave a trail of damage in their paths.

Drought

Shortages of water may result from long, dry spells of weather like the summer of 1995 in Britain. Drought may also occur as a result of human activities such as **deforestation**, **over-grazing**, **urbanisation** and intensive farming using **irrigation**. Countries bordering the Mediterranean such as Spain, which attract large numbers of tourists to their beaches in summer, suffer from severe water shortages.

Coping with environmental hazards

More Economically Developed Countries (MEDCs) are able to cope with natural disasters better than Less Economically Developed Countries (LEDCs) because they have more money available when there is a crisis. For example:

Early warning of a possible disaster
- MEDCs—The United States has a National Hurricane Centre near Miami. Two satellites relay pictures from above the storm and 'Storm Tracker' planes follow the storm.
- LEDCs—Few experts are available. Limited number of scientific instruments available. In Bangladesh only 63 out of 500 shelters were built when a cyclone approached.

Limiting effects
- MEDCs—Thames Barrier to prevent flooding. Dutch Delta Plan (see Unit 6.5). Large buildings in Japan have rubber blocks and springs to allow movement in earthquake.
- LEDCs—Buildings in Mexico City collapsed in the 1995 earthquake; they were not built to sway.

Assistance after disaster
- MEDCs—Rapid repairs to roads, electricity and water supplies using modern expensive equipment.
  Despite all the advanced technology and scientific research in Japan the Kobe earthquake showed that structures such as motorways were not safe. Geophysicists did not know that an earthquake was imminent, despite the government spending £637 million on earthquake research in the last thirty years.
- LEDC—Damage in Philippines not repaired months after Mt. Pinatubo erupted.

1.9 Soils and Ecosystems

Soils

What soil is made of

Soil is the surface material covering the Earth and it is made of **minerals** from the parent material, **organic matter**, called **humus,** decomposed plants and living creatures, **air** and **water**. Soils differ depending on the **parent material**; the **climate** (a very important factor because it will decide the natural vegetation); length of growing season; rainfall and temperatures; amount of **organic material**; the **relief**; the **time** involved.

Soil profiles

The various soil types throughout the world correspond closely with the climatic and vegetation regions. A vertical section through the soil from ground level to the parent rock is called a **soil profile**. The profile consists of different layers, called **horizons**. Figure.1.27 shows two contrasting soil profiles, soil formed in the temperate grasslands regions which is called a **chernozem** soil, and a **podsol,** the soil of the coniferous forest regions. These large regions with similar climates, soils and natural vegetation are called **biomes.**

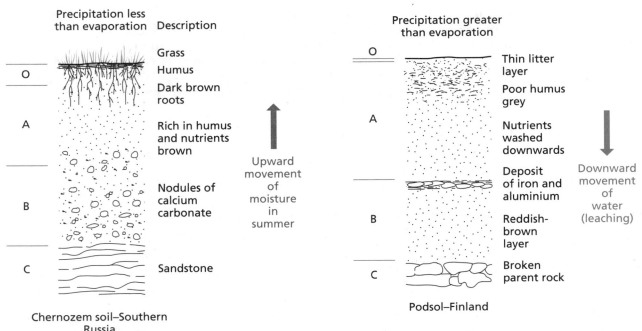

Fig. 1.27 Contrasting soil profiles

Ecosystems

Biomes are very large **ecosystems**. Figure.1.28 shows two examples of biomes. An ecosystem is a community of plants and animals which share the same environment. The life cycles of these plants and animals are linked to one another, to the climate and to the part of the earth's surface they inhabit.

Ecosystems can vary in scale. Examples of small ecosystems are a pond, a tree, a hedgerow and a shingle bank. Larger ecosystems include mountain pastures, woodland,

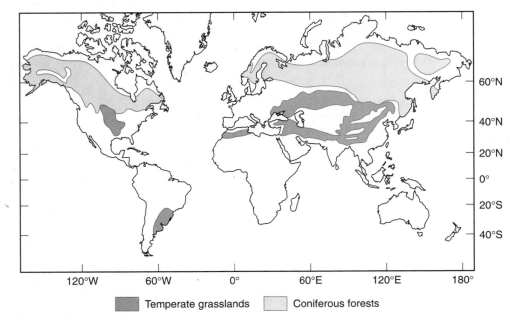

■ Temperate grasslands   □ Coniferous forests

Fig. 1.28 Two vegetation regions

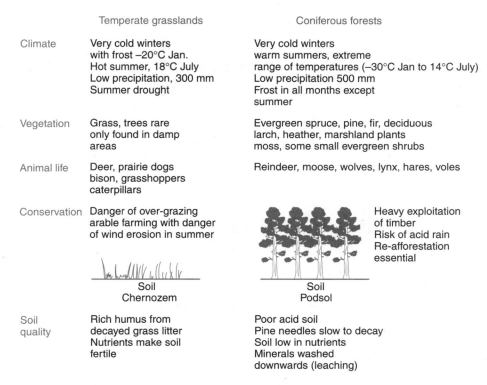

	Temperate grasslands	Coniferous forests
Climate	Very cold winters with frost −20°C Jan. Hot summer, 18°C July Low precipitation, 300 mm Summer drought	Very cold winters warm summers, extreme range of temperatures (−30°C Jan to 14°C July) Low precipitation 500 mm Frost in all months except summer
Vegetation	Grass, trees rare only found in damp areas	Evergreen spruce, pine, fir, deciduous larch, heather, marshland plants moss, some small evergreen shrubs
Animal life	Deer, prairie dogs bison, grasshoppers caterpillars	Reindeer, moose, wolves, lynx, hares, voles
Conservation	Danger of over-grazing arable farming with danger of wind erosion in summer	Heavy exploitation of timber Risk of acid rain Re-afforestation essential
	Soil Chernozem	Soil Podsol
Soil quality	Rich humus from decayed grass litter Nutrients make soil fertile	Poor acid soil Pine needles slow to decay Soil low in nutrients Minerals washed downwards (leaching)

Fig.1.29 Two contrasting world ecosystems

a salt marsh and a heather moor. The largest ecosystems are the global climatic and vegetation regions which include the tundra, tropical rain forests and hot deserts. Figure.1.29 describes the ecosystems of the temperate grasslands and the coniferous forest regions.

Human interference with ecosystems

Ecosystems are very sensitive and the balance between the components is easily upset by human interference (see Units 4.5, 4.6). This interference can take many forms. For example, ecosystems may be damaged when a new road is built, when resources such as rock are removed from a hillside, when new housing development takes place and when natural environments are overrun by tourists. Other examples of human interference with ecosystems include the following:

- The removal of **peat** from moorland for sale as a garden fertiliser. Public awareness of this problem has resulted in firms importing coconut fibre as an alternative fertiliser for gardens.
- Cutting down of **softwood timber** for the paper industry and building. Paper firms are replacing the trees cut down with young saplings. This is known as a **sustainable** development. There is also a world-wide movement to recycle paper to help conserve timber resources.

1.10 Pollution

Pollution is the fouling of the environment by human activities. It can harm or kill living things and make places less pleasant to visit or live in. Oil from a tanker can kill birds, seals and fish. It can also ruin beaches and discourage tourists.

Acid rain

In recent years, there has been growing concern at the damage to plants and fish caused by rainfall which can be as acidic as weak vinegar. Acidity is measured on the **pH scale**. This scale ranges from 0 for solids and liquids that are completely acid, to 14 for high

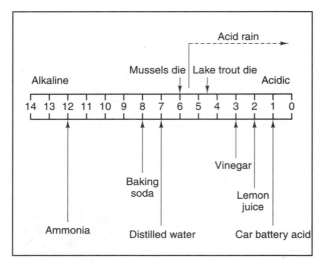

Fig. 1.30 pH values

alkalinity. A pH of 7 is neutral and is the value of distilled water. Normal rainfall is slightly acidic, with a pH value of 5.6, because it contains carbonic acid formed by the reaction of rain water with carbon dioxide in the atmosphere.

Acid rain has pH values of less than 5.6, and the acidity is caused by **sulphur** and **nitrogen** gases in the atmosphere. These gases are emitted from the chimney stacks of power stations, smelters and factories. Nitrogen oxides also come from car exhausts. Some of these gases form as a fine dust in the air and collect on buildings or fall on the soil not far from where they were formed. This type of pollution is called '**dry deposition**'. It eats away at stonework and shortens the life of metals and paints. Many buildings, including the Statue of Liberty, the Canadian Parliament building in Ottawa, the Houses of Parliament in London and Salisbury Cathedral have had to have extensive repairs to stone and metal which has become corroded.

Gases from furnaces which reach the upper air can be carried by the prevailing winds for long distances. During the journey they combine with water vapour in clouds to form weak sulphuric and nitric acids. These fall to the ground as '**acid rain**', or as hail, snow or sleet with an acid content.

This wet deposition can occur up to 2000 kilometres from its source and may not, therefore, originate in the same country as it pollutes, Fig. 1.31. The effects of acid rain are as follows:

1 Coniferous trees turn yellow, the needles fall and the trees die. In Germany about 80% of the fir trees are estimated to be affected in this way.

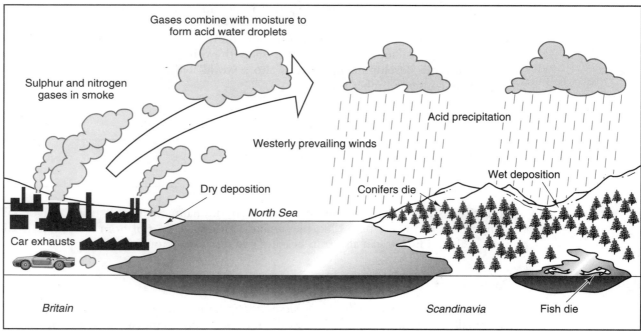

Fig. 1.31 How Britain exports acid rain to Scandinavia

② Polluted water accumulates in lakes, killing fish. In Sweden 9000 lakes are 'dead' and in Norway fish have disappeared from 7000 lakes.

③ Most plant life in the lakes also dies; without green plankton the lakes look abnormally clear.

④ Some mosses and algae grow more vigorously and the food chain in acid lakes is radically changed.

⑤ Acid rain is harmful to amphibians such as frogs.

⑥ Plumbing systems can be corroded, with acid dissolving copper into the water.

Countries affected

The main areas affected are the industrial zones of the northern hemisphere, particularly the north-eastern states of the USA and Eastern Canada, while in Europe acid rain is most severe in Scandinavia, Germany and parts of Central and Eastern Europe. EU measurements show that Britain is responsible for about one-tenth of the sulphur dioxide pollution of the air, more than any other European country.

Acid rain is the cause of a dispute between Canada and the United States. Measuring instruments show that half of all chemical depositions in Canada come from the USA, mainly blown north-east from coal-fired power stations in the midwestern states. In the USA there are complaints about smelters in Mexico, but smelters on both sides of the border generate 1100 tonnes of pollutants each day. The case against acid rain is not completely proven. The acidification of the environment by coniferous trees themselves is important, especially on some rock types. Many experiments are being carried out to identify the ecological disaster which is taking place.

Remedies

In Sweden, one thousand severely affected lakes have been **limed** to reduce acidity temporarily. Liming is expensive, and only a short-term remedy. It is possible to remove most of the sulphur and nitrogen gases before they reach the atmosphere by putting filters in chimneys. It is calculated that this would increase electricity prices by up to 10%. Environmental groups claim that the cost of acid rain is far greater.

The British Generating Boards and the government are installing **filters** at three large power stations as a first measure to reduce acid rain fall-out.

Smog

When polluted dust from car exhausts and chimneys accumulates near the ground, a form of fog called **smog** (**smoke** and **fog**) is formed. This can irritate the eyes and make it difficult for people with respiratory illnesses to breathe. In some cases smog can cause death. Smog is most common in large cities with heavy traffic, such as Los Angeles, Mexico City, Tokyo and Sydney. It occurs when there is no wind and there is an **inversion layer** caused by temperature inversion (temperature rising at a height above the earth's surface instead of falling) Fig. 1.32. The introduction of smokeless fuels and cleaner car exhaust emissions can help to reduce the risk of smog.

Remedies

Countries which suffer from smog are tackling the problem in a variety of ways. Although it is caused by industry as well as by vehicles the emphasis has been on

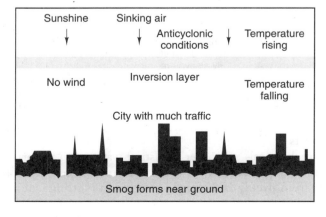

Fig. 1.32 How smog forms

reducing pollution from vehicles.

- **Catalytic converters** Many countries make it compulsory to fit new cars with catalytic converters, which reduce harmful gases from the exhaust.
- **Monitoring exhaust fumes** Older cars in California must pass an annual smog test. 'Smog Dogs' beam infrared light across lines of traffic instantly recording levels of carbon monoxide and hydrocarbons from the exhausts of passing vehicles. In Mexico City 'Green Police' are able to fine drivers of polluting vehicles. Unfortunately, the police are poorly paid and often take a bribe to turn a blind eye.
- **Reducing traffic flows** In Greece traffic has been banned from the centre of Athens. In Italy, Naples and Genoa have imposed two-day bans when the air is highly polluted. In Germany speed limits are reduced during periods of bad pollution. Singapore limits the number of cars on the road by high taxes and a quota scheme for new cars.

Water pollution

Examiner's tip

Make sure you know the reasons why water and air become polluted and how pollution is being tackled.

Pollution of rivers, lakes and the sea on a far greater scale than that from acid rain is caused by chemicals entering drainage basins, or the discharge of untreated sewage, oil and similar pollutants into the sea. In addition, some radioactive materials are also pumped into the sea from nuclear power stations or nuclear reprocessing plants like the one at Sellafield in Cumbria.

The main sources of pollution are farm chemicals, factory effluents, toxic refuse, domestic sewage and oil contamination.

Farm chemicals

Run-off from fertilised fields pollutes waterways and lakes. The main chemicals are nitrates and phosphates, used as fertilisers, and smaller quantities of chemicals used in herbicides and pesticides. Since 1945 the Norfolk Broads have become increasingly polluted, mainly by run-off from the surrounding fields. High nitrate levels cause changes in **food chains** (see Fig. 1.33), destroying wildlife and affecting all but four of the 52 Broads.

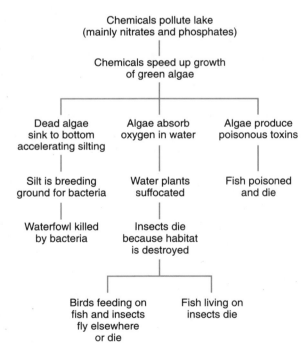

Fig. 1.33 Alterations to a food chain in a polluted lake

Factory effluents

These consist of chemicals and other industrial waste from factories and mine workings. The River Trent is polluted from a number of sources. It collects a great deal of chemical waste from dyeing and bleaching works in Nottingham and Leicester.

Toxic chemicals

Dangerous chemical refuse is usually buried in dumps, but in recent years attention has been drawn to leakage from these dumps. Scientists have identified 1000 man-made chemicals in the Great Lakes of North America, most of which came from dumps in the USA. Like acid rain, this form of pollution does not help USA–Canadian relations.

Domestic sewage

Sewage from urban areas pollutes both drainage basins and the sea. The cheapest way of disposing of sewage is to pipe it, untreated, to the nearest river, or in the case of coastal towns, to pump it a short distance out to sea. Inland towns normally treat raw sewage, so that effluent leaving the works is relatively harmless.

The EU requires sewage outfall pipes from coastal works to extend for at least 500 metres beyond the low water mark. Most outfall pipes in Britain extend only 100 metres, and raw sewage can easily be washed back on to the beaches. Almost half the beaches in England and Wales fail to reach the standard of cleanliness set by the EU. These beaches include those of such well-known resorts as Blackpool, Rhyl, Brighton, Eastbourne and Clacton-on-Sea.

Oil and tar

Oil contamination comes mainly from oil tankers illegally cleaning their tanks. Spillage as the result of shipwreck, although relatively rare, can be quite disastrous. In 1996 the large oil tanker *Sea Empress* ran aground at the entrance to Milford Haven with its oil refineries. Over half the storage tanks leaked more than 65 000 tonnes of oil into the sea. The coastal beaches were seriously polluted with oil and important bird sanctuaries like Skomer Island were affected.

Radioactive waste

Water which is slightly **radioactive** is sometimes discharged from atomic power stations. These discharges are sometimes accidental, but the nuclear reprocessing plant at Sellafield has discharged polluted water deliberately. There have also been leaks which have contaminated local beaches and raised the radioactive level of the Irish Sea.

Summary

---

1 Weather and climate are determined by a number of inter-related factors. Air masses have distinct characteristics which are passed on to areas they cross.

2 Day to day variations in British weather are caused by air masses with differing characteristics.

3 The heat balance of the globe is being altered by the increase of gases in the atmosphere as the result of human activities.

4 A drainage basin is an example of an open system.

5 Upland glaciated regions can have considerable value for tourism but overuse can result in environmental problems.

6 Coastal regions need to be carefully managed to prevent erosion and damage to the environment.

7 Limestone is soluble in rain water and a number of surface and underground features are the result.

8 MEDCs are more able to cope with natural disasters than LEDCs.

9 Ecosystems are very fragile and the balance between the components is easily upset.

10 Pollution can cross international borders and destroy ecosystems.

11 Illegal cleaning of ships' tanks with seawater close to land is often the cause of the patches of tar which pollute beaches around Britain, the Mediterranean and other parts of the world.

Quick test

1.1 Weather and climate

1 The three types of rainfall are ...., ... and ....
2 On a clear calm night in winter the earth's surface cools by ....
3 What does an anemometer measure?
4 Where is a Tm air mass formed?
5 What is the radiant energy that reaches the earth's surface from the sun called?

1.2 Interpretation of weather maps and meteorological information

6 Anticyclones are areas of .... pressure.
7 Using Fig.1.4 on page 28, what were the weather conditions at C?
8 Using Fig.1.4, was the pressure at D high or low?
9 Using Fig.1.4, was there rain, snow or drizzle at A?
10 As low pressure approaches, the barometer ....

1.3 Global warming

11 Outgoing reradiation is absorbed by water vapour and ....
12 Which one of the following releases chlorofluorocarbons (CFCs), fertiliser, aerosols, coal?
13 Why will sea levels rise if global temperatures increase?
14 Changes in the earth's heat balance is called ....
15 Name one fossil fuel.

1.4 The hydrological cycle: drainage basins

16 The seepage of water into the soil is called ....
17 What is transpiration?
18 What is the bombardment of the river bed and sides by debris carried by the stream called?
19 The material deposited by a stream is called ....
20 A storm hydrograph shows .... over a period of time.

1.5 Glacial environments

21 Material carried down by a glacier is called ....
22 What is a snake-like winding ridge of sand and gravel deposited by meltwater streams called?
23 Give one other name for a corrie.
24 What is glacial drift?
25 Which Scottish mountains are popular for skiing?

1.6 Coastal environments

26 How is longshore drift caused?
27 The forward movement of waves is known as the ....
28 Name a British example of a tombolo.
29 How is a natural arch formed?
30 Which government department has overall responsibility for coastal management?

1.7 Limestone and chalk environments

31 Where bare limestone blocks are exposed on the surface a .... may form.

32 What is a stalagmite and where are stalagmites found?

33 The upper surface of a zone of saturated rock is called the ....

34 When chalk rock is tilted .... and .... slopes are formed.

35 Are the Cotswolds made of chalk or limestone?

1.8 Environmental hazards

36 What is a plate?

37 Basic lava cools slowly to form a .... volcano.

38 The point above the seismic focus of an earthquake is called the ....

39 Typhoons move across the Pacific towards ....

40 What does the Richter Scale measure?

1.9 Soils and ecosystems

41 A soil profile consists of different layers called ....

42 Is a chernozem soil found in the tundra or temperate grasslands?

43 What is an ecosystem?

44 Organic matter in the soil decomposed to a dark-coloured material is called ....

45 What is a sustainable development?

1.10 Pollution

46 Which two gases in the atmosphere cause acid rain?

47 Smog may form when there is no wind and temperature inversion causing an .... to form.

48 Which farm chemicals can pollute lakes and waterways?

49 What is fitted to the exhaust of a car to reduce pollution?

50 Name one form of pollution which can affect beaches.

Chapter 2
Population

2.1 The growth of world population

Figure 2.1 shows how rapidly the population of the world has grown since 1750. Before that time, the total population was more or less stable. Over the last 200 years, however, the rate of growth has become increasingly rapid. Estimates suggest that the rate will continue to increase into the 21st century.

Definition of terms

The following terms occur frequently in discussion of issues relating to population:

Population explosion
If there is a sudden decrease in the death rate which is accompanied by an increase in the birth rate overall growth may be very rapid. This is called a population explosion.

Natural increase
Natural increase is the difference between the birth and death rate. This may be positive or negative. For example, if the death rate exceeds the birth rate the total population (ignoring the effects of migration) will fall so that the natural increase has a negative value.

Figure 2.2 shows how the rates of natural increase varied throughout the world in 1995. The most striking feature is the high rate of increase of over 3% in Africa and the Middle East.

E **xaminer's tip**

These definitions are important. They are often used as short questions.

Fig. 2.1 World population growth

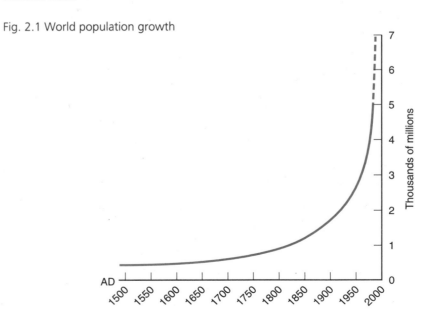

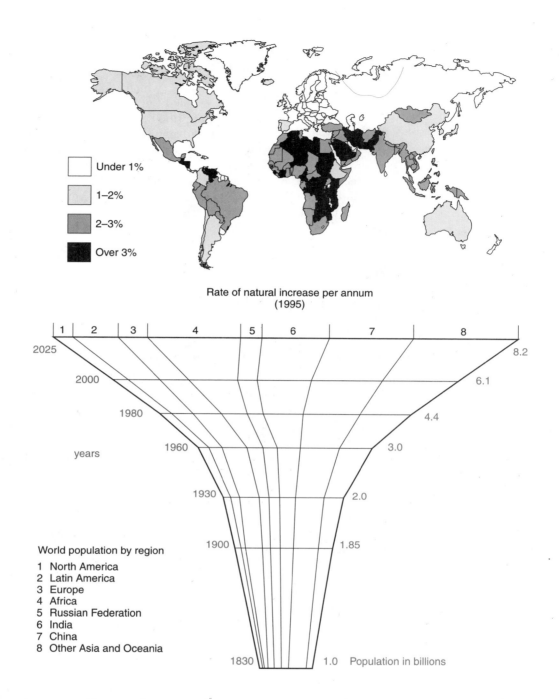

Fig. 2.2 Variable rates of population increase worldwide

The lower part of the figure shows the pattern of population growth since 1830. Different rates of population growth since 1960 in particular will produce major changes in the world pattern of population if estimates are fulfilled. By 2025 it is estimated that Europe and North America will become much less significant in terms of population size.

Population density

Population density is the average number of people living in a particular area, e.g. 500 per square kilometre. Densities may vary significantly within countries, e.g. in Egypt, where the vast amount of people live in the Nile Valley and most of the rest of the country is relatively empty. In the UK the density of population for the country as a whole is 239 per square kilometre. In some inner city areas, however, it reaches over 5000 per square kilometre. This contrasts with a sparsely populated country such as Norway where the overall density is 14 per square kilometre.

Reasons for the rapid increase in population in modern times

1. The middle of the 18th century saw the start of the **agricultural** and **industrial** 'revolutions' in Western Europe, which affected the rest of the world. Scientific developments in farming enabled the production of food crops and meat to be increased tremendously, so the land could support far more people.

2. The new industries required many more workers and raw materials. **New forms of transport** made it possible to collect food supplies and raw materials from any part of the world. Migrants from the industrial countries took the new technology and knowledge to 'empty' lands such as the Pampas and Prairies. They established new nations in North America, South America and Australasia. The new countries themselves began to grow rapidly.

3. Modern developments in science included a vast **increase in medical knowledge**. Fewer infants now die at birth and elderly people live longer. There has, therefore, been a tremendous 'natural increase' of population.

4. **Modern technology and communications** also enable us to offset the worst effects of famine, flood and pestilence, so that fewer people now die from natural hazards.

5. Many societies do not believe in **birth control**, so the population grows rapidly.

Problems of population growth

There were approximately 5734 million people in the world in 1995. The problem is not so much the size of the population, but its **rate of growth**. There has been a population explosion in the 20th century and it is estimated that by the year 2025 the world will have a population of approximately 8200 million people (see Fig. 2.2). At present there are over 12 000 additional mouths to feed every hour and the majority of these are in LEDCs which have little food to spare and cannot afford to buy extra food and resources on world markets.

The main problems are as follows:

1. The world does not have unlimited resources. As the earth becomes the home of more and more people, sources of raw materials will decline and shortages will occur. Eventually some resources, such as oil, may be used up altogether.

2. The MEDCs use up more of the world's resources than the poorer countries, even though their populations are smaller and are increasing more slowly. Per capita income in the United States rose from $7000 to $25 860 between 1955 and 1995. In India it only increased from $170 to $310.

3. The poorer countries which have the most rapid increases in population are unable to increase their food production rapidly. If they borrow money from the rich nations, they are in danger of losing their political independence.

4. Low levels of education and inadequate facilities make it extremely difficult to introduce birth control programmes to some LEDCs.

5. Tradition, the pattern of life in the villages (more children means more breadwinners) and religious beliefs also discourage birth control.

6. Only about one-fifth of the land area of the world can be used for agriculture and habitation. There are vast areas of land, such as the hot deserts, which are likely to remain unproductive and underpopulated for the forseeable future.

7. The difficulty of adequately housing and providing food for the increasing population can lead to unrest, high crime rates and the breakdown of law and order. To some extent this has already happened in parts of South America and Africa.

8. Rapid population growth leads to **increasing urbanisation**. This reduces the amount of farmland and puts pressure on such facilities as recreational areas. It also increases the likelihood of social problems and the deterioration of facilities such as health care.

Dealing with the problems of population growth

Increasing agricultural output

This can be done in two ways:

1. opening up new areas for farming, such as the desert margins and forested areas.

② increasing yields from land already farmed. The Green Revolution (see Unit 4.4) is an example of increasing yields by scientific methods.

Migration
In some countries, less-developed regions can be more fully utilised, for example the interior of Brazil. Migration on a massive scale is unlikely to solve the problem.

Limiting population growth
The Roman Catholic, Hindu and Muslim religions are all opposed to family planning. Some countries, such as India, Thailand and Indonesia have introduced widespread family planning campaigns. China has been even more drastic by encouraging families to have only one child. Eighty-five LEDCs now provide some form of public support for family planning programmes.

Table 2.1 World population (millions)

Country	1960	1990	2010 (projected)
Brazil	73	153	184
China	688	1150	1345
Egypt	26	54	81
Nigeria	52	118	162
U.S.A.	181	251	301
Indonesia	110	181	250
World	3037	5321	7027

2.2 Population change and living standards

Birth and death rates

The population of a country or region is the result of the difference between the birth rate and the death rate. The **birth rate** is the number of live births per 1000 people per year. The **death rate** is the number of deaths per 1000 people per year. In the United Kingdom at the present time the birth rate is 13 per 1000 people whereas the death rate is 11 per 1000 people. This gives a **natural increase** in the population of 0.2% per year. Throughout history birth rates have exceeded death rates except during such hazards as famine and war. Population change is also affected by **migration**, see Unit 2.4.

The demographic transition model

Examiner's tip

This is an important model. Make sure you can describe the different stages shown in Fig. 2.3.

Using past birth and death rate statistics over a long period of time for a number of MEDCs, a model has been developed called the **demographic transition model**. It suggests that all countries pass through similar population stages, Fig. 2.3. After fluctuating high birth and death rates in Stage 1, death rates fall because of better medical care and improved food production. With the birth rate fairly constant, the fall in the death rate results in a rapid population increase in Stage 2 of the model. In Stage 3 birth rates also fall because of family planning and the desire for more material possessions instead of children. In Stage 4 birth and death rates level out. According to the model this sequence of change should apply to LEDCs as they become industrialised and standards of living should rise just as they did in the past for many MEDCs. Present day comparisons between between MEDCs and LEDCs emphasise the different stages they have reached, Fig. 2.4.

Weaknesses in the model

The model assumes that all countries will become industrialised and experience a fall in the death rate in Stage 2. However, some LEDCs in Africa may never become industrialised.

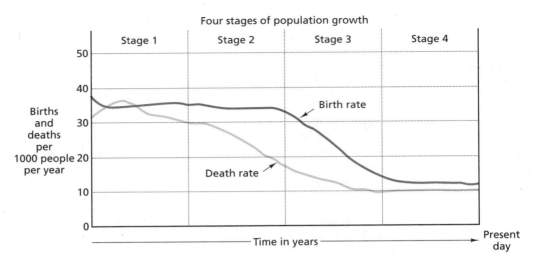

Fig. 2.3 The demographic transition model

The rapid industrialisation of some countries (see Unit 5.10). means that the time scale is being squashed, especially Stages 2 and 3.

There are signs that in some MEDCs the population may decline. In Germany birth and death rates are the same.

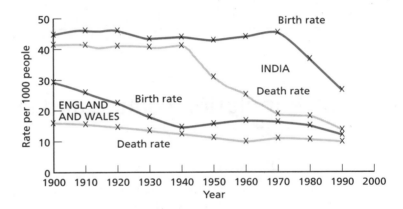

Fig. 2.4 Demographic transition graphs for India and England and Wales 1900–1990

Reasons for changes in birth and death rates

Birth rates are affected by a number of factors:
- Family planning and government incentives to control population numbers. For example, China has a strict one-child-per-family ruling, (which is relaxed in rural areas).
- An increase in the desire for material goods such as refrigerators and cars may result in couples limiting the number of children they have.
- The emancipation of women has resulted in more seeking careers and limiting family size.

Death rates are affected by the following:
- Improved medical care and the supply of drugs.
- Improvements in food supply and quantity.
- Improved sanitation and water supply.
- A reduction in the **infant mortality rate**, i.e. the number of deaths of infants under one year old per 1000 live births in any given year.

Population structure

The **population structure** is the distribution of the population by age groups. It is shown as a **population pyramid**, Fig.2.5. Countries with high birth rates, such as

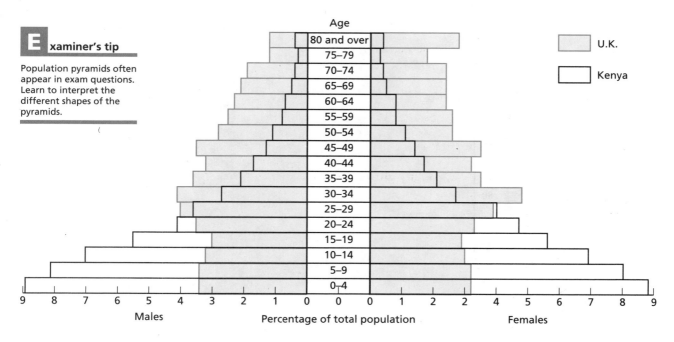

Fig. 2.5 Population structures of Kenya and the UK

Kenya, have a population pyramid with a broad base, tapering in the higher age ranges. There will be a high demand for school places because of the large numbers of children of school age. By contrast the pyramid for the UK is top heavy, due to a high proportion of people of retirement age and of those receiving pensions.

The dependency ratio

The population of a country can be divided into:

- the non-economically active, generally those still at school or college or who have retired,
- the economically active or population of working age.

Those who are non-economically active are dependent on those at work, and this can be shown statistically as a dependency ratio.

$$\frac{\text{children and elderly}}{\text{those of working age}} \times 100 = \text{dependency ratio}$$

In 1991 in the UK there were 11 741 under 16 and 10 598 of pensionable age (i.e. 60 for women, 65 for men), and 35 469 of working age (population figures in thousands). This gives a dependency ratio of 63.0. For every 100 people of working age there were 63 dependent on them. In Kenya in 1989, taking children under 15 and the elderly over 65, the dependency ratio was 111. For every 100 people of working age, 111 were dependent on them. The dependency ratio for LEDCs is much higher than for MEDCs. This is because there is a higher proportion of children in LEDCs.

Living standards

There are a number of indicators which help to measure how developed a country is. Each indicator has its strengths and shortcomings.

- **Gross National Product (GNP)**. This is the total value of all the goods and services produced by a country in one year, plus income from abroad for such things as financial services and company profits. By dividing this sum by the total population of the country the GNP per capita is obtained. To give standardisation this is expressed in US dollars. The GNP is a crude indicator of the standard of living of a country but it ignores a number of other factors that other indicators cover, see below.
- **Gross Domestic Product (GDP)**. This measures the total value of a country's goods and services without adding income from abroad.

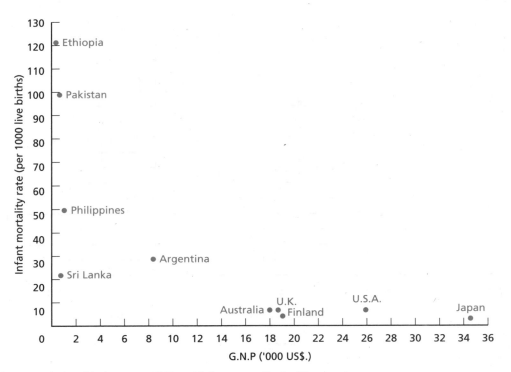

Fig. 2.6 Relationship between GNP and infant mortality in 10 countries

E xaminer's tip

Be prepared to interpret
and analyse graphs and
statistical tables like those
on this page.

- **Infant mortality rate** See Fig. 2.6.
- **Life expectancy** The average number of years a baby born today can expect to live. The male life expectancy rate is generally lower than the female.
- **Calorie intake** This is the average number of calories a person consumes each day. Some people, particularly in more developed countries, eat more than they need. About 2400 calories every day will maintain good health.
- **Other indicators** These include the number of people to each doctor; the number of people per hospital bed and the **literacy rate**, the percentage of the population that can read and write simple sentences. (See Unit 5.7.)
- **Human Development Index** (HDI) In 1990 the United Nations Development Programme published its first estimate of a Human Development Index, which attempts to measure the extent to which a country is developed. It combines statistics on years of schooling, adult literacy and life expectancy with income levels. The HDI gives a better, though far from perfect indicator of living standards. The index is scaled from 0 to 100, with countries scoring over 80 being considered as having a high human development. Scores of 50–79 have medium human development and those under 50 have low human development. Countries can also be placed in rank order using the HDI, see the Table below.

Table 2.2 Some Indicators Applied to 10 countries

Country	GNP	Life Expectancy	Infant Mortality	Literacy	HDI	Rank*
	US $	(Years/Female)	Rate	%	0–100	(175 countries)
Ethiopia	130	52	121	24	23	171
Pakistan	440	59	99	26	31	128
Sri Lanka	640	75	21	87	66	97
Philippines	960	68	50	89	60	100
Argentina	8 060	75	29	95	83	30
Australia	17 980	81	7	99	97	11
UK	18 410	80	7	100	96	18
Finland	19 174	80	5	100	95	5
USA	25 860	80	8	96	98	2
Japan	34 630	82	4	100	98	3

*Canada is ranked as 1 – the most developed country

2.3 Population distribution

The distribution and density of population are uneven at national, continental and world scales. This is because of the interaction of physical, social, economic and political factors.

A growing proportion of the world's population lives in urban areas. The level of urbanisation varies greatly from one country to another. **Migration** is an important factor in the process of **urbanisation**.

75% of the world's population live in LEDCs. It is in these countries that population is growing most quickly. Eighty per cent of people live on 10% of the earth's surface.

World distribution

Figure 2.7 shows the present pattern of uneven distribution. A fifth of the world's population live in China. The populations of India and China make up over 33% of the world total.

The map shows two main clusters. One is in the USA and Europe. The second cluster lies in S.E. Asia, India, China and Japan.

The pattern shown by the map does not neatly match the physical features. It is possible to say, though, that most people live in warm, humid and lowland areas. The pattern reflects all the factors that affect human societies. The three basic factors are:

● **Biological**—age, sex, prevalence and types of diseases
● **Social**—occupation, levels of technology, religion
● **Demographic**—birth rates, death rates, migrations

Economic factors have generally had more effect on the pattern of distribution than physical environmental features. People in MEDCs can manage and control the environment in which they live. The exploitation of resources, the development of new technologies, and the finding of new markets can all lead to changes in distribution. In the USA 70% of the people now live in vast urban areas which have very little direct relationship to the physical environment.

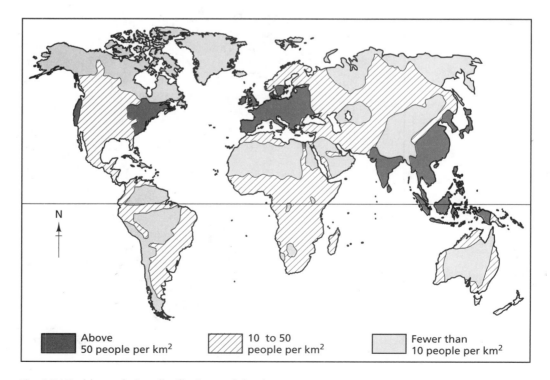

Fig. 2.7 World population distribution and density

Two contrasting examples

Population distribution in the UK

Figure 2.8 shows the distribution of populations in the UK. The average density for the whole area is 239 per square kilometre but there are great variations.

Reasons for the present pattern of distribution are the:

- **physical character** of the country—the north and west, the Highland Zone is the most sparsely populated area
- **early pattern of industrialisation**—new towns and cities were concentrated on or near coalfields
- **dominance of London**—London is the great magnet. It is the financial and international marketing centre. It is also the largest and richest home market, so it has attracted industries and people
- **migration to new areas**—as older industrial regions decline, new areas of dense population have developed, along the south coast in particular. New industries have also been attracted to regions such as East Anglia and this has attracted people.

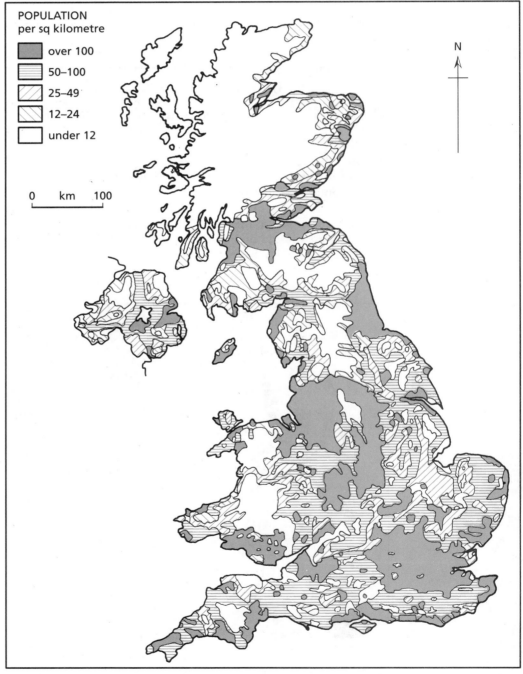

Fig. 2.8 Distribution of population in the UK

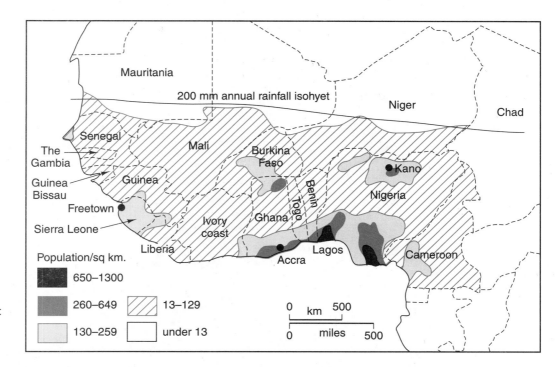

Fig. 2.9 West Africa: Population distribution and density

Population in West Africa

The distribution of population in West Africa is shown in Fig. 2.9. This is an emerging economic region and physical conditions still strongly determine the distribution pattern.

The key influence is **climate**. Human life is mainly concentrated south of a line that represents an annual rainfall of 200mm. North of this the climate is too dry for farming.

The pattern created by climate was reinforced when West Africa was **colonised** by European countries. The rain forest encouraged the growth of commercial crops such as rubber and cocoa. Ports were built on the coast to handle trade with Europe.

Coastal ports and cities have become 'islands' of intense economic activity. They have now become political and administrative centres in which most industrial and commercial activity has been concentrated. They attract migrants from the interior.

The most important process is now **urbanisation**. The number of people living in towns and cities doubles every 10 to 12 years. The cities contain a high proportion of young people.

2.4 Population movement

Types of migration

There are two types of population movement:
- **international migration** from one country to another
- **internal migration** from one part of a country to another part.

The reasons why people migrate are many and varied but they can usually be classified either as **push factors** or **pull factors**.

- **Push factors** come into play when conditions in the home area are such that people feel they need to move to a different area in search of an improvement to their lifestyle. For example, there may be few job opportunities in remote rural areas such as the Central Massif of France or the heathlands of North Germany.
- **Pull factors** take effect when opportunities are offered in another area so that people are drawn towards life in a different place. For example, the countries of western Europe have 'pulled' Turkish workers from their home country for a number of years. The attraction of regular work and high wages contrasts with the poorer living standards in their own country (see Fig. 2.10).

Those who migrate are called **migrants**; the place where they have come from is known as the **source** or **origin**, and the place where they go to is called the **destination**.

People moving out of a country are **emigrants** and when they arrive in their new

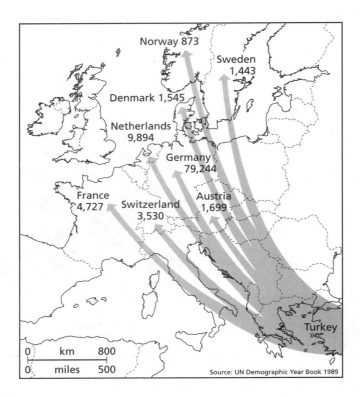

Fig. 2.10 Numbers of long-term immigrants from Turkey in West European countries — 1988

country of destination they become **immigrants** to that country.

The movement of people within a country is called **in-migration**, **out-migration** or **transmigration** (see Unit 6.6) depending upon the direction of movement.

In LEDCs there is still a very definite trend for migrants to move from the rural areas to the urban areas. The possibilities of education, employment, health care, housing, entertainment and a general improvement in the quality of life is an expectation, if not always a reality. The more developed countries have recently reflected a movement of people away from the larger towns and cities to the suburban or semi-rural areas, where there is less congestion and the quality of the environment is better. This movement away from the cities is called **counter-urbanisation** (see Unit 3.3).

The consequences of migration

The movement of people either within a country or to another country, affects both the source and the destination of the migrants in both positive and negative ways:

Source
- the birth rate may be lowered
- there may be less pressure on jobs and certain resources
- migrants may send money back to their families
- new skills may be learned which may eventually be brought back to the area
- labour shortages may be created in some areas of work
- families may be split up, often only the male family members migrate
- those who migrate tend to be those with skills and education
- the average age of the population may increase
- concentrations of communities with a high proportion of older people puts a strain on services and amenities.

Examiner's tip

Relate your knowledge of migration to the process of urbanisation

Destination
- labour shortages are solved
- less attractive jobs not wanted by local people are often taken willingly by migrants
- migrant workers are often prepared to work longer hours than the host population
- new cultures are introduced including foods, music and leisure activities
- population growth is affected as many migrants are of child-bearing age
- in times of recession migrants may be seen as a burden on health and social service provision

- racial tension may result from international migration and resentment can develop
- international migrants are not always prepared to become part of the host culture and ghettos may develop.

Forced migration

People who are forced to leave their home area are known as **refugees**. Refugees seek refuge in another area because of circumstances over which they have no control. These circumstances include:

- war, people leave to escape conflict, e.g. those who left Vietnam
- religious persecution, e.g. European Jews at the time of Hitler's régime
- politics, e.g. Ugandan Asians ordered to leave by Idi Amin
- slavery, e.g. Africans taken to the USA
- accidents, e.g. Chernobyl nuclear disaster and the Bhopal chemical plant explosion in India
- famine, e.g. Ethiopians moving into Sudan
- ethnic cleansing, e.g. Serbia (see Fig. 2.11) and Rwanda
- natural disasters, e.g. earthquakes, volcanic eruptions and floods make thousands homeless every year.

Refugees are often unable to return to their place of origin because of the personal dangers involved, especially if politics, religion or ethnic origin is the cause of their migration. Such people are able to seek **asylum** from their country of destination and if granted, they can remain there as legal citizens.

The 1990s saw a vast increase in numbers seeking asylum and it has become a huge problem for recipient countries. There is debate over judgement for granting asylum, since the recent increase in asylum seekers tends to be due to economic or environmental reasons and not as a result of political persecution. This has led to '**asylum shopping**', where unsuccessful candidates apply to another country and another and so on. While applications are being processed the asylum seekers are supported by the welfare services of the host country. This can be very costly and can divert resources from the resident population. Procedures for granting asylum have been speeded up and tightened up but the confusion over who is a genuine applicant in need of political asylum has sometimes led to wrong decisions being made.

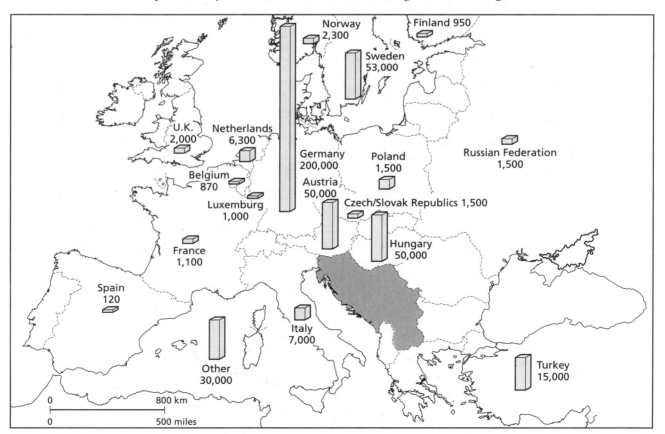

Fig. 2.11 Distribution of refugees from what was Yugoslavia, August 1992

Case study—Chinese migration policy

Migrants from rural poverty are considered the 'engine of China', an inexhaustible supply of cheap labour, a floating population helping to build the country. 'Migration', admits the People's Daily Chinese newspaper, 'has negative effects on transportation, infrastructure, birth control and social order'. Migration is a stabilising force, however, supplying much-needed labour in the cities while minimising the economic strain on the countryside. Migration 'cushions the transformation of the Chinese economy'. The migrants are giant shock-absorbers, flowing from one area of the economy to another.

The opportunity to move around the country is something new to the people of China. Strict social controls used to operate within the country making it difficult for people to move freely from their registered homes. These controls made it virtually impossible for anyone to be able to buy food or get accommodation outside their registered home regions. Reforms within China now mean that people can get a train ticket without a special permit, and buy food and accommodation without government coupons.

Greater freedom of movement has prompted a huge number of people to leave the rural areas and seek jobs in the cities. A combination of **push factors** and **pull factors** is at work.

The push factors include:
- a lack of work in the rural areas where there is a surplus of labour
- wages are very low.

The pull factors are:
- the opportunities of jobs especially in factories and on building sites
- the attraction of higher wages paid to the city dwellers
- an increased demand for women and girls to work as maids and nannies in the wealthy urban areas.

China sets few restrictions on the migration it is encouraging into the industrial cities. Many of the migrants take on poorly paid jobs, but the quality of their life in the city is an improvement on the rural poverty they left behind. Accommodation is expensive and some migrants start off by living on the streets. China's industrial development is dependent upon migrant workers, and they are beginning to benefit from the increasing prosperity of their country. (See Fig. 2.12).

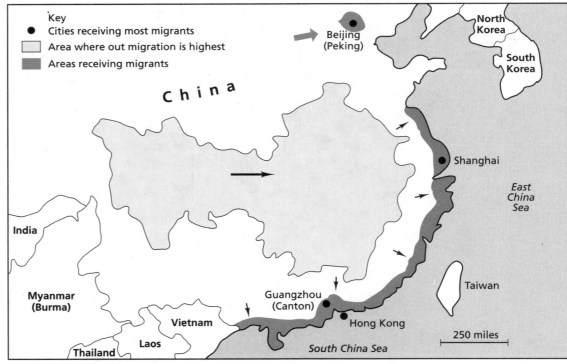

Fig. 2.12 Chinese migration

Summary

1 World population is growing rapidly, especially in LEDCs and this is causing major human and environmental problems.

2 Levels of development are very difficult to measure since a range of indicators must be considered. The Human Development Index is the best measure so far devised.

3 Population is very unevenly distributed throughout the world but urbanisation is a feature common to virtually all countries.

4 People move within their own country or to a different country for a variety of reasons. They may be 'pushed' from their origin due to war, famine or natural disasters. They may be 'pulled' to a new area by the attraction of work, housing, health and social service provision.

Quick test

2.1 The growth of world population
1 What factors produced the population explosion?
2 Define 'natural increase'.
3 Population density is the .... of people living in a particular area.
4 Why do fewer people now die from natural hazards?
5 What proportion of the land area of the world can be used for agriculture and habitation?

2.2 Population change and living standards
6 What factor, apart from birth and death rates, can affect the population size of a country?
7 In which stage of the demographic transition model should the birth rate fall?
8 What is the infant mortality rate?
9 Which have the lowest dependency ratios, MEDCs or LEDCs?
10 What is the literacy rate?

2.3 Population distribution
11 What is the one word that best describes the distribution and density of the population of the world?
12 In which countries of the world are populations generally growing most quickly?
13 What three factors are reflected in distribution patterns?
14 What effect did early industrialisation have upon the present pattern of population distribution in the British Isles?
15 What is the key process affecting the distribution of population in LEDCs today?

2.4 Population movement
16 People who migrate are called ....; where they move from is called the .... or ....; where they go to is called the ....
17 What term describes the movement of people within a country ?
18 Why may racial tension develop from international migration?
19 What are asylum seekers?
20 Why is China encouraging migration whilst most other countries are trying to check population movements?

Chapter 3
Settlement

3.1 Settlement characteristics

Settlements vary in **site**, **size**, **structure** and **function**. The location of settlements and their patterns of growth are related to physical and human factors. In the past studies have concentrated upon *where* settlements grew up and *why* they grew up where they did—that is, their purpose or function.

In order to understand and compare settlements they were classified into different categories. Figure 3.1 shows a commonly agreed basic classification. Despite urbanisation, many of the people of LEDCs still live in rural settlements, while in MEDCs the majority live in urban areas.

Definitions

Hamlet – a cluster of houses without the facilities of a village.
Conurbation – an extensive urban area formed by neighbouring towns and cities merging.
Megalopolis – a very large urban region formed by a cluster of cities – New York to Washington, USA.

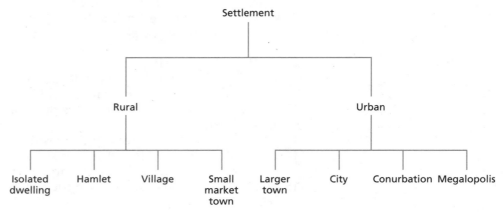

Fig.3.1 A basic classification of settlement types

Types of rural settlements – dispersed and nucleated
Rural settlements may also be classified into two basic types:
- **Dispersed settlements** are those in which individual farms are scattered over the land that is cultivated. Dispersed settlements are characteristic of the highlands of Britain.
- **Nucleated settlements** are those in which farms and other buildings are clustered to form a nucleus from which the village has evolved. Villages centred on village greens and those spread along a main road or street are English examples.

A **dispersed** settlement pattern has developed in Britain where there:

- are very low densities of population (Western Highlands of Scotland)
- is a dependence on livestock farming (Central Wales)
- is specialist intensive farming (market gardening areas)
- are historical reasons, e.g. the Celtic influence (Wales) and the break up of large estates.

A **nucleated** pattern developed where:

- defence was a priority (inside a meander, or on a hill-top)
- people clustered around a water supply (spring line)
- dry sites occurred in marshy areas (the Fens)
- there was a co-operative system of working (open-field farming in manorial system).

Rural settlements may also be classified using other criteria.

A physical classification

Settlements can be classified according to the **physical characteristics** of the site which they occupy and the situations in which they occur. The main physical factors which influenced the sites of villages were:

1. water supply
2. areas of suitable land
3. defensive needs
4. routeways
5. no risk of flooding
6. distance from other villages.

In Britain these factors tend now to be of historical interest only but in many parts of the world these factors are still very important.

Although these classifications seem clear cut, in fact there are many different views of what a rural settlement is, as opposed to an urban one, or what constitutes a village as opposed to a town. As cities, towns and the countryside have become ever more closely inter-related the historical classifications have less meaning and new, more complex, types of settlements have been recognised.

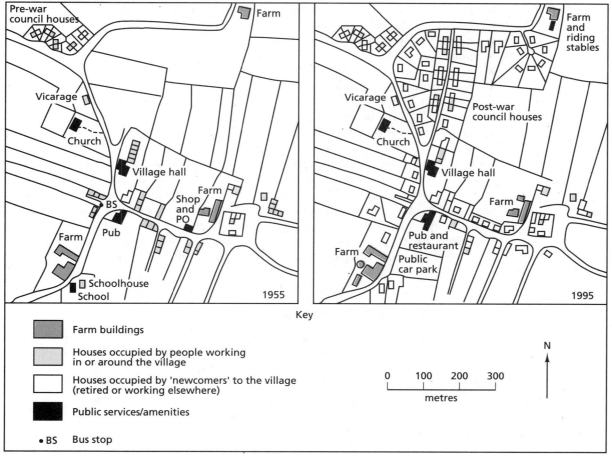

Fig. 3.2 Changes in a village 20km from a city (1955–1995)

Commuter villages

Commuter villages have become an increasingly common feature of urbanised regions throughout the world. People have moved out of the cities and larger towns and have colonised nearby villages that were originally rural in character.

Commuter villages have developed because:

1. There is more money to spend on transport.
2. There is improved public transport—electrified rail lines and motorways.
3. Perceptions of village life attract many people.
4. Decentralisation of industry out of the cities make villages more convenient to live in.

As a result of the development of commuter villages:

1. The social make up of the village has changed
2. The village newcomers often live in separate housing estates.
3. Fewer homes are available for local working families who cannot afford higher home prices.
4. Lower-paid people become concentrated in new council home estates.
5. Village stores are less used because newcomers shop in towns.
6. New services develop for the commuters—restaurants, hairdressers.

These developments are part of the counter-urbanisation process (see Unit 3.3).

Figure 3.2 shows changes in a commuter village between 1955 and 1995. You can see that some of the factors listed above are reflected in the changes in land use and functions shown by the maps.

3.2 The functions of settlements

The function of a town or city relates to its main **economic** and **social activity**. In the past, classifications of settlements were based on their main function, such as:

- defence—e.g. York
- mining—e.g. Wigan
- port—e.g. Grimsby
- market centre—e.g. Norwich
- route centre—e.g. Exeter
- manufacturing—e.g. Coventry
- resort— e.g. Eastbourne
- educational centre—e.g. Cambridge.

At a simple level, these classifications are attractive because they tell you something about the town. In reality, however, the classification is over-simple and in some cases incorrect. York, for example, was a Roman fortress, but for centuries it has been an important religious centre. It also became an important market centre, manufacturing town and a centre of the railway industry. It is now a tourist centre and university city. So this type of classification is inadequate because most towns have a **range of functions** for their inhabitants and for the people who live in the surrounding areas, and the relative importance of the different functions may change significantly over time.

Urban field or urban sphere

Recognising that towns and cities provide services for the areas that surround them (their hinterlands) led to the emergence of the concept of the **urban field**.

The urban field is the area that is economically and socially linked with a town or city. The use of the word 'field' is significant. As with a 'magnetic field', the term suggests that the degree of attraction of the town or city is greatest close to it and decreases steadily in all directions away from the town. Urban fields are also known as **urban spheres** or **spheres of influence**.

Delimiting the urban field

A number of techniques have been developed to identify the areas which are linked to a particular town or city. They include:

1 Analysis of local bus services

In this approach, bus timetables are analysed to work out the frequency of services to villages and towns in an area. The number of buses which pass along particular routes to the main town are shown on a map by lines of breadth proportional to their frequency. That is, the services are shown by means of a flow-line map. This makes it possible to identify the areas from which people travel by bus, and how the pattern for one town links with the flow into neighbouring urban centres.

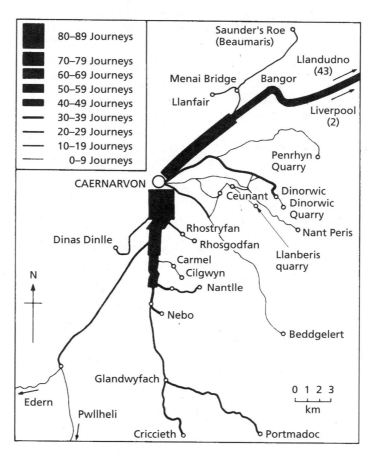

Fig. 3.3 The urban field of Caernarvon as delimited by local bus services

Increased car ownership and the decline in country bus services have made this method much less useful than it was when first used 40 years ago. Figure 3.3, for example, was drawn before the decline of rural services.

2 Analysis of the local newspaper

The number of mentions that different villages or smaller towns receive in a local newspaper published in a larger town can be totalled up over a period of time. **Isolines** can be drawn to show points of equal value on a map of the region served by the newspaper (its circulation area), all the villages with the same number of mentions lying on the same isoline. Usually, the more isolated and more distant villages are the ones which are mentioned least.

3 Mapping the delivery and service areas of town centre shops and offices

The areas to which deliveries are made by furniture shops, electrical goods shops etc. and the areas served by insurance offices, the catchment area of the secondary school or college of further education, and similar services, are mapped to show the extent of the surrounding area which is regularly served by the town or city.

When this technique is used, the lines drawn for each service plotted do not

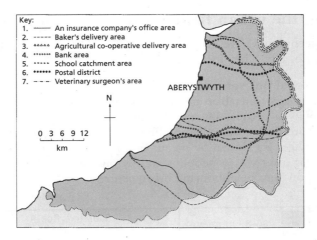

Fig. 3.4 The urban field
of Aberystwyth

coincide; there is no definite boundary to the urban field, Fig. 3.4.

Usually these zones are identified in the field:

● **Zone of dominance**—this area is enclosed by all the services mapped.
● **Zone of competition**—the area covered by some of the services but not by others.
● **Zone of indifference** or **zone of marginal influence**—outside the boundaries shown on the map and so an area where the town has little or no influence.

4 The use of desire-line maps

This technique is based upon a survey of people who live in the hinterland (area with close ties to a place), to find out where they choose to go to buy the goods or get the services they need. Lines are drawn from where the people live to the town which is visited; these are desire lines. When the desire lines have been drawn, the boundaries of the areas of influence of different urban centres can be mapped. This method depends upon questioning a carefully chosen sample of people, Fig. 3.5.

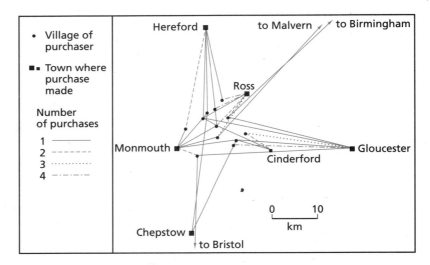

Fig. 3.5 Desire-line diagram related to the purchase of furniture

5 Quantitative analysis

Models have been developed which are based on the idea that the attractiveness of a town depends upon the ease with which it can be visited.

So, for example, the movement between village X and town Y might be expressed as:

● proportional to their populations
● inversely proportional to the distance between them.

This gives a formula:

Movement from X to Y = population X × population Y/(distance X to Y)^2

This formula can be used to determine the boundaries of the urban fields of neighbouring towns B and C. To do this, the **breaking point** is calculated. The breaking point is the place at which, in theory, the shopper changes loyalty from one town to another because it is more convenient to reach.

The formula is:

Breaking point between B and C = distance B to C/1 + [√] population B/population C.

This formula gives the distance of the breaking point from the smaller of the two towns.

Central place theory appears regularly in exams.

Central place theory

Central place theory seeks to explain the relationship of urban settlements to each other. This theory provides a framework for the study of urban settlements throughout the world. Key definitions include:

- **central place**—a settlement which provides one or more services for people living outside it
- **functions**—lower-order functions include the kinds of service provided by a corner shop; higher order functions are the types of service provided by a departmental store
- **threshold population**—the minimum number of people required to support a function economically
- **range of goods or service**—the maximum distance over which people will travel to purchase goods or services offered by a central place
- **hierarchy**—the organisation of central places into a series of orders or grades.

Christaller's ideas

Central place theory was outlined by Walter Christaller. He argued that central places exist because essential services have to be performed for the surrounding area. Ideally each central place would have a circular service area, but since circles do not fit

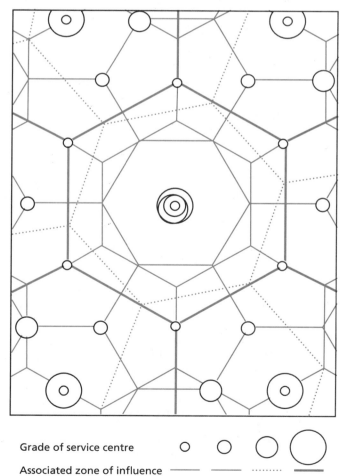

Fig. 3.6 Christaller's theoretical landscape

together neatly, service areas may be seen as **closely fitting hexagons.** Central places compete with each other and the successful centres acquire new functions and so operate at a higher level in the hierarchy. Christaller identified seven levels in the urban hierarchy. The theory is designed to provide an explanation of the size and spacing of settlements as well as of the relationships between the central place and the area it serves, Fig. 3.6.

Summary

It is possible to make four main generalisations:

1 The larger the settlements, the fewer they are in number. So there are many small towns but fewer larger cities.

2 The larger the cities grow in size the greater the distance between them. Villages are nearer to each other than cities are to each other.

3 As a town or city grows in size the number and range of its functions increase. A large city provides many more services than a small town.

4 As the town or city grows in size it will provide increased higher–order functions.

3.3 Urbanisation and the growth of shanty towns

At present, LEDCs are not as urbanised as MEDCs. Despite its huge cities, for example, 80% of the people of India still live in villages, while 80% of the people of Britain live in towns. In LEDCs, however, people are now moving to the cities, which are growing at a faster rate than the cities of MEDCs.

Reasons for urbanisation in LEDCs

E xaminer's tip

Make sure you understand why urbanisation occurs and the problems it creates.

❶ The chief reason is the **decline of the death rate**. Improvements in diet, health, sanitation and so on mean that fewer infants die soon after birth. Better medical services also mean that people live longer. Throughout LEDCs, births now greatly exceed deaths, so there is a rapid population increase. This increase is greater in the cities than in the countryside, because medical and health services are better in the cities, so the cities are growing faster than the rural settlements.

❷ People move from the countryside to the towns because the towns offer **higher standards of living**, higher wages and more varied job opportunities. This is not always so, but is a view firmly held by rural emigrants.

❸ Others leave the countryside because of **natural disasters** such as drought, flood, earthquakes and famine and make for the cities to start a new life.

Effects of urbanisation

❶ **Overcrowding** in the poorer areas of the cities. A survey in India showed, for example, that over half the families lived in single rooms. Migrants making for the cities stay with relatives or people from the same village and this adds to the overcrowding.

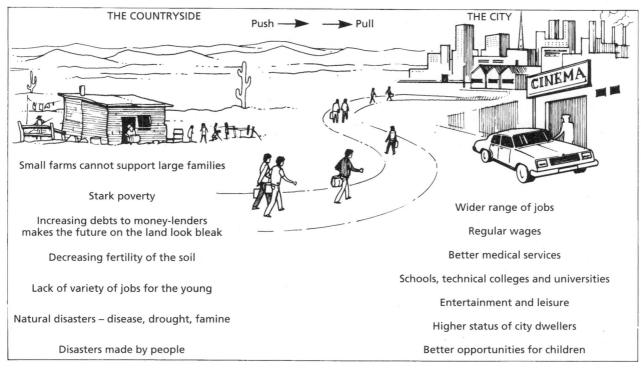

THE COUNTRYSIDE Push ⟶ ⟶ Pull THE CITY

CINEMA

Small farms cannot support large families

Stark poverty

Increasing debts to money-lenders makes the future on the land look bleak

Decreasing fertility of the soil

Lack of variety of jobs for the young

Natural disasters – disease, drought, famine

Disasters made by people

Wider range of jobs

Regular wages

Better medical services

Schools, technical colleges and universities

Entertainment and leisure

Higher status of city dwellers

Better opportunities for children

Fig. 3.7 The push-pull model of migration

Fig. 3.8 A shanty town in Bangladesh

② City authorities are faced with tremendous **housing** and **welfare problems**.
③ Unplanned 'squatter' settlements develop within the cities where there is space (e.g. the *bustees* of Calcutta), or, more usually, on the edges of cities (e.g. the *barriadas* of Lima, Peru). These settlements are called '**shanty towns**'.

Reasons for the growth of shanty towns
The governments and private concerns in LEDCs cannot, as in most MEDCs, meet the demand for houses because:

① LEDCs have little money to spend and this money is needed for major agricultural and industrial projects.

2. The construction industry is concentrated on the development projects, so there are too few resources available for housing schemes.
3. Little subsidised housing is available, because only a small proportion of the population can pay the taxes needed to cover the costs.
4. When subsidised houses are built, many squatter families still cannot afford them.
5. Some migrant workers do not intend to stay permanently in the city, so temporary shanty housing suits them.

Problems

1. Families living in permanent squalor deteriorate in health and vitality.
2. Shanty towns are often built on unsuitable sites, e.g. the ground may be too steep to install a gravity sewer system, or the land so high that an adequate piped-water supply cannot be laid on.
3. There is the danger of contaminated water causing epidemics.
4. Because the shanty towns are on the edges of large cities, people have to travel long distances to work and so use their wages on travel instead of improving their living conditions.
5. Shanty town dwellers do not pay rates or taxes so the city has less money for improvement projects.
6. Overcrowding in squalid conditions on the edges of cities can lead to political and social unrest.

Remedies

Suggestions that have been made to control the spread of unplanned settlements in LEDCs include:

1. building low-cost housing for rent in the cities to rehouse the people living in the poorest areas
2. making shanty towns legal so that people feel more secure
3. demolishing the worst shanty towns but improving the better ones by introducing piped water, sanitation and other basic services
4. giving families land with basic services laid on so that they can build homes
5. building health centres in shanty towns
6. improving public transport so that people can travel to work in other parts of the city
7. increasing birth control education
8. developing the rural areas so that fewer people are attracted to the cities.

Counter-urbanisation

In MEDCs the process of **counter-urbanisation** is becoming increasingly evident. This is the movement of people and employees to small towns and villages outside the city. It was first identified in the USA.

Counter-urbanisation is usually associated with the development of jobs in the distribution and retailing of manufactured foods and in professional and public services **(tertiary)** and the development of jobs involving skills and expertise in the development of ideas **(quaternary)**.

Counter-urbanisation results in the dominance of urban ways of life even in areas relatively remote from the city. It also increases social and economic differences between villages that have become involved in the process and others that are still essentially rural.

3.4 Urban land use

As towns grow, the different functions that they perform tend to separate out into different areas. For example, industries may group together along a riverside or railway to form an industrial zone. As a result it is possible to recognise **functional zones** within every town, which are characterised by distinctive types of land use.

A city model

Towns and cities may be divided into different 'functional regions'. Each type of region has its own character and its own functions to perform. Figure 3.9 is a model of the functional regions of an older town or city.

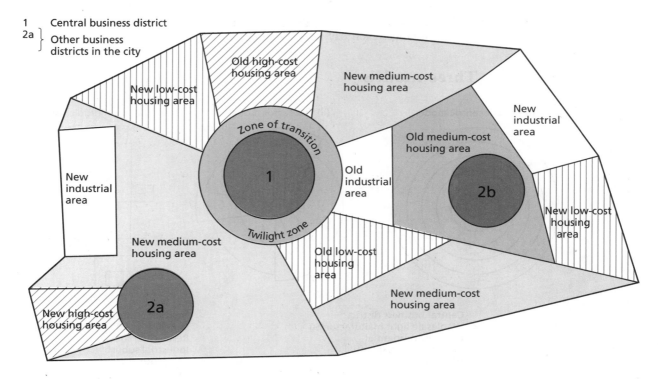

1   Central business district
2a } Other business districts in the city

Fig. 3.9 Model of land-use pattern in an old industrial city

Chief functional zones

①   Central Business District (CBD)—the heart of the city, which contains the chief commercial, shopping and social facilities of the town or city. In the USA it is known as 'downtown', but in Britain we speak of the 'city centre' or 'town centre'.

②   The zone in transition, or the twilight zone—a very mixed area bordering the CBD. It usually contains small industries, e.g. printing works and warehouses. The houses are old and low-cost, often small terraces or tenements. Larger houses in the zone have been converted into offices, e.g. estate agents and insurance companies, or into flats. There is an air of decay and deterioration, which is increased by the presence of demolition sites and rebuilding.

③   Old industrial areas—developed near the town centres. They were established at a time when the convergence of roads and railways made the town centre the most accessible place for industry. Old industrial areas are often found close to railways. Today these areas may also be decaying because the new industries have been located on the edges of the town or city.

④   New industrial areas—these are the result of the suburbanisation of industry. As city centres became congested with traffic, and old industrial premises became out of date, industry began to move to the edge of the city. Modern planned industrial estates provide better premises. They are often located on ring roads or near motorways and so are very accessible. Since managers and workers may also have moved to new estates in the suburbs, it is easy for them to get to work.

⑤   Residential areas—shown in the model divided in two ways:
- into regions of high-, medium- and low-cost housing
- into new and old areas.

The old areas tend to be near the city centre. The grouping of people according to income into different types of residential areas is called **residential segregation**.

⑥ Suburban shopping centres—shown in the model as smaller green circles. They are smaller versions of the CBD and serve a particular part of the town.

⑦ Commuters' zone—not part of the built-up area of the city, but belonging to the city as a whole because it is the region from which workers who live outside the city are drawn to work in the city. Most commuters into cities in MEDCs are professional and white-collar workers who choose to live away from their work. In LEDCs, however, many skilled and semi-skilled workers travel long distances each day to work in cities.

Three models

(i) The concentric model

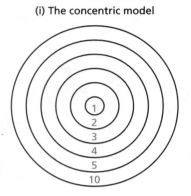

(ii) The sector model

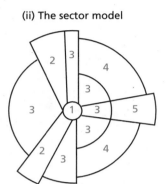

(iii) The multiple-nuclei model

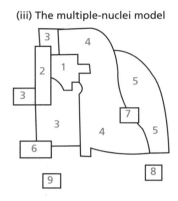

1 Central business district	6 Heavy manufacturing
2 Wholesale light manufacturing	7 Outlying business district
3 Low-cost residential	8 Residential suburb
4 Medium-cost residential	9 Industrial suburb
5 High-cost residential	10 Commuters' zone

Fig. 3.10 The concentric, sector and multiple-nuclei models

For older towns and cities it is usual to consider the functional regions to be arranged in one of three patterns (Fig. 3.10).

① The **concentric** model shows the CBD as the centre of concentric rings—the zone in transition and the old industrial area, then the low-, medium- and high-cost residential rings and finally the outer industrial area.

② The **sector** model is a model in which the different regions are arranged in sectors along the lines of communications radiating from the centre (a little like a dartboard).

③ The **multiple nuclei** model allows for each of the different regions to be arranged in different ways around the CBD.

Apply these models to towns you have studied.

E xaminer's tip

These models and urban models of cities in LEDCs are popular with examiners.

A land-use model for the LEDCs

The rapidly growing cities of the LEDCs have developed function zones that differ from those that characterise MEDC cities, Fig. 3.11. In summary a typical city in an LEDC can be characterised as follows:

① The CBD is similar but competition for space and congestion is even greater, e.g. Cairo.

② The CBD was surrounded in the past by the homes of landowners, merchants and administrators. Some of these have now deteriorated but the better-off still live in this **inner zone** in new high-rise apartments. It is attractive to them because housing quality is good and it is convenient to the CBD.

③ Around this inner zone there is a belt of residential areas which are of poorer quality than those in MEDCs. Many of the houses may be self-built. This is the **middle zone**.

④ A significant difference from MEDC cities is found in the **outer zone**. Instead of wealthy suburbs there is poor quality housing that gets steadily worse away from the city. Shanty towns are located here.

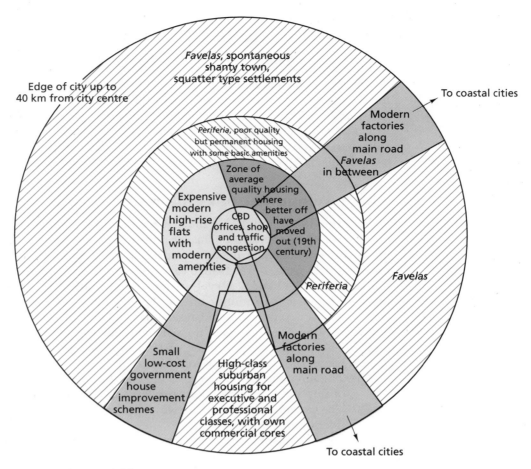

Fig. 3.11 Urban model for LEDCs

⑤ In some cities better-off citizens move to the **suburbs** to avoid the congestion. These are closely knit, carefully guarded communities with their own service centres.

⑥ **Industrial areas** with modern factories have been built along the main roads leading out from the city. Some of this development has been planned; in many cities it is spontaneous.

Changes in urban land use

Towns and cities are dynamic aspects of the landscape and change over time as economic and social factors change. This leads to changes in urban land use; old zones may be replaced and new zones added to the town. For example, in old heavy industrial regions the sites of mines and factories have been flattened and turned into sites for council housing estates or for new light industrial development.

Urban renewal, the replacement of out-of-date housing and industrial regions with new commercial buildings and housing, has involved the clearing of obsolete buildings and the redevelopment of areas to meet the needs of today. Narrow congested roads can be replaced by urban motorways. People can be rehoused in better accommodation. The cleared land can also be redeveloped to provide the greatest possible income for its owners, e.g. by building high-rise blocks of prestige offices.

Renewal, however, causes problems for inner-city people. Cheap housing is demolished and communities are broken up.

The relationship of the functional zones and the patterns of land use may change over time and this may lead to situations of conflict. Over time residential areas may be occupied by groups of lower socio-economic status. This is called **filtering**. In some parts of the city the reverse may happen and areas are taken over by higher socio-economic groups. This is called **gentrification**.

3.5 Urban development and planning

Urban development needs to be carefully planned to provide an attractive environment for the increasing proportion of the world's population that lives in towns and cities. MEDCs have the wealth and planning expertise to carry out major developments successfully. In some cases improvements are needed to correct mistakes made in the past or to redevelop areas which have become derelict because of changing economic circumstances. An example is the dockland region to the east of London.

The development of London's dockland

During the 1960s and 1970s the trade which once passed through London's docks moved away to Rotterdam or smaller ports such as Felixstowe (see Unit 5.5), with their up-to-date container terminals and specialist facilities to deal with bulk cargoes. The London docks from Tower Bridge to Woolwich became a derelict area until 1981 when the **London Docklands Development Corporation** was set up to attract investors to spend large sums of money on the region, backed by Government funds. The aim was to develop commercial and residential buildings in attractive settings close to the City of London. The success of the scheme is due to a number of factors:

1. The extremely high price of land in other parts of central London for new offices or residential development .
2. The proximity of the docks to the City of London and the West End. The Bank of England is only six kilometres from the Isle of Dogs.
3. The potential for leisure activities and scenic views along the dock basins and riverside.
4. Funding of some of the infrastructure by the government.
5. Initiatives taken by entrepreneurs like John Mowlem, whose company built London City Airport.
6. The development of the Dockland Light Railway which will eventually be linked to the Jubilee Line of London's Underground.
7. The setting up of the **Isle of Dogs Enterprise Zone** (Fig. 3.12) to attract industry. Wapping has taken over from Fleet Street as the newspaper centre and several large companies have relocated in office blocks such as Canary Wharf. Residential areas of different types have been developed on both banks of the river.
8. The development of the London City Airport at the Royal Docks, bringing air travel to within 10 kilometres of the City.

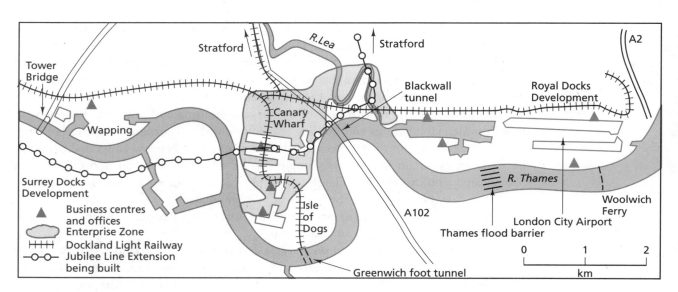

Fig. 3.12 The development of London's dockland

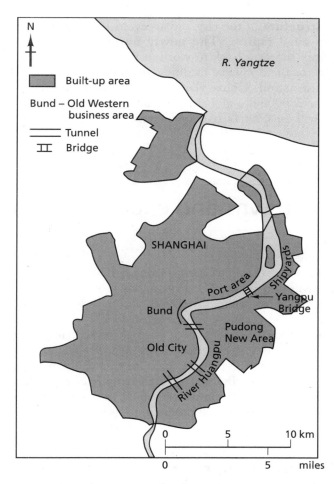

Fig. 3.13 Shanghai showing the Pudong New Area

Development and planning in LEDCs

The poorer LEDCs, such as Ethiopia and Paraguay, do not have the wealth or expertise to undertake major urban development and planning, but the more wealthy LEDCs, such as Venezuela, with its oil income, have implemented development plans for urban areas and housing estates. Other LEDCs with rapid annual economic growth rates such as China, Malaysia and South Korea have ambitious urban development plans which are attracting capital and skilled support from MEDCs. Malaysia, for example, is building a new international airport and has plans for a new capital city by the year 2008. The new capital will be a garden city linked to Kuala Lumpur, the present capital, by a motorway and to the rest of Malaysia and abroad by multi-media communication systems and the latest in satellite and fibre-optic technology.

Case Study: Planning and development in Shanghai

Shanghai, with a population of 13 million, is the second most important port in China. With its deep water harbour Hong Kong remains the busiest port, but Shanghai is catching up fast as an industrial and business centre. During the Communist régime of China under Chairman Mao, Shanghai, a major port in the 1920s and 1930s, went into a period of decline. After Mao's death in 1976 the government began to relax its controls on business and industry and to permit some competition and foreign investment. The turning point for Shanghai came in 1990 when the central government made the Pudong district of the city China's future financial centre. Pudong is on the east side of the Huangpu River (Fig. 3.13), opposite the old colonial centre known as the Bund, once dominated by western firms. The **Pudong New Area**, as it is called, covers over 51 000 hectares and has been carefully planned with industrial parks, factories, office space and housing developments. Investment and technology from overseas has poured in and there are more than 4000 foreign-funded financial and manufacturing companies. One of the attractions for foreign firms is China's **annual economic growth rate** (increase in a country's wealth) of over 9% (U.K. 2.7%) and the rapidly growing market for goods to supply the Chinese population of 1200 million.

The **infrastructure** of the city and access to Pudong from the rest of the Shanghai is being improved rapidly. The newly built Yangpu suspension bridge allows commuters from the west bank to work in Pudong. An airport is planned for Pudong together with road and railway facilities. In Pudong a further 140 high-rise buildings are under construction. China plans for Shanghai to be the national finance centre before the year 2000 and a global centre by 2010. It is possible that both Pudong and Hong Kong will be China's two main business centres at the beginning of the 21st century.

3.6 New towns and expanded towns

Some definitions:
- **New town**—an urban settlement planned and built to ease the housing pressure in existing towns and cities. The new towns provide work as well as homes for the families who live in them. In Britain the new towns were built as the result of Parliament passing the New Towns Act in 1946.
- **Expanded town**—a town where planned growth has occurred according to the Town Development Act (1952). This Act of Parliament encouraged the rapid development of towns in country areas, to ease congestion and housing problems in the cities. Andover and Basingstoke are examples of expanded towns.
- **Overspill**—an excess of population which leaves the city because of overcrowding or as a result of urban renewal programmes (see Unit 3.4). Overspill estates were set up in towns such as Luton to receive families from London.

The development of new towns in Britain

After the Second World War a series of new towns was built. These towns now number over 30 and have a population of about two million.

Towns like Stevenage, Harlow and Crawley were planned to provide new homes and jobs and better surroundings for people living in London. Peterlee, County Durham, was planned to rehouse people from local mining villages and Corby was designed to serve the iron and steel industry of the area. Altogether 14 new towns were developed in areas of high unemployment to attract manufacturing investment. They include Skelmersdale and Warrington in the northwest and East Kilbride and Glenrothes in Scotland.

The first towns that were built, such as Corby and Crawley, are known as Mark 1 new towns. Later, the planning goals were changed and, in particular, traffic-free shopping precincts and larger population targets were built into plans for the next set of towns. The final phase of new town development was the planning of new cities at Telford in Shropshire, in Central Lancashire near Preston and at Milton Keynes, Buckinghamshire. The target population for each of these cities was about 250 000 but only Milton Keynes is likely to achieve anything like this size. Central Lancashire has not been built.

Aims of the new town planners

The new towns were originally intended to be:
1. Limited in size—expected to grow to a population of about 60 000, to be similar in size and character to an old country town, Fig. 3.14. The planners envisaged an **optimum population size** for them. The advantages of keeping the new towns reasonably small were seen to be as follows:
    - people would live within walking or cycling distance of their work
    - everyone would be able to live close to the surrounding countryside
    - it would be possible for a community spirit to develop quickly in the new towns
    - small towns could be built quickly.

    2 Comprehensively planned—providing a markedly better living environment from that of the inner cities.

    3 Socially balanced—with a mixture of age, income and social groups.

    4 Separate from the parent city—to avoid them becoming just suburbs.

    5 Self-contained—so that:
- the towns developed their own identities
- shopping and entertainment facilities needed by the people were provided locally
- new towns had industries which provided work for the inhabitants, so that they would not become commuter or dormitory towns.

Criticisms of new towns and expanded towns

Planners have revised their ideas about how housing and population problems should be solved. They have realised that:

    1 The decline in birth-rate has meant that there is less need for new settlements in Britain.

    2 The movement of industries to the new industrial estates in expanded and new towns has drained the economic life of the inner city areas and has taken jobs away from older towns.

    3 The mass movement of people away from the inner cities to new towns has further accelerated the decline of inner city areas.

    4 Young married couples have found that the cost of living in new towns, especially rents and house prices, is much higher than in the areas from which they moved.

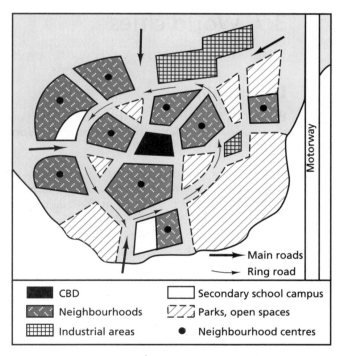

Fig. 3.14 A new-town model

New towns in LEDCs

The planning and building of new towns has been adopted as a strategy to deal with population and housing problems in other parts of the world. In the LEDCs the fundamental reason for building new towns is to relieve overcrowding in the major cities and to cope with rapid urbanisation.

Plans for individual new towns included, as in the UK, the provision of high density housing; the provision of amenities such as mosques, temples, schools and neighbourhood shopping centres; open spaces where possible.

Examples of such planned towns are the Tenth of Ramadan, built in the desert outside Cairo, Tsuen Wan in Hong Kong and Jurong in Singapore (see Fig. 3.15).

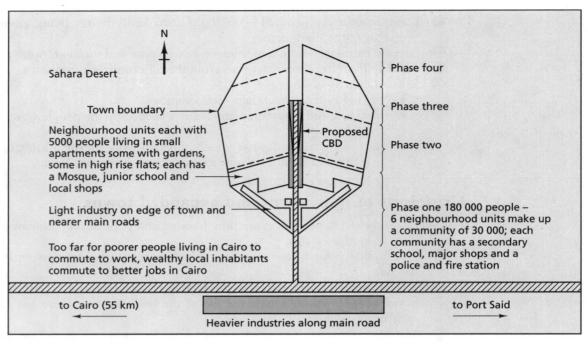

Fig. 3.15 Planned layout of Tenth of Ramadan—a new town near Cairo

3.7 World cities

Distribution

Figure 3.16 shows the distribution of the large cities of the world. The pattern of distribution is of clusters of large cities in North America, Western Europe, China and South East Asia.

Reasons for the distribution

The pattern is the result of two main phases of very rapid urbanisation:

1. In the 19th century industrialisation in what are now the MEDCs led to demand for labour in mines, factories and other industrial activities. Large cities grew as a result of rapid economic development.

2. During the second half of the 20th century many LEDCs gained independence, providing new opportunities for administrative and service jobs, which increased the wealth and importance of the cities. High birth-rates, decreasing death rates and mass migration from rural areas, however, meant that many of the large cities of the LEDCs now have over 1 million people living in illegal squatter settlements or shanty towns.

Changes in distribution

As a result of continuing urbanisation cities with populations of more than 1 million have become common in LEDCs. The number of cities with 5 million and 10 million population has also increased.

Figure 3.17 lists the estimated populations of the ten largest cities in the year 2000. Two of the cities are in the USA but seven are located in LEDCs. This is the result of differential rates of growth of the largest cities. In MEDCs the rate of growth is now much slower than it used to be. This is partly due to low birth rates and effective birth control. It is also the result of strong planning policies and movements out of the large cities—counter-urbanisation (see Unit 3.3).

As well as experiencing differing rates of growth the largest cities in MEDCs also differ markedly from cities in LEDCs in terms of population density. MEDC cities have much lower population densities than the largest cities in LEDCs. The largest cities

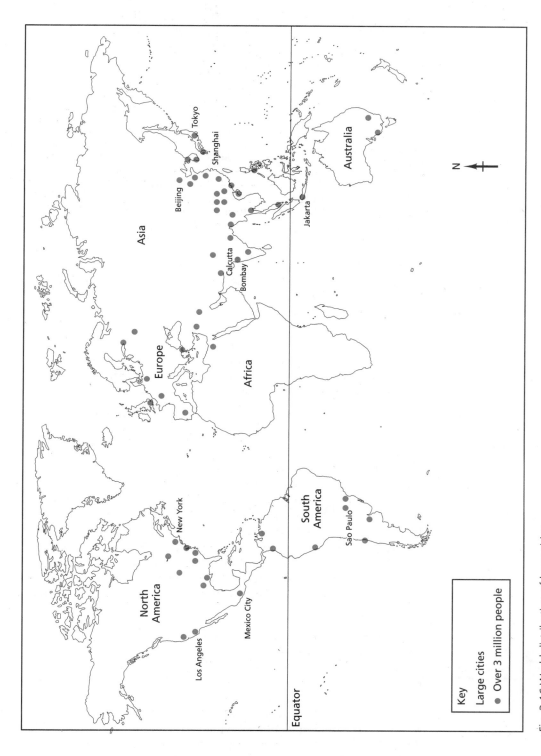

Fig. 3.16 World distribution of large cities

Key

Large cities

● Over 3 million people

Tokyo

Shanghai

Beijing

Asia

Calcutta

Bombay

Jakarta

Australia

Europe

Africa

New York

North America

South America

Mexico City

Sao Paulo

Los Angeles

Equator

N

City	Year 2000
Mexico City	25.6
Sao Paulo	22.1
Tokyo	19.1
Shanghai	17.0
New York	16.8
Calcutta	15.7
Bombay	15.4
Beijing	14.0
Los Angeles	13.9
Jakarta	13.7

Fig. 3.17 Top ten cities (estimated population in millions)

with the lowest population densities are mainly in the USA, such as Los Angeles. Those with the higher population densities are mainly in South East Asia, for example Jakarta in Indonesia.

Global cities

Global cities are the highest order world cities—London, Paris, New York, Tokyo etc. These cities play a key role as headquarters of the international economic system. They are centres for international business and business services.

Global cities house:

- head offices of national and international corporations
- top legal firms and accountants
- the chief marketing organisations
- the most prestigious management consultancy firms.

They are also the centres of economic power and control because they are the key links in the most important world-wide decision making networks.

Although these cities form a distinctive group they differ from one another in a number of ways. For example some are more important politically, e.g. Brussels. Others such as New York and Tokyo are supreme financial and economic centres.

The largest city in the world is Mexico City.

Mexico City

In recent years, Mexico City has become the largest city in the world. It has an estimated population in 1994 of 21 million (15 million at the 1990 census). The city now contains 22% of all Mexicans; 66% of all Mexican students, 70% of the bank and financial organisations in the country, and more than 50% of Mexico's industries. Mexico City has been called the capital of under-development, the capital of pollution, and the capital of slums.

The capital of under-development

Mexico City is a typical LEDC city:

- It contains great extremes of wealth and poverty.
- The population is growing rapidly.
- It is ringed by illegal slum cities.
- It cannot cope efficiently with major disasters.
- It is the capital of a country which has considerable **international debts**.

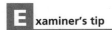

E xaminer's tip

If you have studied another LEDC city, compare it with Mexico City.

The shops of the 'Zona Rosa' in the city centre are as exclusive and expensive as those of Paris and New York. There are also expensive restaurants, magnificent churches and modern office blocks. Yet 2 million people in the city have no running water, 3 million have homes with no sewage system and 40% of the population are unemployed or only have occasional work. The *pepenadores* live by picking over rubbish dumps and selling the reusable bits of metal and plastic they find. Many beggars live and die on the city streets.

The city does not have a well-developed infrastructure and when crises or disasters happen they cannot be handled as well as in a city in a MEDC. The 1985 earthquake disaster highlighted problems of corrupt building companies, poor planning decisions and delays in mounting large-scale rescue operations.

Like many other LEDCs, Mexico is now deeply in debt. The peso has been greatly devalued and the country cannot afford to undertake projects which would help improve its social and economic problems.

The capital of pollution

At the end of the Second World War, the Mexicans decided on a policy of industrialisation, which was concentrated in the cities and in Mexico City in particular. Poor peasants were attracted to the cities and populations increased rapidly. Improved medical care cut the death rate and kept more babies alive. As a result, Mexico City has become a huge industrial centre. There is a permanent cloud of greyish-brown fog over the city. Just breathing in Mexico City is said to be the equivalent of smoking two packets of cigarettes a day. Roughly 30 000 children and 70 000 adults in the city die each year from diseases caused by pollution.

Causes of pollution:
1. 130 000 factories exist in the city area.
2. Pollution laws are not strictly enforced.
3. Neither the factory owners nor the government can afford expensive anti-pollution equipment.
4. Most of the three million cars and 7 000 diesel buses in the city are old and have inefficient engines.
5. The city is 2500 metres above sea level, so the air is thin. As a result, the engines produce extra amounts of carbon monoxide and hydrocarbon pollution.
6. The city is surrounded by mountains, which hold the blanket of fog over the city.

Efforts to reduce pollution:
1. New laws were passed in 1983 to limit factory pollution and to fine factory owners heavily if they break the laws.
2. 'Plan Texcoco', designed to stop the dust storms during which dust and burning pollutants are blown into people's eyes.
3. Pemex, the national petroleum company, has reduced the amount of sulphur in diesel fuel.

The capital of slums

Mexico City has a massive housing problem. The average family size is 5.5 persons and 26% of all families live in single rooms. Even professional people find it difficult to get reasonable accommodation. As a result the city is now ringed with illegal slum cities. These are founded by the *paracaidistas* — the 'parachutists'—who invade private land suddenly and build huts and shacks as quickly as possible. The slums have no services and there are health and political problems for the government (see Fig. 3.18).

Reasons for the population growth
1. Rapid immigration into the city as a result of industrialisation.
2. 'Push' from the country areas, where there is extreme poverty.
3. A high birth rate.
4. Ineffective population control—90% of the people are Roman Catholic.
5. Decline in the death rate from 9.6 to 6.7 per 1000 during the 1970s.

Effects of the growth of the city
1. Mexico City has lost 75% of the woodland in its region since 1945, and this has reduced the amount of water available.
2. More water has to be pumped from the sub-soil, and parts of the city have now sunk 110 metres.
3. Traffic congestion—a six-lane orbital motorway, called the *Periferico* has been built, on which there are massive traffic jams.
4. Public services, especially sewerage, are inadequate.
5. 50% of the people have no medical services.
6. Government departments are bureaucratic and slow, some are corrupt. As a result the problems grow faster than solutions can be found for them.

Fig. 3.18 Mexico City: Slum dwellings behind better housing

3.8 Urban issues

The sheer size, rates of growth and changes that have occurred in large cities have inevitably resulted in major urban problems. Some issues are specific to the older cities of the MEDCs, others are distinctive of rapidly growing LEDC cities. There are also general issues that are common to all cities.

Some of these issues and the solutions applied to them have already been identified and examined in earlier units of this chapter. It is important that you do not confine your revision of urban issues to this unit alone.

Urban issues in MEDCs

Figure 3.19 illustrates the range of urban issues faced by large cities in MEDCs. Not all the cities face all these problems at any one time and the severity of a particular problem varies from city to city. Nevertheless, it is possible to develop a theoretical model that is relevant to cities in more developed economies.

Case Study: Phoenix, Arizona

Phoenix is the largest city in Arizona and is one of the fastest growing cities of the American South West. It now has a population of over 1 million and it sprawls over a wider area than Los Angeles. When the information provided by Fig. 3.19 is applied to Phoenix the result is shown in Fig. 3.20. The politicians intended to build Phoenix as a city close to nature (the Sonoran Desert), a pleasure to live in and sustainable. A major issue that Phoenix and other western cities such as Denver, Las Vegas and Salt Lake City have to face is that of water supply. Advanced technology has enabled the Americans to pipe water hundreds of miles to the growing cities. The hot desert climate means that families have their own swimming pools while some estates for the wealthy have been built on the edges of artificial lakes. Vast quantities of water are consumed daily but in Las Vegas for example the limit of water supply will be reached within ten years.

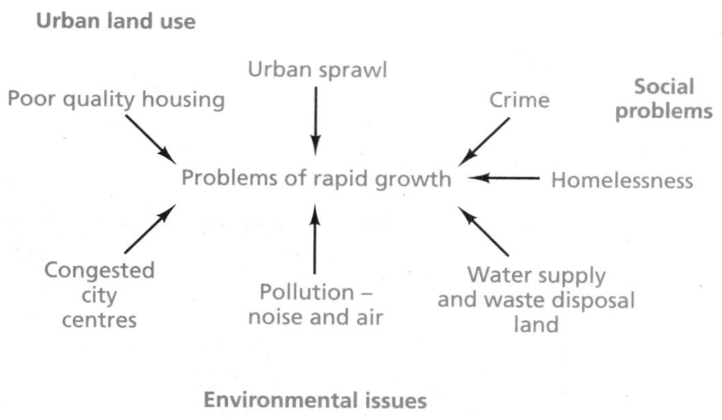

Urban land use

Poor quality housing   Urban sprawl   Crime   **Social problems**

Problems of rapid growth ← Homelessness

Congested city centres   Pollution – noise and air   Water supply and waste disposal land

Environmental issues

Fig. 3.19 The range of urban issues faced by large cities in MEDCs

Land use	• Phoenix eats up open space at the rate of 1 hectare every 2 hours • Urban sprawl–Scottsdale suburb has grown from pop. 2000 (1950) to 130 000 and is now 3 times the physical size of San Francisco • Open space within the city is disappearing as the city becomes more built up – there are not enough parks
Social problems	• Because people want low taxes there is not enough money for Education • The 'inner city' is characterised by crime and racial conflict • Huge gulfs have appeared between rich and poor causing social problems • New suburbs are being built as 'gated' communities to try to keep out crime
Environmental issues	• The urban site is congested with traffic; serious traffic jams are common • Poor quality air alerts are common. Phoenix air is among the dirtiest in the USA • Water supply limits are being reached • The rapid growth of the airport has caused noise pollution for parts of the city.

Fig. 3.20 Urban issues in Phoenix, Arizona

Urban issues in LEDCs

Some key issues are shared with the large cities of the MEDCs. Traffic congestion, for example, is a major problem for most cities in many LEDCs.

The decay of inner city areas and the serious deterioration of formerly good quality residential areas is also common. This decay within the city is paralleled by the development of shanty towns and unplanned residential development on the rural—urban fringes (see Unit 3.3). The poor quality environment raises problems of health, education, availability of clean water, employment and the disposal of waste. Where these problems are not tackled effectively it can lead to political unrest.

The problem for many LEDCs is that the rate of urban growth is very rapid. Furthermore, the problems are so great when compared with the limited amount of investment capital available that major progress is very difficult or virtually impossible. As debtor nations, many LEDCs have to conform to strict financial controls recommended by the World Bank or official Aid Agencies, which makes it even more difficult to achieve adequate investment.

Summary

1 There is no clear boundary between urban and rural settlement and the process of urbanisation is further fudging the division.

2 Central place theory provides a framework for understanding the pattern of relationships between settlements.

3 Urbanisation is a common feature of LEDCs and has resulted in the creation of large unplanned settlements with severe economic and social problems.

4 Urban structure is the result of the spatial relationships that exist between the chief land-use zones of the town or city; it is demonstrated by different economic conditions.

5 Urban planning influences how towns and cities grow and adapt to new social and economic conditions.

6 New towns have been planned in MEDCs and LEDCs as an important way of helping to solve the housing and economic problems of cities.

7 The present distribution of large cities in the world is the result of two main phases of urbanisation.

8 The sheer size, rates of growth and changes that have occurred in large cities have inevitably resulted in major urban problems.

Quick test

3.1 Settlement characteristics
1 What are the two basic types into which rural settlements may be classified?
2 What kind of settlement pattern is encouraged by a dependence on livestock farming?
3 What is the 'site' of a village?
4 What effect has public transport had upon the character of some rural settlements located conveniently near cities?
5 What is likely to happen to services in a village when it becomes a commuter village?

3.2 The functions of settlements
6 What is the area that surrounds a town for which the town provides services called?
7 Why is the analysis of bus services of limited use as a way of mapping a town's sphere of influence?
8 What is the theory called that seeks to explain the relationship of urban settlements to each other?
9 What is the 'urban hierarchy'?
10 What is the 'range of a good'?

3.3 Urbanisation and the growth of shanty towns
11 Are LEDCs more urbanised than MEDCs at present?
12 In what way does the 'push—pull' model of migration help to explain the process of urbanisation?

13 What is another name for a shanty town?

14 Name three ways in which health conditions could be improved in shanty towns.

15 What is 'counter-urbanisation'?

3.4 Urban land use

16 Define a functional zone or region.

17 In the USA the Central Business District is known as ....

18 What is the grouping of people according to income and status into different types of residential areas called?

19 In an LEDC city, the functional region that surrounds the CBD is known as the ....

20 What is urban renewal?

3.5 Urban development and planning

21 Why is urban planning necessary?

22 Why has so much urban development and planning focused on the inner city?

23 State two key aims of central city redevelopment as far as traffic is concerned?

24 Why is there generally less effective urban development and planning in the rapidly growing LEDC cities?

25 Name an important type of urban redevelopment that may be located outside the city itself.

3.6 New towns and expanded towns

26 What is meant by 'overspill'?

27 Give three reasons why the first British New Towns were planned to grow to a population of about 60 000.

28 Name the planned new city which was built near London.

29 State one way in which New Town development damaged existing city areas.

30 What is the fundamental reason for the development of planned New Towns in LEDCs?

3.7 World cities

31 Name the only city in Africa with a population of more than 5 million.

32 Give three important reasons why large cities in LEDCs have grown so rapidly during the 20th century.

33 Give three important reasons why large cities in MEDCs are growing at a slower rate than cities in LEDCs.

34 Give one other significant difference between large cities in LEDCs and MEDCs.

35 Why has Mexico City been called 'the capital of pollution'?

3.8 Urban issues

36 State two major issues common to larger cities in MEDCs and LEDCs.

37 What problems do the large cities create for areas which surround them?

38 What are the chief causes of the problems large cities now face?

39 Why is water supply a major problem for cities in both MEDCs and LEDCs?

40 Why do LEDC cities find it difficult to solve traffic congestion?

Chapter 4
Agriculture

4.1 Farming as a system

A system is a set of objects or parts linked together in a way we can recognise. The system has one or more functions to perform; in other words it has a purpose or a job to do. Systems in geography are **open systems**, which means they need a supply of energy to keep them going. By adjusting to changing conditions the system is kept in a **state of equilibrium** or balance.

A farm satisfies this definition of a system.

1. It is made up of a set of parts—the farm buildings, the fields, the silage bins and the machinery. These parts are linked together, e.g. the grass cut from the fields may be stored in the silage bins until it is used as cattle feed in winter.

2. The system has a purpose—the production of food, fibres and raw materials for industry.

3. The farm needs supplies of energy to keep it going. The basic form of energy is the sun which promotes plant growth, but the farm workers also provide energy to make the system work.

4. Farmers often have to adjust the ways in which they manage and run their farms. These adjustments are the result of new farming techniques and the availability of new equipment and machinery. Farmers may also be affected by

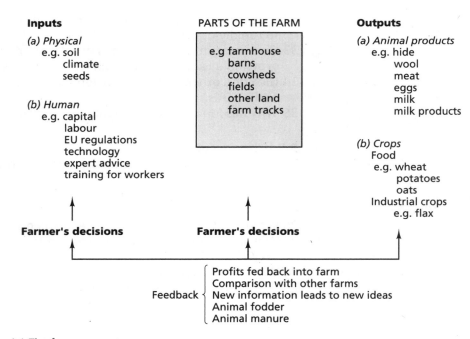

Fig. 4.1 The farm as a system

changes in consumer demand, government policy or other regulations. For example, farmers of the European Union (EU) have to adjust to the demands of the Common Agricultural Policy (CAP) (see Unit 4.8).

Figure 4.1 illustrates the way in which we can look at the farm as an open system. The key factors in determining how the system will operate are the physical environment and the decisions made by the farmer. The inputs, outputs and feedback are directly linked to the physical environment and the decisions made by the farmer.

The physical environment

Examiner's tip

Make sure you understand what is meant by the physical or natural environment (rocks, soil, rain, aspect, temperature, etc.)

The physical environment influences considerably the nature of farming practised in different places. In Britain, for example, the mild winters and substantial rainfall make grass the most suitable crop to be grown in the western part of the country. Conversely, the sunny summers, lower rainfall totals and flat land of eastern England are physical factors which are much more favourable to arable farming.

Relief and geology also have their effects. In Scotland, for example, 70% of the land area is unsuitable for farming. Even on a single farm, variations in geology and slope can produce different land uses. On a farm in southern England you may find cattle-rearing for milk production concentrated on the rich wet meadows and low-lying fields with heavy clay soil, while cereal crops are grown on the lighter, better drained and more fertile soils of the hillside.

The farmer as decision-maker

The success of a farm is dependent largely upon the ability of its farmer to make the right decisions. A farmer must decide:
- how best to use the available land
- how much money and other resources can be invested
- which products will bring the greatest return.

As well as these long-term judgements, day-to-day decisions include when to start harvesting, when to time the lambing season or when to sell the animals.

When the farmer makes the right decisions the farm is successful and a profit is made. The profit is the income remaining after all the production costs have been paid. The farmer then has to decide what proportion of the profit should be reinvested in the farm (new machinery, the repair and modernisation of buildings) and how much can be saved or spent on the family.

Inputs and outputs

Inputs are the raw materials of farming. They include physical inputs such as soil quality, climate, animal breeds and seeds, and some human inputs, especially the labour needed to work the land. The capital or money available, as an input to maintain and improve the farm, may be directly related to the feedback in terms of the profit made by the farmer in the previous year.

Outputs are the products of the farm, which may be animals, animal products or crops. Outputs such as animal feed and animal manure may also become an input through the feedback process.

Feedback

Farmers have to constantly assess how well their farm is operating. Evidence comes partly from how high or low profits are. A farmer will also compare operations with other farmers and get expert advice from the agricultural advisory services (ADAS), from farming journals, from the National Farmers Union (NFU) and radio broadcasts. From experience and new knowledge, the farmer may change decisions and practices from time to time, to try to make the farm system operate more effectively and more profitably. In recent times there has been an increase in consumer demand for organically produced meat and vegetables which has encouraged some farmers to change their style of production completely, so that chemicals and inorganic fertilisers are no longer used on the soil or the crops.

Ostrich farming has recently gained in importance as a direct result of a decrease in demand for red meat for health reasons. Ostrich has the same texture as beef, but it is less likely to lead to illness such as heart disease since the fat content is much lower. Some farmers have opted for herds of water buffalo and deer since the BSE scare; the meat is similar to beef but there is no trace of BSE in these breeds.

A hill farm in Wales

Fig 4.2 shows an example of a farm as a system, using a hill farm in mid–Wales. The area where the farm is situated is an upland plateau with thin acid soils. The annual precipitation is high (1500mm), due to the height of the land (above 300m) and the westerly location; there is some snowfall in winter. Summers are cool with an average temperature of 13.5°C and winters are mild with an average temperature of 4.5°C in December.

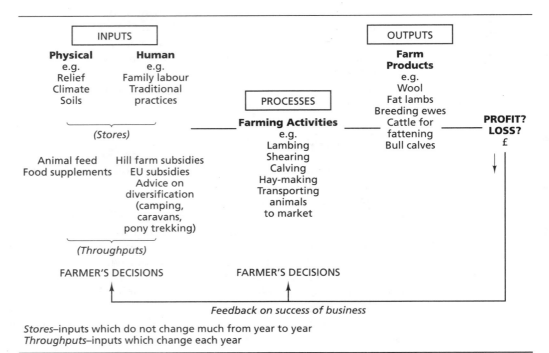

Fig. 4.2 A hill farm system

Main features
- The main crop is grass.
- Sheep rearing is the main activity on exposed moorlands.
- Cattle may be reared in sheltered parts and sold to lowland farms for fattening.
- Farms are small and usually still family run.
- Government grants and EU subsidies help farmers to survive in these **marginal** areas.
- Some farmers try to diversify by opening up their land as camp and caravan sites; pony trekking holidays may also be offered.

Problems
In spite of EU and government help the marginal farmlands have to contend with a number of problems.
- Richer farmlands rear sheep more successfully. This competition may mean a reduction in subsidies which would severely affect all hill farmers.
- Bad weather in the lambing season can have a drastic effect on the number of lambs that survive, which in turn affects the farmers' annual profit.
- The traditional economy is in decline; it is unattractive to many young people who move to the urban areas for work. The old farms are bought up as retirement or holiday homes.
  These factors could equally well apply to a hill farm in other parts of Britain such as the Lake District or north Yorkshire.

4.2 Farming contrasts

Types of farming

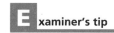

Farming activities can be classified according to a number of different characteristics.

1 Specialisation
i) **Arable** farming is the ploughing and cultivation of land for the production of crops.
ii) **Pastoral** farming is the rearing of animals that feed on grass and other vegetation.
iii) **Mixed** farming is where crops are grown and livestock is also reared.

2 Intensity of land use
i) In **intensive** farming large amounts of capital and/or labour are applied to the land.
ii) In **extensive** farming large areas of land are worked by a small labour force. The extensive cultivation of crops usually requires the use of modern machinery.

3 Economic level
i) In **commercial** farming the farm outputs are produced for sale.
ii) In **subsistence** farming the farm produce is mostly consumed by the farming family within the local community.

4 Land tenure
i) In **sedentary** farming the farmer is settled and uses the same area of land to farm at all times.
ii) In **nomadic** farming the farmer moves over large areas of land with the people of the community and the animals, in search of feeding grounds and water supplies.

Farming can also be classified by the method of production used, for example:
- **factory farming**, in which livestock are kept inside in small units to produce high outputs at competitive prices
- **plantation agriculture**, in which one cash crop is grown on a large estate with a high level of organisation and administration
- **shifting cultivation** or **slash and burn**, in which community groups settle, clear the land and cultivate it for a number of years until the soil is exhausted. They then move to a new site and repeat the process. The old site is allowed to recover and not usually revisited for 20 or 30 years.

Contrasting farming activities

The following case studies of farming in East Anglia, Denmark and India will allow you to contrast farming activities in three different locations where different physical and human factors have influenced the types and methods of agricultural production.

Farming in East Anglia
East Anglia is a low plateau bordered in the west by a chalk scarp (the East Anglian Heights) which is broken by the Breckland, a low-lying sand and gravel area covered by heath. The plateau is plastered with glacial deposits, boulder clays, sands and gravels. Two distinctive areas are the Fens, which are made up of very fertile silt and peat deposits, and the Broads, shallow lakes formed by the drowning of peat workings from medieval times (see Fig. 4.3).

Main features
The farming success of the area results from a combination of the following factors.
1. The glacial deposits have been broken down to form fertile soils, e.g. the richer glacial soils are important for cereals and sugar beet; the heavy boulder clay soils are used for beef and dairy cattle.
2. The drier and sunnier climate of eastern England suits arable production.
3. This is the chief arable farming area of England.

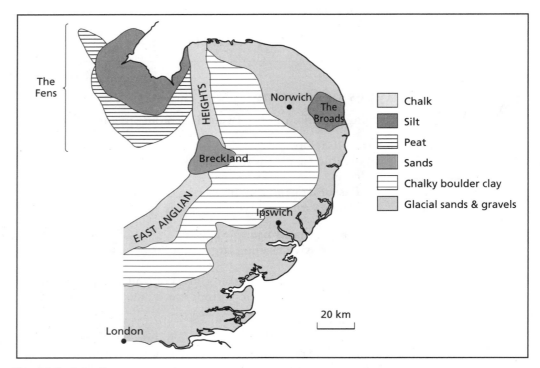

Fig. 4.3 East Anglia

④ Wheat is sown in the autumn and barley is sown in the spring.

⑤ The flat low-lying areas allow farmers to use efficient mechanised techniques.

⑥ Cereals are grown in rotation with valuable cash crops such as potatoes, sugar beet and vegetables.

⑦ The 'waste' from the sugar beet processing is returned to the farms as animal fodder.

⑧ The beet is lifted in the autumn which fits in well with the 'off-peak' period for cereal production.

⑨ There is easy access to London and the towns of the East Midlands to market crops and animal products.

⑩ The growth of the frozen food industry means a ready market for vegetables.

⑪ Industries have developed in the area which have a close link with farming, e.g. brewing, milling, mustard and shoemaking in Norwich; fertiliser manufacture and agricultural equipment in Ipswich.

Problems

However, the farmers in East Anglia also have some problems to contend with:

- Cold north–east winds and late springs can affect yields.
- Large mechanised farms require a great deal of capital.
- Although few labourers are needed, farms have to compete with higher wages offered in towns.
- In order to maintain efficiency and profitability, farmers have to keep up with new research and techniques.
- Modern farming methods have lead to recent criticism with regard to loss of hedgerows and habitat.

Farming in Denmark

The map Fig.4.4 shows the general distribution of soil types and associated farming regions in Denmark. Like East Anglia, the soils are derived from glacial deposits. East Jutland and the islands are the most fertile areas with a boulder clay cover containing lime from the chalk bedrock. Western Jutland consists of morainic hills and sandy outwash material which forms heathland and marshes. The climate of Denmark is also similar to that of East Anglia but with more severe winters. The January average is 0°C with 18°C in July. Rainfall averages 558mm.

The relief and climate therefore favours arable farming as in East Anglia, but Denmark is famous for animal products such as butter and bacon, the output from pastoral farming activities.

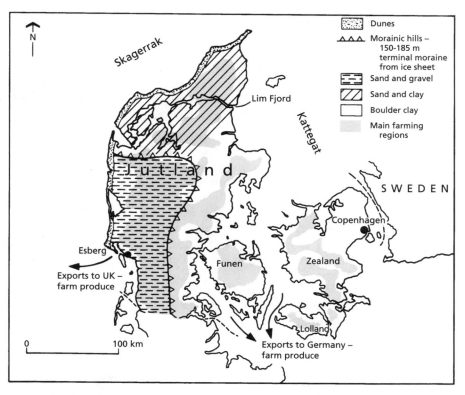

Fig. 4.4 Denmark: soils and farming areas

Denmark's farming changed from wheat growing in 1880, when government policy caused farmers to move towards a highly organised dairy industry. This move was partly prompted by the competition from the newly developing wheat producing areas of North America (the Prairies) and partly due to the fact that a potential market for dairy products was evident in the nearby industrial countries of Germany and Britain.

Strategies for success

In order to make a success of the change in direction of farming a number of strategies have been adopted:

1. The use of fertilisers, a balanced rotation of crops and other scientific methods, has made the boulder clay highly productive.
2. A highly developed co-operative movement has made small-scale farming efficient and productive.
3. The co-operative system allows for standardisation of produce, very important for the consumer.
4. The co-operatives have large-scale buying and selling powers.
5. The co-operatives undertake mechanised processing of milk, eggs and bacon.
6. Government inspections maintain standards and help to uphold the quality and reputation of the produce overseas.
7. Selective breeding has developed cattle and pigs which produce more of what the consumer demands so there is less wastage.
8. Animals are fed on the fodder crops grown in Denmark.
9. High schools provide education for young people and train farmers in up-to-date methods.
10. There are close links between farming and industry, e.g. dairy engineering, milling and brewing.

The majority of Danish farms are small—between 5 and 30 ha. Three quarters of the land area is cultivated; barley is the most important crop and is grown mainly for animal feed. Other fodder crops include beet, hay, clover and oil seed rape. Ninety percent of the total crop yield is used for livestock fodder. Although only 5% of the workforce is directly employed in farming, the scientific methods used and the efficient co-operative system means that over one third of Denmark's exports are food products. Britain and Germany are still Denmark's main customers; all three countries are in the European Union so trading has been reinforced in the last 20 to 30 years.

Farming in India

Farming in India is based on the rhythm of climate created by monsoons. The monsoon climate is experienced in south-east Asia and northern Australia and is caused by the reversal of winds. In winter, most monsoon regions experience dry conditions as the winds blow from the land to the sea. Heavy rainfall occurs in summer as a result of moisture-laden onshore winds blowing onto the land mass. The two periods of monsoon each year give India four seasons.

The dry north-east monsoon gives:
- a 'cool' season in January and February
- a 'hot' season from March to June.

The wet south-west monsoon provides:
- a 'hot-wet' season from June to September
- cold, showery weather from October to December.

As a result of the climate it is usual for two crops a year to be grown because the winter temperatures are high enough for temperate crops to be grown. However, the 'hot' season without rain makes irrigation necessary. There are three main methods of irrigation:
- **tank irrigation**, in which the water is stored in small reservoirs and ponds
- **wells**, in which the water may be raised by tubes or in the traditional way by oxen
- **canal** irrigation—now the most widely used form, with new projects continually being developed.

Examiner's tip

Remember that irrigation is not limited to LEDCs. It is also very important in MEDCs such as USA.

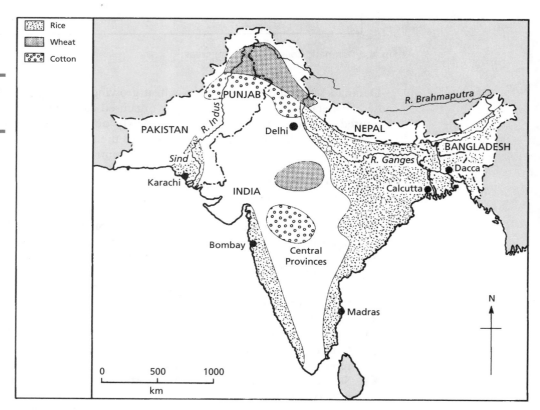

Fig. 4.5 India, Pakistan and Bangladesh: distribution of important crops

Rice is the chief crop and the basic diet for many people. Figure 4.5 shows that rice is grown on the coastal plain and in the Ganges valley. India is the world's second most important producer of rice after China. Wheat is grown in the drier areas and millet in areas where the soils are poorer. Other important crops include jute (used for making sacking, rope etc.), tea and linseed; for each of these crops, India is amongst the world's top three producers.

Rice farming is a very important part of many people's lives in India; Fig. 4.6 shows the annual cycle of a rice farmer. Generally, the rice produced on the farm is consumed by the family. The quiet period on the farms lasts from March to May so many men look for work in the cities during that time to boost the family income.

Problems

Farming in India produces lower yields than in Europe, for example, as Indian farmers have a number of problems to overcome.

1. The soil is poor with little humus and minerals are washed out by the monsoon rains.
2. Farms are small (0.25 ha) and divided into scattered strips making the use of machinery almost impossible.
3. Animal dung is burned as fuel and not used to manure the land.
4. Since the cow is a sacred animal to Hindus, they are allowed to wander in large numbers, eating the food resources.
5. Since farmers are poor they are unable to afford better seed, better tools and better fertilisers.

However, rice yields are better than they used to be as a result of the progress of the 'Green Revolution' (see Unit 4.4).

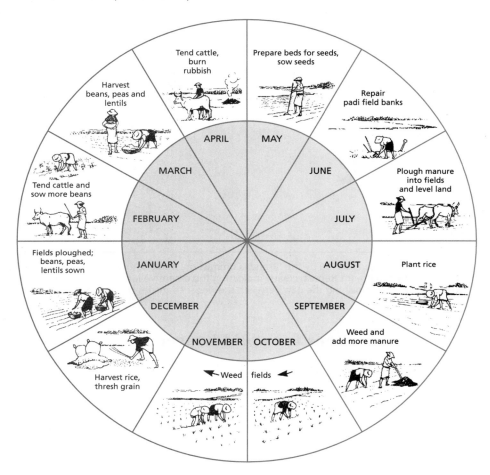

Fig. 4.6 The rice farmer's year

4.3 Food supplies

There is sufficient food produced on a global scale to feed the world's population adequately. Grain production alone would give each person 3000 calories a day in food consumption. The fact that hunger is a problem in many areas is due to the unequal distribution of food supplies, not to a shortage of food produced. Food is considered a commodity to be bought and sold, not a basic human right. This has led to a situation of surplus food supplies in many agriculturally efficient countries, while other countries suffer a food deficit. In general, the areas where food shortages are greatest are the less economically developed countries (LEDCs) seen on map Fig. 4.7; these countries contain two thirds of the world's population.

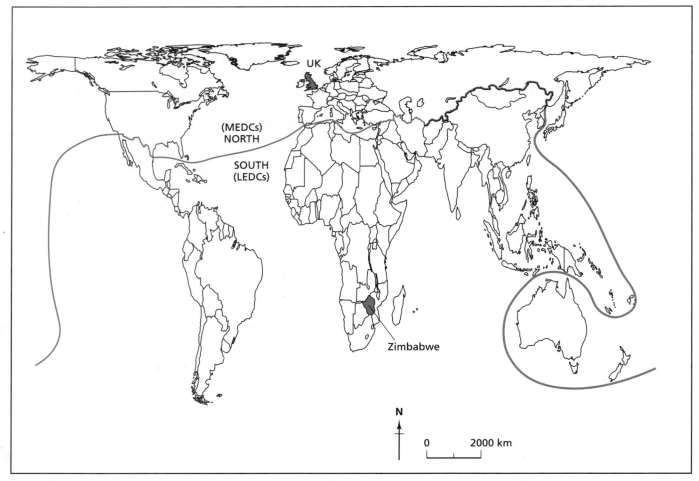

Fig. 4.7 This map was first produced in 1980 by the 'Brandt Commission' and is known as the Peter's Projection. It emphasises the 'north' 'south' divide highlighted by the Brandt Report, clearly indicating the extensive land area included in the 'south'. The Brandt Report attempted to focus on ways of diminishing the gap between the richer countries of the 'north' and the poorer countries of the 'south' (see Fig. 4.9)

Reasons for world hunger

1. Population growth has outstripped increases in food production in some LEDCs.
2. There is limited availability of new land for farming.
3. There is limited access to water resources for farming.
4. Poor harvests and natural disasters, such as drought and flood, disrupt farming and destroy seed and food reserves.
5. Overfishing in some areas has reduced the supply of fish as food.
6. Some farmers are poorly educated and are not given the opportunity to adapt to modern scientific approaches to farming.
7. Transport systems and communications are not well developed and food supplies are not efficiently distributed in many LEDCs. People in one region may be short of food, while another region may have a food surplus.
8. Fertilisers are expensive, many being oil-based, and beyond the reach of many farmers.
9. World food prices have increased to the extent that poorer countries cannot afford to buy extra food on the world markets.
10. Development projects such as irrigation and flood control schemes are very expensive and many LEDCs are heavily in debt.
11. Best land is often taken for cash crops; e.g. hungry people grow tea for export to earn foreign currency to pay foreign debts.
12. Cash from crops goes to the men who often spend it away from the farm; most farming is done by women who do not receive the money.

The circle of poverty

Many farmers in LEDCs find themselves in a circle or cycle of poverty (see Fig. 4.8). Because they have poor food supplies they suffer from malnutrition. This means they are not fit enough to work very hard, so the farmwork is not done properly and the crops give poor yields. Consequently the family has poor food supplies.

The cycle can also be shown in terms of farming techniques. Since the farmer is poor, modern tools, improved seeds and fertilisers cannot be bought. As a result, yields are low and there is little surplus for sale. This means there is very little cash available and no chance of saving. Without savings, farmers are too poor to buy modern tools and seed.

In many LEDCs it is therefore very difficult to improve food supplies.

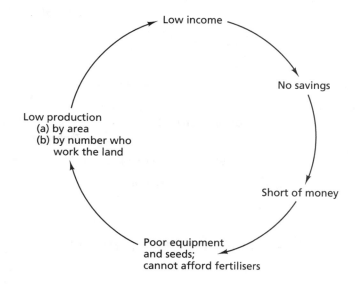

Fig. 4.8 The circle of poverty for farmers in LEDCs

Effects of inadequate food supplies

People are healthy when they have a balanced diet of nutrients—carbohydrates, proteins, fats, minerals and salts. In LEDCs, some foods are very expensive or scarce, especially foods which are high in protein. Even where people have enough food to eat, they may not be healthy because their diet is not balanced. A shortage of proteins or vitamins will cause deficiency diseases such as kwashiorkor, beriberi, rickets and night-blindness.

Many LEDCs are too poor to spend much money on health services and preventative medicine. As a result, the general health level is not as high as in the more economically developed countries (MEDCs) and people have a lower capacity for work. Where health standards are generally low, people are more susceptible to illness and infectious diseases spread rapidly. Diseases such as measles and tuberculosis, easily contained in MEDCs, can cause death to large numbers of people. The spread of AIDS is now a serious problem too, especially in African countries (see Fig. 4.9).

Life expectancy

Poor diets and the illnesses linked with this mean that people living in LEDCs generally have shorter lives than people in the MEDCs. It is possible to work out average life expectancy for different parts of the world. For 37 of the richest countries of the world the average life expectancy is 72 years, for the poorest 31 countries of the world it is 45 years.

Nevertheless, death rates have declined in many countries due to the effects of better food supplies and better medical care, relative to what was available before. This has resulted in the increase in world population; this increase puts more pressure on food supplies. Birth rates have often remained stable or even decreased in some LEDCs. Infant mortality has also declined in many LEDCs although it still remains higher than in most MEDCs. Figure 4.9 compares some statistics for the UK and Zimbabwe to indicate the trends which are evident around the world.

UK and Zimbabwe statistics compared

		1950–55		1970–75		1990–95	
INFANT MORTALITY (per 1000)	UK	28		17		8	
	Zimbabwe	120		93		55	
BIRTH RATE (per 1000)	UK	16		15		14	
	Zimbabwe	52		49		40	
DEATH RATE (per 1000)	UK	12		12		12	
	Zimbabwe	23		15		9	
		Male	Female	Male	Female	Male	Female
LIFE EXPECTANCY	UK	67	72	69	75	73	79
	Zimbabwe	40	43	50	53	59	63

1990s

Doctors per head of population	UK	1 to 667
	Zimbabwe	1 to 7100
GDP spent on health	UK	6.6%
	Zimbabwe	3.2%

In 1991 28.5% of the work force of Zimbabwe was reported to be HIV positive

Fig. 4.9 UK and Zimbabwe statistics compared

Examiner's tip

Compare the changes that took place between 1950 and 1995 in the UK and Zimbabwe, as shown by the indicators in Fig. 4.9.

4.4 The Green Revolution

The 'Green Revolution' is the term given to the programme of plant breeding which produced new **high-yielding** (or **heavy-yielding) varieties (HYV)** of crops which led to great increases in food production.

Mexico developed a new wheat strain in the 1960s which trebled the yield of wheat.

New rice strains grown in the Philippines (IR8) more than trebled rice yields.

There has since been plant breeding to produce high yielding maize, sorghum and potatoes.

Features and effects of the Green Revolution

- Extension of irrigation so water is available at the time and place it is needed for the crops
- Wider use of fertilisers and pesticides to protect the crops
- Up to four times the yield from the same land
- Shorter growing period so multiple cropping is possible
- New industries developed to supply fertilisers to the farmers, creating more employment
- Rural electrification followed the extension of irrigation (needed to operate pumps), bringing an increase in the standard of living of village dwellers.

The success of the Green Revolution is summarised in Fig. 4.10, which shows a model of agricultural development as a consequence of improved inputs.

Problems

There have, however, been problems associated with the Green Revolution:

1. Fertilisers and seeds are sometimes too expensive for poorer farmers to buy without getting into debt.
2. High yields mean there is more grain available which in turn means prices are lower.
3. HYV grains are rich in carbohydrate but a balanced diet needs protein foods such as peas and lentils.
4. Fertilisers sometimes have to be imported using valuable currency.

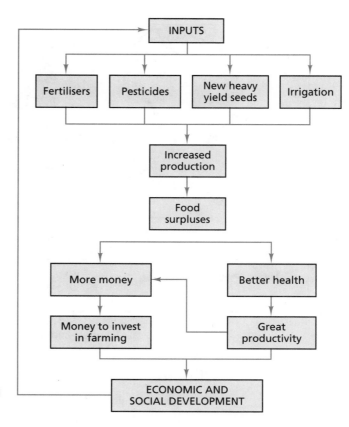

Fig. 4.10 A model of agricultural development

5. Increased use of machinery leads to a decrease in employment.
6. People find some HYV grains less palatable.
7. Dwarf varieties provide little straw and thatch which is widely needed on the farm.
8. Landless or small farmers have been unable to compete and have added to the drift of people into the towns.
9. Increased irrigation can lead to the spread of water-borne diseases such as bilharzia.
10. The use of fertilisers and chemicals has an environmental impact on land and water.

It is clear that the positive aspects of the Green Revolution have not been enjoyed by all farmers and in some cases the gap between rich and poor farmers has widened.

There has been considerable success in South Asia with improved rice yields, where the farming initiatives have been backed by government funding. HYVs have had little impact in Africa, where drier conditions are experienced, but research continues.

The Green Revolution should not be seen as an event but as a process which is evolving to suit the needs of farmers in a variety of environments. Current research into micro-biological techniques could lead to further improvements for farmers in difficult rural environments in both LEDCs and MEDCs in the near future. Current moves in plant and animal breeding have been termed the **Gene Revolution**.

4.5 Savanna lands

The savanna or tropical grasslands, are located between the Tropic of Cancer and the Tropic of Capricorn, north and south of the tropical forest zones (see Fig 4.11).
The main areas are:
1. The *llanos* of Venezuela
2. The *campos* of Brazil
3. Parts of Africa including the Sahel
4. Parts of northern Australia.

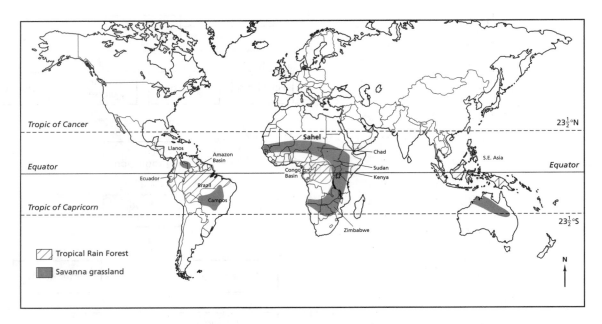

Fig. 4.11 Tropical rain forest and savanna grassland regions

Climate

● Convectional rain falls in the summer when the sun is most powerful.
● Winters are dry, with trade winds blowing from the north-east in the northern hemisphere, and from the south-west south of the Equator.
● Temperatures are high, reaching a peak before the summer rains begin.

See climate graph for Bulawayo, Zimbabwe Fig. 4.12

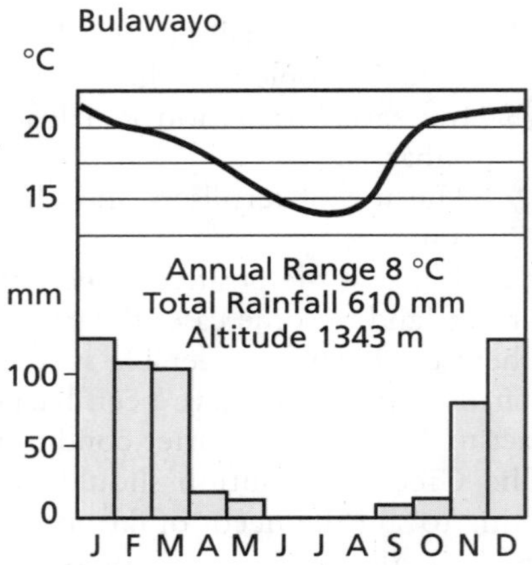

Bulawayo

Annual Range 8 °C
Total Rainfall 610 mm
Altitude 1343 m

Fig. 4.12 Climate graph for Bulawayo, Zimbabwe

Vegetation

● The true savanna is a parkland with scattered trees and grass.
● Trees are adapted to retain moisture, e.g. acacia branches are long to shade the roots; the baobab has thick bark and holds moisture in its trunk; bushes are thorny with narrow leaves to reduce transpiration.
● Elephant grass can grow to a height of 5 metres but most grasses are short and coarse.
● Grasses die down in the dry season but grow quickly when the rains come.
● Near the tropical rain forests there are extensive patches of woodland.
● On the desert fringes there are only a few stunted trees because the rainfall is so low.

Soils

- Soils are not very fertile.
- Soils are mainly red laterites with the nutrients leached out.
- Soils are porous so irrigation is difficult.

Farming

Cattle rearing is the traditional way of life of many people in the savanna lands. Large-scale stock rearing is particularly important in South America and Queensland, Australia.

Crops are also grown including corn, cotton, groundnuts and tobacco.

The tropical grasslands, especially in Africa, are the home of herds of animals such as the zebra, giraffe, elephant, gazelle and wildebeest. As a result, these areas have become popular tourist destinations.

The Sahel

The Sahel region of Africa stretches across the continent on the southern edge of the Sahara desert and takes in parts of all the following countries: Mauritania, Mali, Niger, Chad, Sudan, Ethiopia, Senegal, Burkina Faso, Benin and Nigeria.

The rainfall varies on average from 100mm per annum on the desert edges to 500mm on the southern side of the region. These rainfall totals hide the large variations which may occur from year to year. Since 1968 the actual rainfall has been well below average and the result has been a prolonged and severe drought.

The drought has meant that the peoples of the region have not been able to grow their staple (basic) foods – millet and sorghum. The cattle pastures have been over-grazed and the bare patches of land have encouraged soil erosion which in time, destroys the pastures. Trees are cut down for fuel and, again, the bare patches of land lead to soil erosion. The result has been **desertification** of the region and traditional ways of life have been damaged.

Reasons for desertification

Desertification simply means the spread of desert-like conditions into areas which formerly supported a vegetation cover. It can be brought about in several ways:

- A decrease in rainfall means fewer plants will grow.
- Too many animals graze too little pasture which eventually leaves the ground bare.
- Trees are cut down for fuel too quickly to be replaced by natural regrowth; bare ground is exposed.
- Land is taken for cash crops pushing the landless farmers on to more marginal land.
- Marginal land is overcultivated and the soil soon becomes exhausted and laid bare.
- Bare soils are soon subjected to soil erosion.
- Increasing demands for water reduces the available supply.
- A lowering of the water table may result after prolonged drought and with increased demand for water.

There is strong evidence to indicate that desertification is not a permanent situation in which land is lost forever from farming. Rather, it is a state of temporary land degradation which may be rectified by good land management techniques in sympathy with the local climatic conditions and the needs of the local communities.

The plants of the Sahel are well adapted to the unpredictable climate, and the people who have traditionally lived in the area for generations have adapted their lifestyle to their physical environment.

Some of the peoples of Sudan and Ethiopia have been particularly affected by the apparent spread of the desert which has gradually reduced their ability to farm the land and feed themselves. Famine has been the long-term result, causing disease and death. People have migrated from the worst-hit areas, sometimes abandoning farming altogether and moving to the towns.

While climate has played a part in the human suffering of the Sahel, it must be remembered that conditions have been accentuated by civil wars. These always affect the poorest sectors of the community more than any other.

Examiner's tip

Draw a systems model to show the processes involved in desertification. Identify which are physical and which are human factors.

4.6 Tropical rain forest ecosystem

The regions of tropical rain forest lie within approximately 5° north and south of the Equator. They are also commonly called the equatorial rain forests.

The main areas are:

1. the coastal regions of Ecuador and Colombia
2. the lowlands of the river Amazon
3. West Africa and the Congo basin
4. Malaysia, Indonesia and New Guinea.

Climate

- Temperatures are high and uniform, with a yearly range of only a few degrees.
- The diurnal range can reach 7°C.
- There is high humidity.
- Heavy convectional rain falls every afternoon.
- Rainfall is at its highest when the sun is at its highest (in March and April, and September and October)

(See climate graph for Singapore, Fig. 4.13.)

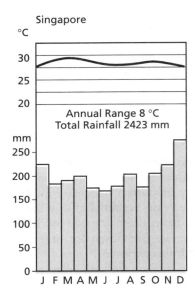

Fig. 4.13 Climate graph for Singapore

Vegetation

- There is dense forest, sometimes called **selva**.
- The thousands of plant species include valuable hardwoods such as ebony and mahogany.
- A canopy layer of tall trees with high branches shades the lower layers from the fierce sun.
- Tree roots form thick plank-buttresses at ground level.
- Shorter trees form an intermediate layer below the canopy.
- Lianas (rope-like climbers) hang from the trees.
- Orchids grow out of crevices in the tree trunks.
- At ground level there are ferns and mosses; it is dark and damp as the sunlight cannot filter through.
- Mangrove forests grow along low-lying muddy coasts. Trees are short with a tangle of roots which trap the mud and extend the mangrove swamp.
- There is no seasonal rhythm; some plants will be in bud next to plants in flower, while others will be shedding leaves.

(See Fig. 4.14.)

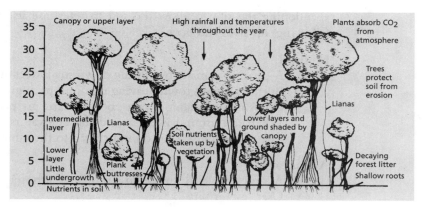

Fig. 4.14 The equatorial rain forest ecosystem

Soils

- High temperatures and high humidity cause chemical weathering and leaching
- Soils contain iron; these are fertile when first planted but rapidly lose fertility.

The rain forest ecosystem

(See also Units 1.9, 6.1 and 6.6.) An ecosystem is a community of plants and animals which share the same environment. Figure. 4.15 shows a model of the tropical rain forest ecosystem.

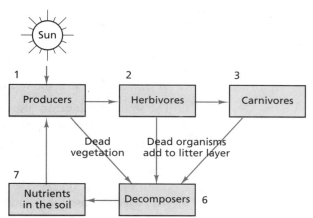

Fig. 4.15 Model of an ecosystem

- Sunlight provides energy for the system.
- This energy is converted by the plants into food—the process of photosynthesis.
- The **producers (1)** are the plants, e.g. the trees.
- The **herbivores (2)**—e.g. insects, caterpillars, monkeys—feed on the plants.
- The **carnivores (3)**—e.g. jaguar, ocelot, puma—feed on the herbivores and on each other.
- The **decomposers (6)**—e.g. fungi, bacteria—quickly break down the dead material from groups 1, 2, and 3 in the high temperatures and rainfall.
- The **nutrients (7)** or plant foods are formed from the decomposed materials and together with water help the producers to grow and so the cycle begins again.

Traditional ways of life

In the past, people lived in the tropical forests either by collecting or gathering food such as berries and fruit and hunting fish, birds and animals or by growing food as **shifting cultivators**.

Shifting cultivation

This is a method of subsistence farming practised in the humid tropics. It involves clearing and cultivating small plots of land for two or three harvests and then abandoning the site to allow the soil to refertilise itself. It is sometimes called 'bush-fallowing' or 'slash and burn'.

Method

1. A clearing is made by cutting down small trees and bushes.
2. Burning undergrowth leaving tree stumps in ground.
3. Crops such as manioc, yams, beans, maize are planted in ashes.
4. When the ground is exhausted the cultivators repeat the operation in another part of the forest; they do not return to the same site for 20 or 30 years.

Advantages

1. Allows people to survive in a hostile environment
2. Uses soil fertility
3. Avoids erosion
4. Does not require expensive or elaborate tools.

Disadvantages

1. Few people per hectare. A family of five may need 20 ha to survive.
2. Diet is limited and no animals can be kept
3. Original vegetation is eventually replaced with poorer secondary growth.

Recent changes

Better communications have opened up some of the forest areas, such as the Amazon lowlands, and people have become sedentary, growing subsistence crops and cattle ranching.

The hunters and gatherers face the end of their traditional way of life because:

- Less land is available for hunting and fishing as areas are opened up by modern developers.
- They catch diseases from the new settlers, from which they are not immune.
- It is planned that some of the forest dwellers will be concentrated in forest reservations so that the rest of the land can be developed.

The shifting cultivators also find their way of life threatened.

- Modern timber and ranching projects are pushing into the forest and taking over land formerly used by the cultivators.
- Medical care is now reaching remote villages and fewer people are dying young. The population is increasing but traditional farming techniques cannot keep up with the extra food needs.
- In order to raise their standard of living, some are now growing cash crops such as cotton and sugar and giving up traditional farming.

4.7 Tropical food and forest products

The tropical regions yield valuable products which have provided the basis of trading for long periods of time. After the Industrial Revolution raw materials and food were in great demand for the developing industries and growing urban populations of European countries in particular. Many European countries therefore established tropical colonies to meet some of these needs. Cotton, rubber, timber and minerals provided cheap raw materials for industry; and foods such as sugar, cocoa, tea and fruit supplied the needs of the urban dwellers.

Although most of the tropical colonies are now independent nations their economies still reflect the old colonial links.

Plantation agriculture

Food products were often grown on plantations, most of which were managed by people from the colonising country. The main plantation crops are tea, coffee, cocoa, bananas, rubber, palm oil, sugar cane.

- This is a highly organised form of agriculture, involving the growing of one crop in tropical or sub-tropical regions.
- Plantations are usually large, 400 ha or more for a rubber plantation, and need a large labour force for cultivating, picking, processing etc.
- The crop grown is often processed on or near the plantation and then shipped to Europe, North America or one of the other industrialised parts of the world.

Advantages
- The quality of the crop and product is high.
- Care is taken with the crop to improve output and keep down diseases.
- It is efficient; capital investment provides the expert knowledge and methods.
- A steady supply of the crop for the market can be achieved by staggered planting.
- It provides employment for large numbers of people who are not skilled.
- Workers are often provided with housing, schools and health care.

Disadvantages
- The crop can be attacked by disease, pests or storms and all profits lost.
- Produce and profits are often sent overseas.
- The soil may become poor and erosion can then occur.
- Overseas supervision can cause political tension.
- Local people are often exploited.
- The need for more labour has resulted in immigration, which causes social problems, e.g. Indians working on sugar plantations in South Africa.
- Fluctuations in world prices often cause supply and demand problems.
- Cash crops are sometimes grown at the expense of food crops.

Recent changes
- Change of ownership: such plantations are sometimes taken over by governments when countries become independent.
- There has been an increase in smallholdings for such crops as cocoa.
- Government-sponsored plantations use money borrowed from overseas.

Examiner's tip

Find out more about plantation agriculture with a specific case study of a plantation.

A food exporting tropical country—Sri Lanka

Sri Lanka is an island about half the size of England. It lies between 5° and 9° north of the Equator, so it is well located to grow tropical crops.

Sri Lanka consists of a mountain core, rising to over 2400m, surrounded by coastal lowlands. Different types of crop can be grown at different altitudes: coconuts on the coastal plain, rice on the lowlands, rubber in the foothills, tea in the hills (See Fig. 4.16).

Temperatures are high all year due to latitude. Sri Lanka's rainfall varies from 5180mm in parts of the 'wet zone', to less than 1000mm in parts of the 'dry zone'. The 'dry zone' covers 75% of the country. There is a summer drought and unreliable rainfall. The 'wet zone' is where the commercial farming is found.

Although technology has produced substitutes for many tropical products, tropical foodstuffs are still in demand by MEDCs.

Chief exports
Food crops form one third of the value of Sri Lanka's exports; tea is the most important, then rubber, coconut products (copra, desiccated coconut, coconut oil) and spices (cinnamon and cloves).

Sri Lanka was a British colony—Ceylon—and the tea industry is still mainly British owned.

Chief imports
Petroleum, machinery and transport equipment are Sri Lanka's main imports. Sri Lanka is a crossroads for world shipping so it is easy to export agricultural produce all over the world, e.g. tea to the USA, UK and Australia.

Forest products in a tropical country—Malaysia

Malaysia is a federation of 13 states which became a new nation in 1963. The states were formerly British colonies. Two of the states, Sabah and Sarawak, are in northern Borneo (see Fig. 4.17).

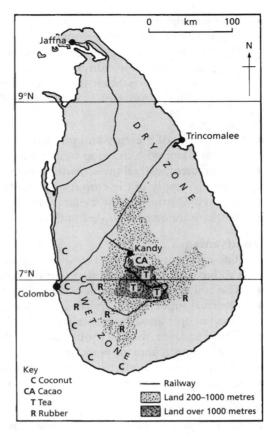

Fig. 4.16 Sri Lanka: Export crops

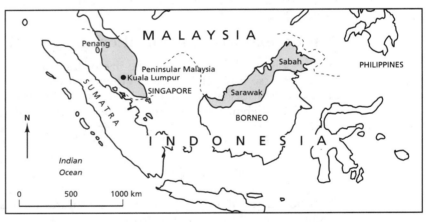

Fig. 4.17 Malaysia and neighbouring countries

Relief

- The Malay Peninsula has very little flat land and the mountains rise to over 2100m.
- Borneo has coastal lowlands with a highland core rising to 4090m.

Climate

- Temperatures are high, averaging 32°C all year.
- Rain falls throughout the year; the annual average is 2540mm.
- The wettest areas receive 6580mm a year.
- This is a monotonous climate, with constant high humidity.

Vegetation

- There are mangrove swamps in coastal areas.
- Evergreen forests grow on land up to 600m.
- A high canopy of trees reaches 50-60m in height.
- The middle layer of shade-loving trees grow to 6-15m in height.

- There is a ground layer of bamboo, mosses, ferns and other large-leaved plants.
- Land between 600m and 1250m supports chestnut and oak forests.
- Small gnarled trees up to 5m high and covered in mosses and lichens are found on land above 1250m.

Economic exploitation of the forest

The forests or 'jungle' were first seen as a barrier to economic development by the British, who wished to exploit the vast tin resources of Malaysia. Roads and railways had to be cut through dense forests to link mining centres with the ports.

In 1878 the British introduced rubber to Malaysia, establishing plantations on the western side of the Malay Peninsula using the already established road, rail and port links. Hardwood forests were cut and burned to make room for the new plantations, for at that time such timber was of no commercial importance.

The chief forest products today are rubber, palm oil, timber and copra.

Rubber

- Malaysia produces 25% of the world's rubber (Thailand is now the world's major producer of rubber).
- Half of Malaysia's rubber is still produced on plantations which are now government run.
- Half is now produced by farmers with smallholdings on the eastern side of the peninsula.
- Smallholders grow crops for home consumption as well as rubber as a cash crop.
- Smallholders are given financial support by the government to protect their interests.
- Production is dependent on world prices which fluctuate greatly, and synthetic products have reduced demand.
- There has been a recent revival in the industry due to the AIDS scare and the increased use of condoms; Malaysia claims to produce 60% of the world's condoms.

Palm oil

- Coconut palms are grown on sandy soils near the sea
- Malaysia is now the world's largest producer of palm oil.
- Palm oil is now a more important export product than rubber.

Timber

- Timber is cut from the edges of the tropical forest up to a height of 600m.
- Forests yield a variety of high-quality hardwoods.
- On the peninsula timber is moved by road.
- In Sabah and Sarawak logs are floated down rivers.
- Most towns have sawmills and timber yards.
- Cutting is carefully controlled as tree cover controls groundwater flow, protecting the soil from erosion.
- Two-thirds of Malaysia's forests remain untouched; the mountainous terrain makes access difficult and rural-urban drift has led to a labour shortage.

4 .8 Agriculture in the European Union

The Common Agricultural Policy (CAP)

The Common Agricultural Policy came into being in 1962 with the aim of achieving five goals:

1. To increase agricultural productivity
2. To ensure a fair standard of living for farmers and farm workers
3. To check price fluctuations
4. To ensure that supplies of farm produce were available when needed
5. To guarantee supplies to consumers at reasonable prices.

When CAP was established there were six members of what was then called the

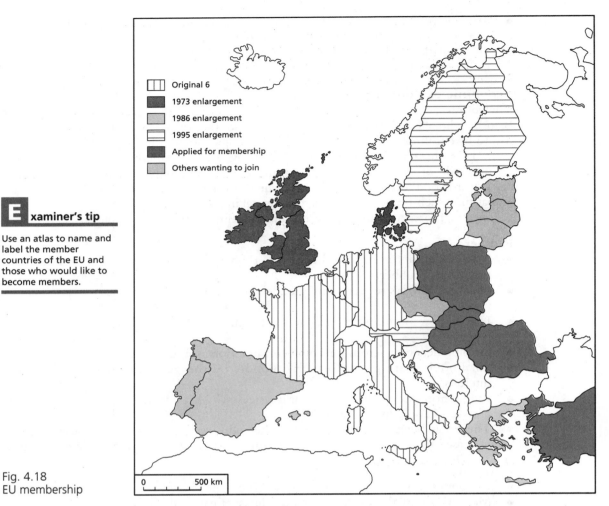

Fig. 4.18
EU membership

European Economic Community or EEC (see map Fig 4.18). Five goals were set in order to address the main problems identified in the agricultural sectors of the six member countries. The main problems were as follows.

Fragmentation

In some countries the laws of inheritance mean that land is divided equally among heirs. In time this leads to a situation where farms consist of tiny scattered strips. It is difficult to use machinery on small strips of land and farmers waste time travelling to tend each plot of land. There has been a big effort to consolidate plots of land and increase farm size; considerable progress has been made in France, Germany and the Netherlands (see Fig. 4.19). Spain, Portugal and Greece which joined the EEC much later still have some way to go to achieve land consolidation.

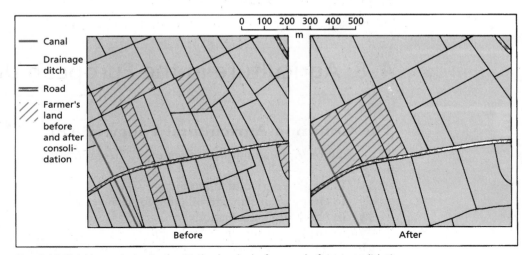

Fig. 4.19 Field boundaries in the Netherlands, before and after consolidation

Small size of farms

Farm sizes are traditionally small in many European countries, partly as a result of the division of the land as mentioned under fragmentation. Small farms are generally not very efficient unless they are intensively cultivated, such as market gardening in the Netherlands. Figure 4.20 shows that farm size still varies considerably between the member states.

Country	% of workforce employed in	Average farm
Belgium	2.6	17.3
Denmark	5.1	32.5
Ireland	13.7	22.7
France	5.5	30.7
Greece	21.3	5.3
Italy	7.3	7.7
Luxembourg	3.0	33.2
Netherlands	3.9	17.2
Portugal	11.6	8.3
Spain	10.2	16.0
United Kingdom	1.0	68.9
Germany	3.5	17.6
Austria	6.7	13.1
Finland	8.6	13.5
Sweden	3.6	30.4

Fig. 4.20
Average farm size and employment in agriculture in the countries of the EU

The latifundia system

Farms in southern Italy, Spain and Portugal have traditionally been organised under the latifundia system. This means that the farms are run as large estates by agents of the landowner who usually lives some distance away, very often in one of the large cities. The estates are worked by landless farm workers who are paid a wage for their work in the same way as if they worked in a factory or a shop. They have no say in the management of the farm.

Money from the *Cassa per il Mezzogiorno* (Fund for the South) has brought about widespread land reform in Italy. Here, large estates have been taken from absentee landowners and redistributed amongst the previously landless farm workers, with the result that output has increased. Reform has been slower in Spain and Portugal since they only joined the EEC in 1986 whereas Italy was a founder member in 1957.

Changes to the EU and the CAP

All member countries have to abide by the CAP; there are now 15 member states belonging to what is now known as the European Union (EU) (see map Fig. 4.18). Inevitably, goals set down in 1962 for the six original member countries, will not necessarily be relevant to the new members 30 or 40 years later, and a series of changes to the CAP have been imposed as time has gone on.

There have been many difficulties for the EU in trying to achieve the five original goals, and what has been achieved so far has not made the CAP popular in the majority of EU countries. The problems have arisen because all member states have had to comply with the CAP but in fact there are **wide differences in farming conditions** among the member countries. For example:

- Farming in the UK is more highly mechanised and more efficient than farming in France or Portugal.
- Some countries are important exporters of agricultural produce, e.g. Denmark and Ireland.
- Some countries are largely importers of agricultural produce, e.g. UK and Germany.

- Farming is more important to the economy of some member states, e.g. in Greece 21% of the workforce is employed in agriculture whereas in Luxembourg the figure is only 3%.

Most of the CAP funds are spent supporting EU farmers through a complex system of guaranteed prices. The price of farm products is set sufficiently high to encourage farmers to produce a surplus. High prices benefit the large farmer, while allowing the inefficient small producer to stay in operation.

Problems that have arisen

While most of the original goals have been achieved, some believe that the price has been too high:

- Food surpluses have been created (milk and wine 'lakes', butter, grain and beef 'mountains').
- These surpluses must be stored, incurring high costs.
- Surpluses are sometimes sold cheaply to other countries, affecting prices internally and internationally.
- The prices paid to EU farmers are often higher than world prices; as a result EU food is comparatively expensive.
- Price cuts severely affect marginal farmers, with contributory social and economic impacts.
- Some of the farming methods adopted have greatly affected the environment.

Solutions to the problems

In the 1980s and 1990s reforms were introduced to try to solve some of the problems created:

- Gradual reductions were made in the subsidies paid to farmers to reduce the possibility of overproduction.
- Quotas were introduced to regulate milk production and the production of beef and sheep.
- A 'set-aside' policy was brought in. Farmers were paid to leave land fallow, to create woodland, or to make other use of farmland, e.g. golf courses, caravan sites, farm tourist attractions.
- There was an emphasis on stewardship (management in the country's interest). Farmers were paid to conserve and restore five types of vulnerable landscape:
  (i) chalk grassland
  (ii) lowland heath
  (iii) coastal vegetation
  (iv) river meadows and marshes
  (v) hill and heather moorland.

Examiner's tip

Find out more about some of the changes in this list. Draw a chart to illustrate what you discover.

Changes to the environment

In the interests of efficiency of farm production as stressed by the CAP, farming practices began to change the landscape quite dramatically (see Fig 4.21):

- Hedgerows were removed to enlarge fields.
- Woodland was cut down to extend areas of cultivation.
- Moorlands were lost to cultivation.
- Wetlands were drained to extend fields.
- Heathlands were planted.
- There was a loss of habitat.
- Plant and animal species were lost.
- An increased use of chemicals and fertilisers affected soils, vegetation and water supplies.

Environmentally Sensitive Areas (ESAs)

The need to reduce farm output in the EU came at a time when more and more people were beginning to show a concern for the environment, and politicians were forced to take action. Combining the need to reduce farm output with pressure to address landscape conservation means it is now possible for farmers to obtain financial incentives to farm in an 'environmentally friendly' way. Areas in England and Wales considered to be under particular threat from farming practices, and being of historical and habitat importance, have been designated Environmentally Sensitive Areas (ESAs), as shown on the map Fig. 4.22.

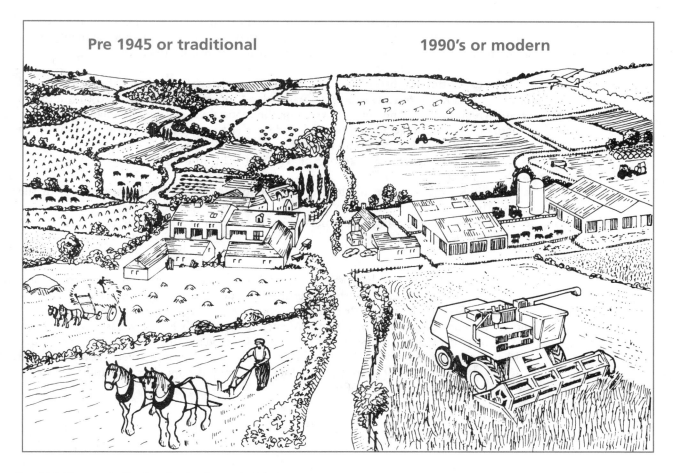

Fig. 4.21 Changes in the farming landscape in Britain

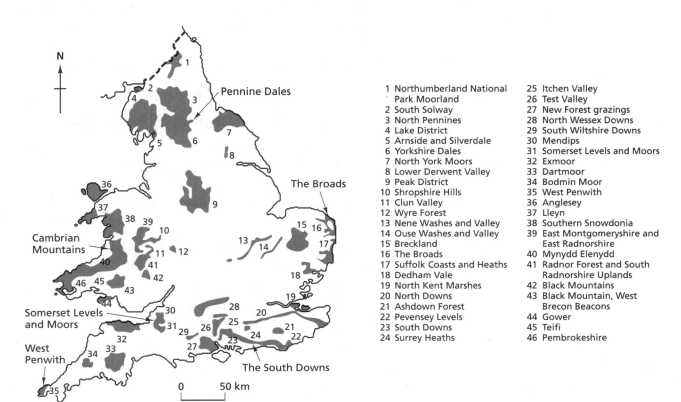

1 Northumberland National	25 Itchen Valley
Park Moorland	26 Test Valley
2 South Solway	27 New Forest grazings
3 North Pennines	28 North Wessex Downs
4 Lake District	29 South Wiltshire Downs
5 Arnside and Silverdale	30 Mendips
6 Yorkshire Dales	31 Somerset Levels and Moors
7 North York Moors	32 Exmoor
8 Lower Derwent Valley	33 Dartmoor
9 Peak District	34 Bodmin Moor
10 Shropshire Hills	35 West Penwith
11 Clun Valley	36 Anglesey
12 Wyre Forest	37 Lleyn
13 Nene Washes and Valley	38 Southern Snowdonia
14 Ouse Washes and Valley	39 East Montgomeryshire and
15 Breckland	East Radnorshire
16 The Broads	40 Mynydd Elenydd
17 Suffolk Coasts and Heaths	41 Radnor Forest and South
18 Dedham Vale	Radnorshire Uplands
19 North Kent Marshes	42 Black Mountains
20 North Downs	43 Black Mountain, West
21 Ashdown Forest	Brecon Beacons
22 Pevensey Levels	44 Gower
23 South Downs	45 Teifi
24 Surrey Heaths	46 Pembrokeshire

Fig. 4.22 Environmentally Sensitive Areas (ESAs) in England and Wales

Farmers in ESAs can opt to receive a payment if they agree to maintain the current state of the landscape of their farm. However, they can receive a higher payment if they agree to actively restore the landscape to its former status, by replanting hedgerows and digging ponds for example.

Farmers in the South Downs ESA are encouraged to take land out of cultivation and return it to animal grazing—sheep in particular—to restore the downland to the grassy sward which people generally believe to be the 'natural vegetation' for chalk areas. Such practices do encourage regrowth of a wide variety of grasses and flowers and attract many species of birds, insects and butterflies.

Other farmers have moved to organic farming. This in itself

- cares for the landscape being farmed
- provides an alternative method of production to deal with the restrictions of the CAP
- ties in with increasing consumer demand for produce which is not treated with chemicals of any kind.

Agribusiness

The reforms of the CAP have taken their toll on some farmers, who have found it a struggle to stay in business without getting into debt to purchase new machinery or new land. Some farmers in Britain have sold out to large companies who run farms along the lines of business organisations; such an approach is known as **agribusiness**. Farms owned by agribusiness organisations grow, process, store and pack the produce which is marketed direct to large retailing chains such as supermarkets, restaurants and fast food outlets. High standards are maintained, since the retailers demand high-grade produce and uniform quality of produce.

Summary

1 Farming can be seen as a system in which a set of inputs go through processes which result in a set of outputs. The outputs form the feedback which then become part of the inputs to drive the system on.

2 Farming can be classified according to a number of different criteria.

3 Food production and food supply is unevenly distributed across the world.

4 The Green Revolution brought about increased food supplies for some LEDCs.

5 Tropical grasslands support cattle ranching and crop production, but the unreliable rainfall can cause human suffering if drought prevents food production over a long period of time.

6 The traditional way of life is dying out in the tropical rain forests as they are developed for timber and cattle ranching activities.

7 Tropical regions of the world supply valuable products for industry as well as for food.

8 The CAP has resulted in the reorganisation of farming within the member states. The achievement of the CAP's original goals brought problems which are gradually being addressed by reforms to the CAP being imposed on member states.

Quick test

4.1 Farming as a system
1 What is the collective term for a set of inputs, processes and outputs?
2 What physical factors will influence a farmer's decision about how to use the land?
3 If a farm is successful, the farmer will make a .... at the end of the year.
4 What sort of activities do some hill farmers engage in to supplement their income from farming?
5 Engaging in activities other than farming is called ....

4.2 Farming contrasts
6 Large amounts of capital and/or labour applied to the land is called .... farming.
7 What is the difference between commercial farming and subsistence farming?
8 What are the fertile soils of East Anglia derived from?
9 Why did Denmark change from being an arable farming country to being one famous for animal products?
10 What type of climate is experienced in India?

4.3 Food supplies
11 If sufficient food is produced world wide to feed the world's population, why is it that some people suffer from hunger?
12 When farmers in LEDCs find it hard to increase their food supplies they can be said to be trapped in a ....of ....
13 What proportion of the world's population live in LEDCs?
14 What should a balanced diet consist of?
15 Why is life expectancy in LEDCs generally shorter than for MEDCs?

4.4 The Green Revolution
16 What does HYV mean?
17 Why was the term 'green' used to describe this process?
18 Which four inputs have increased production in the model of agricultural development?
19 Why has the Green Revolution had little impact on African cultivation?
20 New plant and animal breeding experiments have been called the ....

4.5 Savanna lands
21 What are the winter months like in the savanna regions?
22 How are plants adapted to periods of low rainfall?
23 Which savanna areas are important for commercial cattle rearing?
24 Where is the Sahel?
25 What does desertification mean?

4.6 Tropical rain forest ecosystem
26 When can you expect rainfall in the tropical rain forest regions?
27 What is the name given to the dense tropical forest?
28 What is an ecosystem?
29 What is shifting cultivation?
30 Which activities threaten the traditional ways of life of the tropical forests?

4.7 Tropical food and forest products
31 Name the main plantation crops.
32 Where is commercial farming found in Sri Lanka?
33 What British interests still remain in the production of crops in Sri Lanka?
34 Which product was originally exploited by the British in Malaysia?
35 Why does two-thirds of Malaysia's tropical forest remain untouched?

4.8 Agriculture in the EU
36 What does CAP stand for?
37 What were the three basic problems which originally affected the efficiency of farming in the EU?
38 Which foodstuffs in particular have been overproduced creating surpluses?
39 Leaving land out of cultivation is called ……………….. ………………..
40 Why have some areas in England and Wales been designated ESAs?

Chapter 5
Industry and development

5.1 Location of industry

The location of industry is the spatial distribution of industrial activity, that is, where manufacturing plants and other industries are sited.

Industrialists wish to make the maximum profit. To do this they seek to produce their goods at the lowest cost, to sell as widely as possible and to distribute their goods as efficiently as possible. Industries are located at the most advantageous place to achieve these goals.

Factors in industrial location

1 Raw materials
One way of reducing transport costs is to locate industry near the source of its raw materials (i.e. the materials used in the manufacturing process). This is a key consideration in the case of industries which use vast amounts of bulky raw materials.

Examiner's tip

Learn the factors of location and apply them to an industry in your area.

2 Fuel and power
Industries need a form of energy which will drive the machinery. When industries were dependent upon coal as a source of power, the main manufacturing regions in Britain grew up on the chief coalfields. Today there is much greater freedom of location for many industries, because they depend upon electricity which is widely distributed.

3 Markets
The markets are the places where there is a demand for an industry's products. Manufacturing industries are drawn towards their major markets because this reduces transport costs. The advantages of a market location include:
- reducing the problem of packing and transporting goods which are bulky and therefore expensive to transport
- the location of a factory in a large centre of population which is an important market will probably mean that a labour supply (work force) is available
- the presence of a large works in an area which forms an important market gives the product good publicity.

4 Transport
The availability of a transport system to link production with market outlets used to be a major cost consideration when locating an industry, especially when water and rail transport were the dominant methods of moving goods. New forms of transport and improved transport networks have reduced the overall cost of moving goods for the producer. Road links in particular have allowed industry greater freedom in choice of

location. Motorway intersections are very attractive to some types of industrial production; the motorway network provides easy access to a variety of destinations for the collection and distribution of goods.

5 Labour
The location of industry is influenced by both:
- the availability of a suitably sized labour force
- the quality of the labour available.

At one time, most factory workers were skilled, but today many workers are only semi-skilled and carry out routine assembling jobs or simple machine processes. However, new industries based on modern technology still require highly skilled workers, who need special training.

Some industries are based upon the availability of **cheap labour**. At one time British workers earned comparatively high wages and some companies moved their production operations to less developed countries to exploit cheap labour. However, a series of economic recessions has meant that British labour is competitive again, and foreign investment—especially from Japanese firms—has been attracted to parts of Britain where labour is available.

Other industries seek **well-disciplined workers** who are unlikely to interrupt production through strikes. Some countries do not allow workers to belong to trade unions so the threat of disruption is highly unlikely. However, the working conditions of people in some countries would not be tolerated by workers in other parts of the world.

Labour is therefore a very complex factor of location often involving ethical and moral issues, not simply cost factors.

6 Capital
Large amounts of money are needed to buy raw materials and to run and promote an industry.
- **Fixed capital** is money invested in buildings and machinery.
- **Circulating capital** is money which is tied up in stocks of raw materials and half-finished goods.

Lack of capital in LEDCs is a major reason why some of these countries find it difficult to expand their industrial output.

7 Land
Some industries require a particular type of location in terms of site and land. For example a car assembly plant needs a very large area of flat land so will be looking for a location where land is relatively cheap.

Oil refineries also need large areas of land; but in addition they require easy access to the crude oil, which is usually shipped in very large tankers so a site near a deep water port is essential.

8 Perception
When a new industry is being established, a decision has to be made to develop one particular site in preference to others. The decision is the result of judgements made by those with the power and authority to make such decisions, and is based upon the advantages the chosen site is perceived to have.

Location of traditional industries in Britain
- Coal was the dominant form of fuel and power.
- Large industries needed to be located at coalfields or near a location to which coal could be transported easily.
- Traditional industries were located according to the needs of the time.
- Industries remain in traditional areas, even though the original factors of their location are no longer relevant; this is called **industrial inertia.**
- Relocation is often too expensive to consider.

Location of modern industries
- Industries which have grown up in this century are mainly **consumer industries**.
- Consumer goods include TVs, fridges, washing machines, hi-fi equipment.

- Modern industries which can be powered by electricity and are not tied to a particular location are called **footloose industries.**

The influence of Government policy

In Britain, as in other countries with long established manufacturing industries, the decline of the traditional industries has led to a decline in the prosperity of the regions where these were once found. In order to try to help the people in these regions a number of government initiatives have been established over the years these include the following.

- Setting up trading/industrial estates
- Financial incentives offered to companies to locate in areas of high unemployment
- Restriction of developments in the most favoured areas (e.g. London and the south-east)
- Enterprise Zones designated to encourage a variety of new industrial and commercial activities. New developments in such areas are often exempt from the usual planning processes and may also be eligible for grants and other incentives
- Seeking foreign investment from firms such as Toyota and Nissan
- Encouraging new projects in derelict areas, e.g. the docklands of London and Liverpool.

The EU also allocates money for the revival of the poorest areas within the EU. Areas are designated at different levels depending upon their particular needs and funds can be applied for accordingly, see Fig. 5.1.

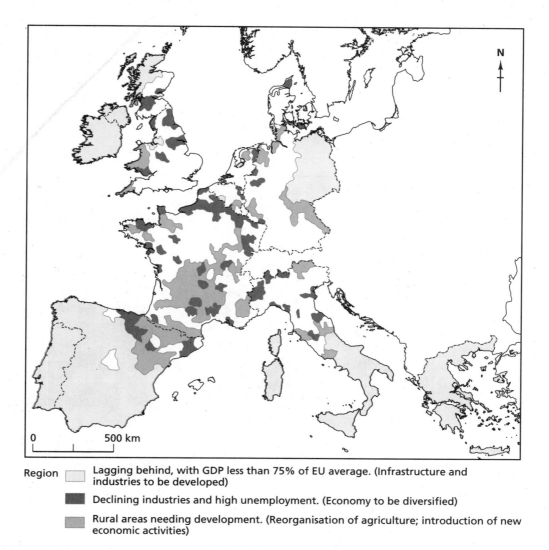

Region ☐ Lagging behind, with GDP less than 75% of EU average. (Infrastructure and industries to be developed)

■ Declining industries and high unemployment. (Economy to be diversified)

▨ Rural areas needing development. (Reorganisation of agriculture; introduction of new economic activities)

Fig. 5.1 Regions eligible under the EU Structural Funds 1994–95

Problems created by industrial development

Major industrial development can create environmental problems such as traffic congestion, pollution and waste disposal. In addition there are the social and economic problems created in the older industrial regions where unemployment is still high.

5.2 An old-established industrial region

The growth of an industrial region

During the 19th century the coalfields of northern France, Belgium and the Ruhr valley in Germany were developed, together with iron ore resources in Lorraine, Luxembourg and the Ruhr. The coal and iron, with local limestone, provided the raw materials for the iron and steel industry which grew up on each of the coalfields. Canals and railways were built to link the works with their raw materials and to waterways such as the Meuse and Rhine.

As the iron and steel industry grew, so did settlements for the miners, factory workers and their families. A belt of almost continuous urban development formed along the Franco-Belgian coalfield from Northern France to Liège in Belgium, with separate clusters in southern Luxembourg and the Rhine–Ruhr region.

Heavy industries using **iron and steel products** also grew up on the coalfields, using steam-driven machinery. Other industries were attracted to the region, such as **engineering and chemicals**.

The traditional textile industry of Flanders was mechanised, and moved to the coalfield where power was cheap. Production of **cotton cloth** took the place of linen and Lille, Douai and Valenciennes became cotton cities. The ports of Antwerp and Rotterdam, linked to the region by canals and rivers, made the import of raw cotton

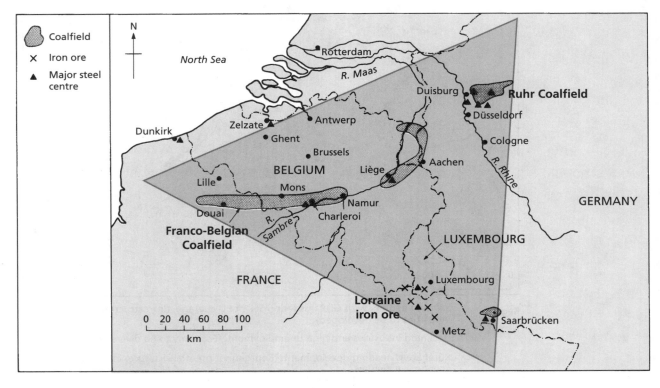

Fig. 5.2 The heavy industrial triangle

and the export of finished goods relatively cheap and easy.

At the beginning of the 20th century this was the most important heavy industrial region in Western Europe. It is sometimes described as the **heavy industrial triangle** (see Fig. 5.2), and acted as a magnet to other industries.

Industrial change

The region has lost some, but not all, of its industrial importance in the last 50 years. There has been a rapid decline in coal production and the steel industry has also reduced its output.

The decline in coal production is partly because new sources of energy, particularly oil and natural gas, are being used instead. Cheaper coal can be imported from the USA and Poland. Steel production has declined because of the increase in cheap steel imports from countries like Brazil and North Korea.

Modern steel plants have been built on the coast at Dunkirk in France and close to the coast at Zelzate in Belgium. This **trend towards coastal sites** is also to be found in other West European countries, including the Netherlands and Germany. These new sites have facilities for importing overseas ore and coal and exporting finished steel products.

The textile industry has also had to change to meet competition from cheap cloth made in mills in India and other Asian countries. The number of workers has nearly halved since 1954, following the introduction of automatic machinery and more efficient working methods. The **engineering**, **chemical** and **metal-smelting** industries which grew up during the industrial revolution are still an important feature of the heavy industrial triangle. Like the steel industry, they have reduced their labour force and changed their products to meet the needs of modern industry. For example, the metallurgical region of Liège produces castings for machine tools, and special steels required by the electronics industry.

Industrial inertia

The heavy industries of the triangle have remained, despite the fact that many of the reasons why they grew up there no longer apply. This is an example of **industrial inertia**. They have stayed because it is expensive to move, difficult to find a suitable labour force elsewhere and many of their customers are also in the same region. In the Ruhr, for example, coking coal is still available from the coalfield, but local iron ore was exhausted many years ago. Ore must now be imported through Rotterdam, which increases costs, even though it can be carried by barge and does not need to be transported by rail. Despite these higher costs, the steelworks at Rheinhausen, Dortmund and Duisburg continue in production and the Rhine–Ruhr region remains the most important centre for heavy industry in Germany.

Footloose industries

As the heavy industries of this region have declined, unemployment has risen, giving rise to concern about the consequent social distress. 'Footloose' industries have been encouraged to set up factories and bring new life into the heavy industrial triangle.

Footloose industries are those which are not tied to a particular location because of high transport costs for raw materials or the need for local supplies of energy. For example, the car industry requires hundreds of components which can be made in factories using relatively small amounts of raw materials and machinery run by electricity. The finished components, such as radiators, windscreens and tyres, are mainly light and easily transported. Both car assembly plants and component manufacturers are footloose and can choose from a variety of sites, preferring those with a suitable labour force and good distribution facilities to the markets.

Footloose industries have been attracted to the heavy industrial triangle by the long industrial tradition of the region, a ready supply of labour and good transport facilities. The governments of France, Belgium and Germany have spent considerable sums of money building new industrial premises, providing grants to attract new industries and cleaning up many of the eyesores such as tip heaps which are a legacy of the industrial revolution. As a result, footloose industries have been established in the triangle. They include car component factories in the Lille–Douai area, pharmaceutical goods at Liège and Opel cars near Bochum in the Ruhr.

5.3 Industrial growth and decline

In the course of the Industrial Revolution, major new industrial regions grew up. The industries which expanded rapidly were largely heavy industries, producing goods which were heavy and bulky compared with other products. The most important industry was the manufacture of iron and steel, upon which other industries such as shipbuilding, locomotive engineering and boiler-making depended. The coal and iron mining industries are classed as **primary industries**, because they make available natural resources suitably processed for other industries. Iron and steel manufacturing, shipbuilding and other types of heavy engineering are **secondary industries**, because they are concerned with processing raw materials to produce goods.

It is the coalfield-based heavy industrial regions that have now declined in Britain.

A declining heavy industrial region—north-east England

Decline

The industrial strength of north-east England was originally based upon the coal obtained from the Northumberland and Durham coalfield. The chief industries were coal mining and exporting, shipbuilding, iron and steel making, engineering and chemicals. Apart from the chemical industry the traditional industries have now declined.

The chemical industry centres on Billingham (ICI). It uses coal by-products, chemicals from the Tees saltfield and by-products from the oil refineries on Teesmouth. Major products are paints, fertilisers, explosives, plastics and Terylene (at Wilton).

Some of the basic industries have been in decline for more than 50 years, but their demise has accelerated in the last twenty.

Reasons for the decline of regions such as the north east include:

1. The disappearance of traditional markets—coal is far less important a fuel than it once was; there is a surplus of shipping in the world, so shipbuilding has declined.
2. Inability to compete with new industrial regions which have significantly lower production costs, e.g. the steel industry of Brazil, the Japanese shipbuilding industry.
3. Failure to invest in modern machinery and production techniques.
4. Inability to attract new industries to the old regions because of the unattractive appearance of the old industrial landscapes, with sub-standard housing, a polluted environment, and large areas of derelict land.

Regeneration

Many efforts have been made to revitalise the region. Obsolete housing has been removed and replaced by new estates. Planned new towns such as Washington have been built to provide more attractive environments to which industries from other parts of Britain and from overseas have been attracted, e.g. the Nissan works at Washington.

Much of the **urban redevelopment** has focused upon Newcastle, the economic capital of the region, and upon Gateshead, which lies immediately south of the River Tyne. In 1977 the Newcastle and Gateshead Inner City Partnership was set up. It was intended to tackle the economic, social and environmental difficulties faced by the two inner city areas. The inner city areas suffered from:

- poor housing conditions
- a declining and ageing population
- high unemployment
- many families having very low incomes
- a higher crime rate than in other parts of the region.

The aim of the partnership was to make inner city areas places where people would want to live and work.

In Newcastle itself there had been major redevelopment of the Central Business District and new housing estates built nearby even before the partnership began. City transport has now greatly improved with the building of the Metro system and the Metrocentre. Economic development has focused upon the creation of enterprise workshops, offices built for new and expanding industries, and the fostering of tourism. The Inner City Partnership has an action programme to attract new industries and jobs into the inner cities. Run down industrial areas have been improved, new access roads built and grants made available to improve factories. The heart of the old industrial region was the River Tyne, and the old riverside wharf has been cleaned up and landscaped. Moorings have also been provided for leisure and residential uses.

The region has been classified by the government as a **Development Area**, and money has been provided to diversify employment and attract new industries to the area. Tyne and Wear is also an **Urban Development Corporation** with government grants; there are **private investments** to provide houses, offices and industrial buildings.

An example of a growing industrial region

One of the few rapidly growing industrial regions of Britain lies to the west of London, along the M4 motorway. It is not a completely built-up urban region as the old industrial regions were. The new region is a corridor within which new industries are clustered in and around the main towns, such as Swindon and Reading.

The M4 motorway was opened in December 1971. It links London with South Wales and the West Country, making journeys between London and Cardiff, Newport and Bristol much quicker, but it does more than this. Patterns of travel have changed significantly and it is now possible to live in the countryside near Swindon and to commute to London daily.

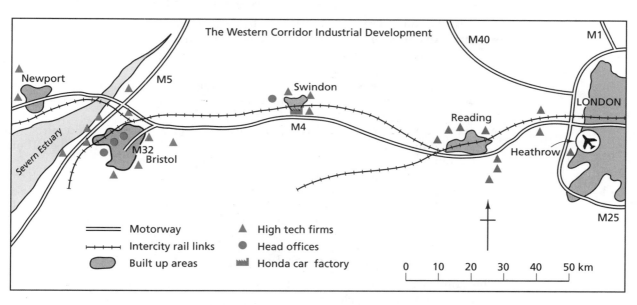

Fig. 5.3 High-tech firms and head-offices along the M4

The motorway has been a magnet for new industries. This is because:
1. Modern footloose industries are not bound to specific locations.
2. Industries located near the M4 have easy access to the chief British market, London.
3. The motorways with which the M4 links give easy access to other parts of Britain.
4. London's Heathrow Airport is conveniently close to the M4, so business journeys to the USA, Europe and other major markets are easy.
5. Many factories are built in the countryside on 'greenfield' sites.
6. New industries such as microelectronics need to attract highly skilled scientific staff, who can be recruited from the universities of London and the south.
7. It is an attractive region in which to live for American, Japanese and German managers of factories owned by foreign firms.

As a result, the M4 corridor is a developing and prosperous industrial region.

5.4 Service industries

A service industry is one that provides a facility or service, instead of manufacturing goods. Service industries belong to the category of **tertiary industry**, which is now the chief source of employment in Britain and most other more economically developed countries. Important categories of service industries are:

Examiner's tip

Make sure you know many examples of service sector industries

- government, national security and defence
- health and education services
- transport services for both goods and people: road, rail, air and sea
- wholesale distribution of bulk goods, broken down into smaller lots and sent to retailers
- retailing: the selling of products to the consumer
- building and construction work
- communications: transmitting and receiving information and messages; telecommunications, satellites, internet.
- banking and finance; at all levels from the local branch of the bank to the commodity markets where international trading is carried out
- entertainment: leisure and tourism; the fastest growing sector of all the service industries
- personal services: jobs which serve the customer directly, e.g. hairdressers, cleaners.

Factors affecting the distribution of service industries

The distribution of service industries can be determined by a number of factors:

- **attractiveness of location**, e.g. the people of the South Wales valleys have fewer doctors than do parts of the south east of England, because fewer doctors wish to live in an old industrial region
- **demand for the service**, e.g. in areas of high unemployment there may be less demand for beauty salons than in a more affluent area: the services provided are expensive and are non-essential
- many services are concentrated in the capital city or other major urban areas because the **large populations** can support a wide variety of services, e.g. London has numerous theatres, concert halls and sporting facilities
- clustering or **agglomeration** is also a feature of service industries which attract allied activities; these are made more efficient and more economic by their nearness to each other, e.g. the commodities markets, international banks and the Stock Exchange all cluster in the City of London.

Problems of uneven distribution

The concentration of service industries in a few major urban centres may cause considerable problems including:

- traffic congestion
- commercial enterprises being able to afford higher prices for land, thus displacing the residential population
- the character of the city centre changing when high-rise commercial blocks replace traditional buildings
- high buildings needing deep foundations which has sometimes led to the destruction of archaeological sites.

In Britain the government has influenced the location of some service industries by dispersing national offices away from London. For example, the Royal Mint is now in Llantrisant and the Motor Vehicle Licensing Department in Swansea. This has had the twofold effect of dispersing the concentration of services, as well as creating employment in South Wales where the decline of the traditional industries has been a big problem.

An example of decentralisation

One example of a development which has taken activities away from centres in London is the building, with government approval, of the National Exhibition Centre (NEC)

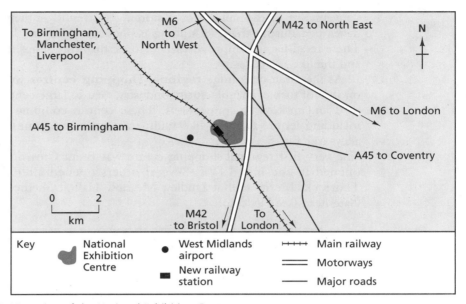

Fig. 5.4 Location of the National Exhibition Centre

on the edge of Birmingham. It has been built on a 125 ha site between Birmingham and Coventry. The advantages of this location are shown in Fig. 5.4.

The building of the NEC has stimulated other activities in the region. Shops, offices, banks, motels and hotel accommodation were needed nearby. Hotels in Birmingham and Coventry have expanded and new ones have been built to meet the needs of visitors. A railway station has been built on the London–Birmingham–Manchester–Liverpool line and the airport has become busier.

Birmingham has become a centre for national and international events.

The retailing revolution

Changes in retailing since the 1970s shows another way that decentralisation has occurred. There has been a drift away from the traditional pattern of shoppers converging on a high street or town centre, to out-of-town locations.

The first **out-of-town superstores** or **hypermarkets** of the 1970s took advantage of cheaper land on the urban fringe and provided extensive parking facilities for customers. At the same time the old central business districts (CBDs) of towns and cities were becoming congested with inadequate parking and out of date shopping facilities.

Shoppers were now more mobile and more affluent and were soon attracted to the

Fig. 5.5 View of Lakeside regional shopping centre, Essex

convenience of the out-of-town stores. As a result, numerous non-food **retail parks** developed during the 1980s along easily accessible road links on the edge of towns. These retail parks comprised carpet stores, furniture shops, garden centres, DIY centres and the like.

At the same time huge **regional shopping centres** were being constructed, often on sites of former manufacturing industry, near to large centres of population with good road and motorway connections. These centres combine everything under one roof including leisure facilities like multi-screen cinemas, amusement arcades and bowling alleys (see Fig. 5.5).

The very first regional shopping centre was Brent Cross in north-west London which opened in the mid 1970s. Several others opened after this including Lakeside at Thurrock, Merry Hill at Dudley, Meadow Hall at Sheffield and the Metro Centre at Gateshead (see Fig. 5.6).

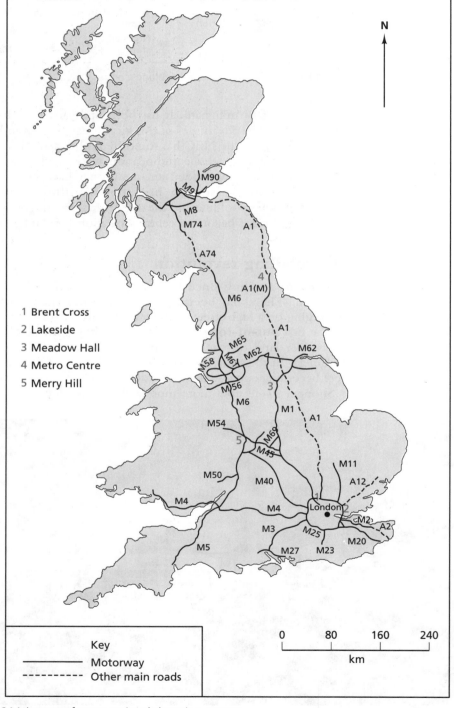

Fig. 5.6 Major out-of-town regional shopping centres

Recent out-of-town centres often combine a fast-food outlet such as McDonald's with large chain stores such as Tesco's and Marks and Spencer.

It is becoming more difficult to get planning permission for such developments and local councils will sometimes only give consent if the retailers pay for necessary road improvements.

Local councils are very aware of the impact that the out-of-town centres have had on some of the old high street shops and old city centres. As a result many CBDs have upgraded their facilities by building covered shopping centres or malls, like the chain of Arndale Centres, and care has been taken to improve the general inner city environment (car parking, seating, trees and plants) to try to win back the customers lost to the retail parks (see Fig. 5.7).

Fig. 5.7 A town-centre pedestrian precinct in Hull

5.5 Ports

Model of a port

Figure 5.8 shows the chief conditions that favour the expansion of modern ports. Since ships have increased in size tremendously in recent years, deep-water approaches are needed in which there is no great range between high and low tides to force ships to wait for the tide. Dock fees are high and modern ships are very expensive to run, so rapid turn-around is vital.

The dock itself needs basins large enough to take the ships or terminal jetties at which they can tie up. They also need to provide repair and maintenance docks. In addition to the usual warehouses and sheds, modern ports require space for the storage of bulk cargoes and containerised general cargoes.

Since industries develop where raw materials are landed, an industrial area is needed near the docks which is large enough to allow for the expansion of industry. Two other important factors are also shown on the model. One is the need for efficient, rapid transport to distribute the imports and to bring cargoes to the docks for export. The other is the advantage of having an industrial hinterland so that return cargoes are

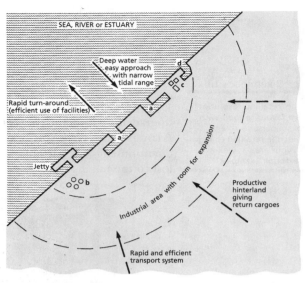

Fig. 5.8 Model of a port

a Large, well-equipped dock basins
b Facilities for handling bulk cargoes (e.g. oil)
c Facilities for handling containers
d Repair and maintenance docks

available to keep ships working profitably.

In recent years ways in which goods are handled at ports have changed fundamentally. At one time every item of cargo had to be handled separately. Many were lifted on and off ships in nets and the process involved a large labour force.

These old techniques have now been replaced by **containers**. These are weatherproof boxes of a standard size, normally 2.4 metres wide, 2.4 metres high and 6 metres long. This is an internationally agreed size so equipment can handle containers from any part of the world. The containers are packed at the point of production. They can then be shifted rapidly to any destination by river, rail or road. **Ro Ro (roll-on roll-off)** facilities have also improved. These facilities allow trucks to drive on and off ferries which have movable doors front and back.

Freeports

A freeport is a port with free trade zones within it that is open to all countries. Goods can be made or assembled without payment of import or export duties in the free trade zones. Profits can also be sent back to a parent company in another country without paying tax. Both Singapore and Hong Kong are freeports. High tech industries assemble their products in the free trade zones and then sell their products at very competitive prices.

A container port—Felixstowe

The increase in the use of containers and changes in the UK's trading pattern with the rest of the world have resulted in the rapid growth of the port of Felixstowe on the east coast in Suffolk. Felixstowe has a tremendous advantage over the traditional ports such as Liverpool because it faces European ports around the North Sea. the first container terminal opened in Felixstowe in 1967. At that time it was a very small port with a limited amount of trade but in the last thirty years it has become the largest deep sea container port in the UK and the fourth largest in Europe. It is also the second Ro Ro port, after Dover, in the UK. In 1996 it handled 1.4 million containers, an average of over 3,800 per day. One third of the port's trade is with North America, one third with the Far East and the rest with other parts of the world, particularly Europe.

The reasons for Felixstowe's success include:

● Its position. Since Britain joined the EU the volume of trade with Europe has grown significantly.

● Improvements to the A14 road and motorway links have made the transfer of goods between Felixstowe and major British cities more efficient.

● Felixstowe has a compact site which enables it to compete successfully with Rotterdam and Hamburg where the container terminals are dispersed. (See Fig. 5.9)

● It developed as a container port before traditional ports accepted the new

Fig. 5.9
The port of Felixstowe

technology, and so was able to build up new trading links swiftly and with very little competition.

- It is a privately owned port which has established good industrial relations while ignoring the conditions of work and wages operating in the traditional ports. As a result labour costs are low and ships can be turned round more cheaply.
- Its deep water facilities attract large container ships which can turn round quickly by off-loading all their containers and so avoid deviating to other European container ports.

This has made Felixstowe a busy **transhipment port**. Containers to and from other European ports, including those in Scaninavia, Spain and Portugal, are off-loaded at Felixstowe for onward shipment.

An entrepôt port—Rotterdam

Rotterdam is the busiest port in the world and continues to grow as new docks are added and the approach channel is deepened to take larger ships. It owes its importance to its position at the mouth of the River Rhine, as the terminal for the network of inland waterways in Western Europe. It is predominantly an **entrepôt port**, that is, most of the cargoes handled at Rotterdam are in transit, bound for destinations elsewhere. Ocean-going ships arrive to off-load grain, iron ore and other goods into steel barges which carry them to factories in other parts of western and central Europe. Manufactured goods from the industrial regions such as Mannheim, which are destined for overseas markets, move in the opposite direction.

Port industries

Like many other ports, Rotterdam has developed industries based partly on the needs of shipping using the port, such as shipbuilding and marine engineering, and partly on raw materials which enter the port, such as oil refining, chemicals and flour milling. Oil refineries and petrochemical works line the south side of the **New Waterway**, causing oil spillage and air pollution problems, which the oil companies are attempting to solve.

Reasons for Rotterdam's importance

Here is a summary of the reasons why Rotterdam is such an important port:
1. It is a natural gateway to the Rhine and the connecting waterways of western Europe.
2. There is a large hinterland stretching as far as Switzerland and Austria and including the Ruhr industrial region.
3. It has kept up with port technology. Europoort has been built, largely on reclaimed land, and transit facilities have been improved.
4. It has highly developed port-based industries, such as oil refineries, chemical plants and shipbuilding and repair yards.
5. The dredging of a deep water channel allows ships of up to 300 000 tonnes to enter the port.

E xaminer's tip

Draw a sketch map to show the position of Rotterdam in relation to the Rhine valley and neighbouring countries. Annotate your map to explain why the port is so important.

5.6 Regional contrasts

Different regions have developed in different ways according to how people have interacted with the physical environment of the region. Regions evolve and change as society changes, and regions sometimes have to radically reform their structures in order to cope with imposed changes. The following section looks at several different regions so that you can compare and contrast the ways the regions have coped with the situations facing them.

South Wales

In the past the industrial areas of Wales depended upon two major industries: coal mining and steel production. In recent years the number of mines has decreased rapidly and famous coal mining areas such as the Rhondda valleys have lost their industrial base completely. Only one deep coal mine remains in production in South Wales.

There are still two **integrated steel works** in Wales: at Margam near Port Talbot and Llanwern near Newport. Figure 5.10 shows the factors which led to the establishment of the Llanwern works.

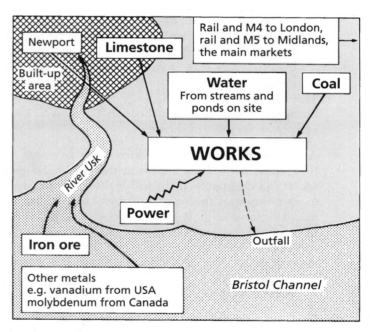

Fig. 5.10 Llanwern steelworks, Newport

Infrastructure

Since the 1950s major efforts have been made to improve the infrastructure of the region to make South Wales a more attractive location to industrialists and financiers. The infrastructure is the basic framework upon which industry operates, e.g. power supply, water supply, sewage, road network. The Severn Bridges and the M4 motorway made South Wales more accessible from London and the south-east, including direct motorway links with Heathrow and Gatwick airports. Within South Wales, the Heads of the Valleys road links South Wales with the M50 and the M5 to give access to the Midlands and then on to the north of England and Scotland.

The Welsh Development Agency (WDA)
The WDA was set up in 1976 to:
  ❶   further the economic development of Wales

2 promote industrial efficiency in Wales
3 encourage the improvement of the environment.
(See Fig. 5.11).

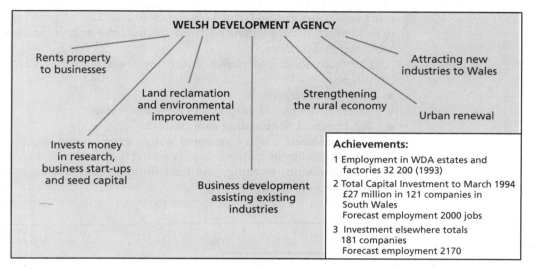

Fig. 5.11 Chief activities of the WDA

These aims are achieved by:
- helping small and medium sized industries which are now the driving force of the economy
- making large grants to attract overseas electronic and other growth industries. The size of the grants is a secret but the South Korean firm of Lucky Goldstar is thought to have been given about £200 million in 1996 to manufacture electronic equipment in Newport, South Wales. 6000 workers will be employed when the plant is built. If the grant estimate is correct this would amount to a government subsidy of around £30 000 for each job created
- encouraging communities to help themselves by involving the local people in decision making
- a special drive to create job opportunities for the disabled
- land reclamation schemes
- urban renewal projects including better housing, modern factories, shopping centres and leisure centres
- the removal of coal tips and the cleansing of industrial sites poisoned by factory waste.

How successful are these efforts?
The Welsh economy has attracted large amounts of regional aid (see Fig. 5.12) and is one of the fastest growing of all the regions of the UK. Cardiff is attracting a number of new financial and business firms, and over 40 new Japanese owned plants have been located in Wales. One new problem results from that success: there is now a shortage of good industrial property, especially in south-east Wales.

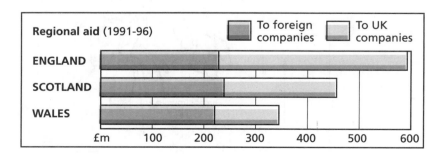

Fig. 5.12 Regional aid, UK, 1991–1996

The Scottish Highlands and Islands

The rugged landscape of the Scottish Highlands makes farming and accessibility difficult in the region. Farming is confined to the hills, mostly sheep with some crops grown for feedstuffs. Crofting is found on the islands and along the west coast. These are traditionally run family farms keeping a few animals and growing some crops for home use. Income is supplemented from fishing, the textile industry (tweed cloth and knitwear) and tourism.

The main source of power in the region is hydroelectricity due to the physical advantages:

- heavy precipitation
- extensive lochs and deep valleys for water storage
- hard bedrock for building dam facilities
- steep gradients which give stored water the thrust required to turn the turbines.

The availability of hydroelectric power (HEP) has encouraged some heavy industry such as aluminium smelting, and light industries are also to be found in a variety of locations (see Fig. 5.13).

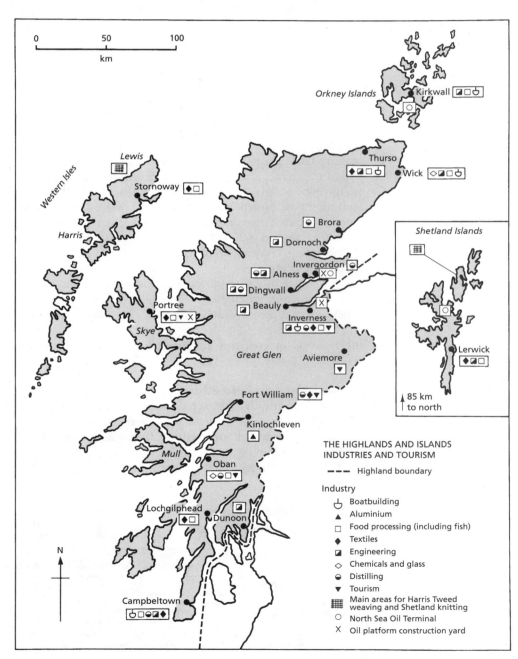

Examiner's tip

List and learn the towns with distilling, tourism and textile industries.

Fig. 5.13 The Highlands and Islands industries and tourism

The rapid development of oil and natural gas in the North Sea and the large-scale investment in terminals in the Shetlands, Orkneys and north-east Scotland have brought employment to these areas and elsewhere.

The oil has also brought with it new problems of pollution, land conservation and long-term planning.

The Forestry Commission has helped to regenerate many Highland forests which, with the spectacular scenery, help to attract tourists into the region. The Scottish Tourist Board has encouraged the building of new hotels and facilities in the Highlands to bring tourist money into the area.

Aviemore in the Cairngorms has been developed as a winter sports centre and Fort William is an important tourist centre at the foot of Ben Nevis (see Unit 1.5).

Tourism in the region is likely to expand with improvements to roads, ferries, accommodation and recreational facilities.

Problems

- **depopulation**—there is little to hold people in the region; the population total is only about 5% of Scotland's total with a higher proportion of older residents
- **loss of young people**—the proportion of young people is falling especially in the more remote areas. Better job opportunities, higher wages and city attractions are the urban 'pulls'
- **main towns and services**—lie on the eastern side of the region which consequently have very extensive hinterlands
- **transport and communications**—costs can be high because of the distances involved, restricting the development of road, ferry and air transport
- **power**—HEP schemes mean that electricity is widely available. However distribution to remote areas can be expensive. The service is run at a loss to encourage people to stay and industries to move into the region.

Regional aid

Government aid has been available in the region since the 1960s, and new enterprises were promoted by the Highlands and Islands Development Board. In 1991 this was replaced by a new board, Highlands and Islands Enterprise (HIE), to target areas of high unemployment. It operates through Local Enterprise Companies (LECs) which are responsible for development in their areas.

The Highlands and Islands are eligible for maximum aid from the EU because of the limited extent of the development. Emphasis is put on developing communications, energy and water supply, research and vocational training (see Fig.5.1).

Randstad, Holland

Randstad or 'ring city' is the core region of the Netherlands and contrasts with the periphery made up of the eastern provinces. The Netherlands has a population of 15.5 million of which 89% live in urban areas. Just under 6 million of this population is concentrated in two loops of built-up land, which include Haarlem, Amsterdam and Utrecht in the north and The Hague and Rotterdam in the south. In the centre of these urban loops is the 'green heart', a fertile area of farmland including the well known bulb fields and intensive horticultural areas (see Fig. 5.14).

The growth of Randstad has produced a number of planning problems for the Dutch:

- Green-heart farmland has been lost to housing.
- The dune coastline is suffering from excess pressure due to urban populations seeking recreation space.
- Some of the woodlands north of Utrecht have also been lost to urban sprawl.
- Inner cities have become run down as people move to wealthier suburbs.
- Good road and rail links have encouraged long-distance commuting; this in turn leads to the spread of low-density suburbs which then encroach on other landscapes.

Solutions to the problems

- The 'green heart' is now protected for farming and recreation with little additional building allowed.
- Inner city urban renewal projects have been set up while other types of building development have been restricted.

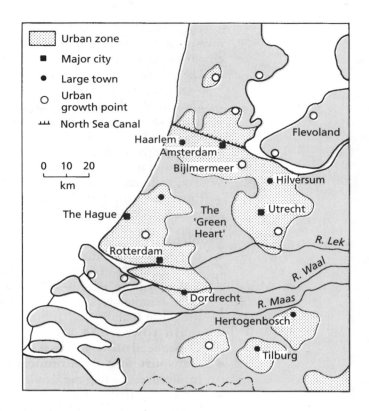

Fig. 5.14 Randstad, Holland

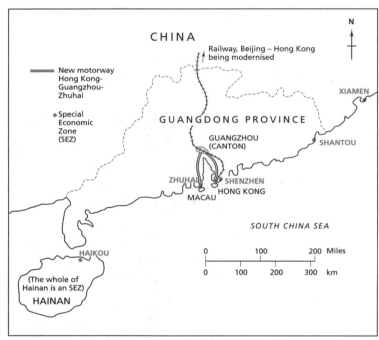

Fig. 5.15 A new industrial region

- Satellite towns or 'growth points' have been designated for new house-building, and fast rail links to the parent city provide a good service for commuters.
- Incentives are offered to industry to locate in the eastern provinces; manufacturing has increased but services are still based mainly in Randstad.

An industrial region in an LEDC

Guangdong Province in south-east China is a rapidly developing industrial region which attracts migrants from the rest of China. It is estimated that the growth of industry along the coast has flooded the area with ten million migrants, of whom about one million sleep on the streets of the rapidly expanding cities.

The former British colony of Hong Kong, returned to China on 1 July 1997, has a population of over six million. It is no longer important for the manufacture of cheap consumer products such as plastic handbags. Today the major industries are the production of textiles and clothing and the manufacture of electrical machinery and high-tech goods such as computers. Hong Kong has the largest container port in Asia which acts as an important trade gateway for China.

The Communist government of China has permitted the rapid growth of capitalist enterprises in recent years. To encourage foreign companies China established five Special Economic Zones (SEZs) in the 1980s (Fig. 5.15). Favourite growth industries—such as those making telecommunication equipment, consumer electronics, precision machinery, chemicals and pharmaceuticals—are attracted by large subsidies and exemption from taxes. The Shenzhen SEZ, inland from Hong Kong, was formed in 1978. By the mid-1990s it was an industrial city of three to four million with the highest incomes in China. Haikou on Hainan Island, the largest of the SEZs is being transformed from a region of farms and fishing villages into an international centre of light and heavy industry, trade and tourism.

Development in the region has been hampered by the poor infrastructure. International companies have built two new coal-fired power stations for the Shenzhen SEZ and a modern highway now connects Hong Kong, Guangzhou (Canton) and Zhuhai. The railway between Hong Kong and Beijing is also being modernised. As incomes rise in China and people have more spending power, the industrialisation of Guandong Province and the rest of China will accelerate.

5.7 The development gap

Definitions

The advanced industrial nations of the world such as Japan and the USA are said to be more economically developed countries or MEDCs. In contrast, most of the countries which make up Africa, Asia and Central and South America are said to be less economically developed countries or LEDCs. (See map Fig. 4.7, indicating the location of MEDCs and LEDCs)

The **development gap** is the difference in economic activity and wealth which exists between the MEDCs and the LEDCs. The gap is largely because the LEDCs have a limited industrial base. Some LEDCs have poor resources but in many, the resources are not fully used because inefficient methods of production are still employed.

Characteristics of LEDCs

The degree of development of a country is difficult to define and measure but the following are **general** characteristics which typify the LEDCs:
- little modern industry
- high birth rate
- farming is the chief economic activity
- few are employed in the service sector
- low educational and technological levels
- poverty
- poor diets which lead to malnutrition
- underdeveloped transport facilities
- lack of basic services such as clean water and adequate housing.

Measures of development

One difficulty in defining and measuring the level of development of a country is that we are not always comparing like with like. As a result there are a number of ways used to show development called **indicators**. These are described in Unit 2.2. Diagrams to illustrate some of these indicators are shown in Fig. 5.16.

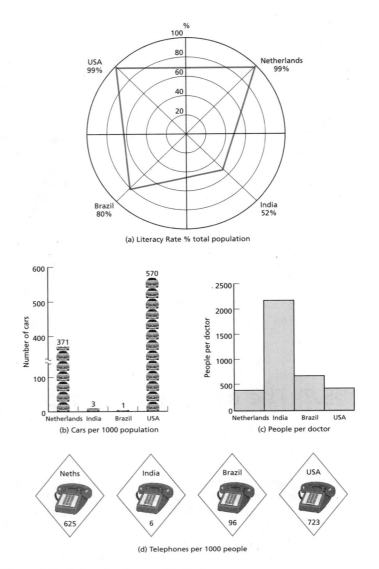

Fig. 5.16 Ways of displaying development indicators

A model of underdevelopment

The model, Fig. 5.17, was designed to describe and explain the process of development. It simplifies the situation to help us understand why some countries remain poor, and why LEDCs do not have enough capital to invest and bring about development more quickly. It is called the 'vicious circle' because it is so difficult for the LEDCs to break out of the circle.

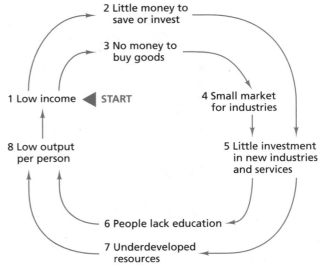

Fig. 5.17 The vicious circle of development

How development may be achieved

Three main needs have been identified as a basis for development:

1 **Industrialisation** is seen as the chief agent of change, although this tends to be a 'western' perspective. It is not necessarily appropriate for all LEDCs especially when we remember the state of declining manufacture in many of the MEDCs and the social consequences of the resulting high unemployment.

Increasing industrialisation can also severely affect the environment, e.g. fossil fuel emissions.

2 **Capital**: vast amounts of money are needed to help the LEDCs' progress. This may come from international aid or from investment by large international companies (see Units 5.9 and 5.10).

3 **Trade agreements**: these guarantee markets and fair prices for goods from the LEDCs.

Several approaches have been used to achieve more rapid development:

- **National Plans** give a country clear goals and purpose. Tanzania and India are two countries which have adopted National Plans.
- **Export stimulation** or **export substitution policies**: countries can decide whether to export raw materials to earn money to buy goods they need, or to spend less on imports by making things themselves for the home market.
- **Intermediate technology**: (see Unit 6.8) traditional crafts and industries may be expanded and modernised to avoid importing more expensive goods, e.g. the textile industry in India.
- **Revolution**: some countries have turned their backs on the western economic system and have tried to change their futures through revolution, e.g. Ethiopia and Cuba.
- The **rapid development of industry** (see Unit 5.8).

5.8 Establishing new industries

Many LEDC governments see industrialisation as the key to economic growth, believing that income and job opportunities will grow with the development of manufacturing as was the case for western Europe, the USA and Japan.

Obstacles to industrialisation in LEDCs

1 limited capital
2 limited managerial expertise
3 shortage of skilled labour
4 limited local markets
5 trade barriers; MEDCs often impose **import duties** to restrict the import of manufactured goods, e.g. Ghana cannot afford to export chocolate to the UK, but the UK manufactures chocolate from cocoa beans grown in Ghana
6 poor infrastructures on which to build modern industry:
   - electrical power and basic services needed by factories are not readily available
   - information technology networks do not compare with those of MEDCs
   - transport networks are not well developed; this hinders collection and distribution of goods; causes communities to remain in isolation; accentuates the problems caused by natural hazards and other disasters; limits the possibilities of raising standards of living throughout the country.

A model of industrialisation

In South America it is possible to recognise three stages of industrialisation:

Stage 1—The start of industrialisation
- low-technology industries are developed to process exports, e.g. manufacture of corned beef in Argentina and Uruguay

- low-technology industries are developed to make basic goods for the local market, e.g. bottled drinks, cigarettes, clothes
- factories are run by immigrants/multinationals from MEDCs who import machinery and skilled workers (see Unit 5.9 for an explanation of 'multinationals')
- the possibility of factory employment draws people from the countryside to the towns.

Stage 2—Import substitution
- new factories are built to make things which were previously imported, e.g. toys, clothes, cars
- more work for local people is created
- products are cheaper than imports as local wages are lower than in MEDCs
- import bills are cut making the LEDC economically stronger.

Stage 3—Export promotion and the manufacture of capital goods
- the range of manufactured goods widens and capital goods such as factory machinery and building equipment are made.

All the countries in South America have experienced Stage 1 and have moved on to Stage 2. Brazil and Argentina have entered the third stage.

These stages of industrialisation also apply in other LEDCs such as China.

Problems of industrialisation

1. foreign debts build up
2. there is little benefit if multinational companies (see Unit 5.9) take their profits out of the country
3. the 'pull' to the urban areas creates pressure on housing and other services
4. production is not always efficient
5. prices are sometimes higher than imported goods
6. there is traffic congestion and pollution.

The effects of industrialisation

1. since so many concessions have to be made to industry, taxes are not adding to the wealth of the nation, although personal incomes are increased and the demand for goods and services is boosted
2. new technology often means fewer jobs are created than was anticipated
3. factory products kill off traditional skills and handicrafts
4. new consumer industries add to health problems by increasing smoking and alcoholism
5. the gap between rich and poor has often widened rather than closed.

The chief industrial areas of South America can be identified from Fig. 5.18.

Tiger economies, NICs and the Pacific Rim

The industrial development of certain countries, especially those of south-east Asia has had a great effect on the pattern of manufacturing since the 1960s. Japan has been the role-model for industrial expansion with its massive growth in manufacturing since the end of World War Two. The subsequent development of the 'tiger economies' (so called because of their aggressive approach to market competition and international trading) has been achieved by planning, investment and hard work; strategies which were the basis of success for Japan.

There are three countries which share the label 'tiger economies': Singapore, Taiwan and South Korea (see Fig. 5.19). When Hong Kong was a British colony it made a fourth 'tiger'. It is no longer a separate country but it maintains its importance as an economic centre. They are also referred to as **newly industrialised countries** or **NICs**. However, the list of NICs is longer since many countries, such as Thailand, Indonesia, Malaysia, Mexico and Brazil, are striving to develop their manufacturing base.

The success of the 'tiger economies' has been due to a combination of factors:
- long hours worked and a plentiful labour supply
- education and training to improve the quality of the workers

Examiner's tip

Make a list of other NICs and what they manufacture.

Fig. 5.18 Chief industrial core areas of South America

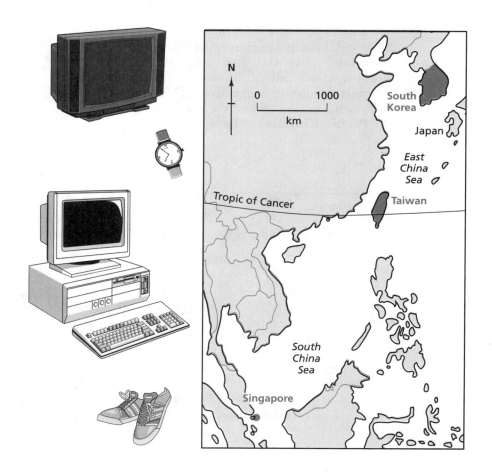

Fig. 5.19 The three 'tigers' and some of their products

- large injections of capital for machinery and equipment partly financed by high savings rates
- a rapid increase in production as the result of good management and the acceptance of ideas from abroad
- low labour costs compared with those in Japan and other MEDCs
- the business leadership of **overseas Chinese**, except in South Korea. The overseas Chinese dominate business throughout south-east Asia.

However, as with any success story, there are always associated problems which for the 'tiger economies' include:

- working conditions, which in some factories are very poor
- health and safety conditions for the workers are frequently overlooked
- the environment has been neglected in the pursuit of economic growth; air, water and noise pollution are particular problems
- wages have risen so labour is more expensive; multinational companies look for new production locations
- the infrastructure has not kept up with industrial development, except in Singapore
- strong currencies mean exports become more expensive
- world economic recessions in the 1980s led to a drop in consumer demand for goods.

Nevertheless it is clear that the economies of the countries of south-east Asia have grown more rapidly than any other region in recent times (see Fig. 5.20). There is a strong feeling that the growth areas of the 21st century will be those countries which border the Pacific Ocean, the south-east Asian countries having set an example which others are keen to follow. China is beginning to develop its industrial potential and with its huge population, one fifth of the world total, it has an immense internal market to satisfy. This area of dynamic growth around the Pacific is called the **Pacific Rim** and can be seen in Fig. 5.21.

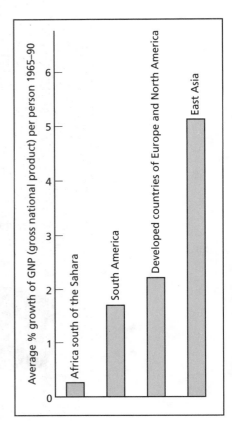

Fig. 5.20 World economic growth

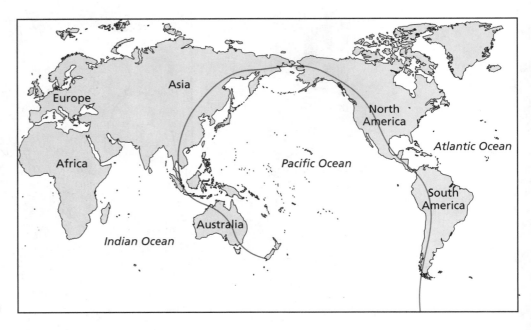

Fig. 5.21 The Pacific Rim

New industries in MEDCs

The establishment of new industries is also a concern for the MEDCs. Declining manufacturing and peripheral locations mean that many governments there are also trying to establish new industries. This is in order to spread the wealth of the country and maintain jobs and services for the people who live in these regions (see Units 5.1 and 5.6). In Britain, for example, the government has encouraged foreign investment and many Japanese, South Korean and other Asian companies now have manufacturing plants here.

Toyota at Derby

Toyota was keen to establish a car manufacturing plant in Europe because of the size of the potential market. Also, EU regulations state that 60% of a foreign car has to be made in an EU country if it is to be sold within the EU.

Fig. 5.22 Toyota site, Burnaston, during and after construction of the plant

Before deciding to build at Burnaston, an old airfield near Derby (see Fig. 5.22), the Toyota company investigated the potential of 28 different UK sites. These were some of the criteria which had to be fulfilled:

- 'greenfield' site, minimum size 100ha
- not in south-east England since land prices and wage levels would be too high
- good communication links
- skilled labour force nearby
- pleasant environment both in terms of attractive landscape and social provisions such as housing, schools, entertainment and sports facilities
- financial incentives offered by the government and local authorities.

Very detailed questionnaires were sent to all 28 possible locations; the Toyota company was very thorough in its research before making a final choice. A shortlist of three sites was selected but Burnaston was chosen ahead of the others because:

- a pool of skilled labour lived within three-quarters of an hour commuting time
- highly skilled workers had recently lost their jobs at Rolls-Royce Aero
- there was no competition for this labour force from other Japanese firms

E xaminer's tip

Make a case study of another overseas company which has factories in Britain. A good case study can earn you high marks in the exam.

- good access existed to the West Midlands car component industry
- there was total co-operation for the development from Derbyshire County Council
- a substantial grant was provided by the British government.

At the same time, Toyota chose a site on Deeside to produce the engines. Both plants produced their first outputs in 1992, three years after the company made the decisions to build. When fully operational the Burnaston plant should employ 3000 people and the engine plant 300. Of course there is considerable extra indirect employment generated from investment projects of this scale.

5.9 International trade and trans-national corporations

International trade

Trading is the exchange of goods between people. Trading has been part of human life for centuries as different groups of people, producing different goods from each other, exchange surpluses to satisfy the needs of their own lifestyles. At first raw materials were swapped, for example grain might be exchanged for animals. Latterly, goods have been exchanged for money and groups of people and countries have become wealthy as a result of trading between themselves and among other nations, which is called **international trade**.

Traditional patterns of international trade reflected the colonial ties of the European countries with their colonies in Africa, South America and Asia. The industrial revolution created a manufacturing sector ready to process many of the raw materials readily available in the colonies. This pattern of exchange has dominated international trade for much of the 20th century. It has contributed towards the disparities now recognised between the MEDCs and the LEDCs. Raw materials were sent from the colonies and manufactured into goods of a much higher value than in a raw state. For example, you would probably not know what to do with a bale of cotton and would certainly not be prepared to give very much, if any, money for it as it is. However, once that cotton is manufactured into a pair of jeans or a tee shirt, you would probably be very happy to part with your hard earned cash to own some new clothes.

LEDCs sometimes feel they are caught in a trade trap and destined to be kept from developing their own manufacturing industries by the policies of the MEDCs. The MEDCs sometimes impose trade barriers to protect their own industries which effectively limits the import of manufactured goods. Alternatively, if access to a raw material is denied, then MEDCs can look for another supplier or seek a substitute—for example, clothes can be made from a wide variety of synthetic materials.

However, it is possible to escape from the trap, India has managed to establish its own very successful textile industry and has stopped exporting large quantities of raw cotton. Instead, it exports a wide variety of clothing and other goods manufactured from cotton. This move severely affected employment in the Lancashire cotton industry. Demand declined as the cotton items manufactured in Lancashire were more expensive than those arriving from India. Factories had to close, causing a lot of hardship in the area.

Other countries have also managed to escape the trap as is clearly demonstrated by the success of the NICs . The success of the 'tiger economies' has had quite an impact on the pattern of international trade. This is why the 'Pacific Rim' is forecast as being the focus of world trade in the 21st century, a move away from the old domination of trade between Europe and North America (see Unit 5.8).

Trans-national corporations

International trade is not only affected by the way national governments or trade organisations impose policies. It is also influenced by the ways in which very large international companies choose to operate their businesses. Such companies are called **trans-national corporations (TNCs)** or **multinational corporations (MNCs)**. As the names imply these companies operate across (trans) national boundaries and in many (multi) different countries (see Fig. 5.23).

TNCs seek out locations which will allow them to produce their goods at the best possible price to make the biggest possible profit, as does any industrialist (see Unit 5.1). TNCs can be criticised for changing their location of production at very short notice, severely affecting the local employment structure with knock-on social implications.

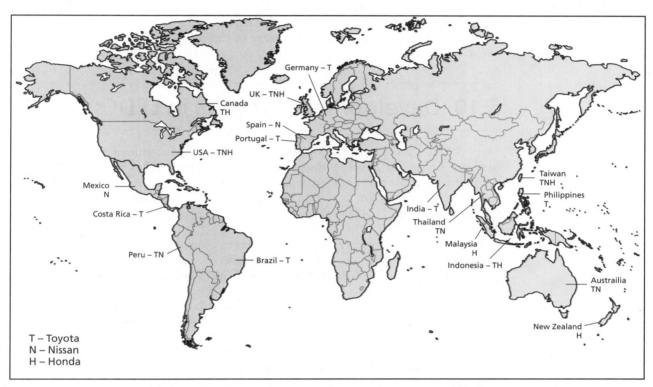

5.23 Japanese car companies are TNCs. This map shows the location of vehicle manufacturing plants for three Japanese car companies

Examples of TNCs

Mattel Toys, for example, who make the 'Barbie Doll', had a production plant in Japan in 1958 as wages in Japan at that time were quite low. By 1965 cheaper labour was found in Hong Kong so production was shifted away from Japan. Factories were also opened in Taiwan, Mexico and South Korea. In 1975 the Mexican workers went on strike for higher wages so Mattel closed the plant. Then in 1977 the Korean plant was closed when workers there asked for higher wages and better working conditions. Production was shifted to the Philippines where labour was still cheap and where there were no trade unions. This pattern is one paralleled by many TNCs.

On the other hand, the presence of TNCs can promote the expansion of local economies and can greatly improve the standard of living of a local community.
Unilever owns and operates plantations in a number of LEDCs for the raw materials it needs to produce a wide variety of goods.

Plantation workers are provided with housing, schools and medical care and the wages they earn are spent within the local community creating trade and employment.

Advantages brought by TNCs

- employment created
- reliable income for workers
- training and skills of workers improved
- resources developed
- infrastructure developed
- investment increased

- local economy improved
- healthcare and social benefits for workers including provision of schools.

Disadvantages of TNCs
- pollution and environmental damage caused
- profits go out of the country
- trade unions often not recognised
- poor working conditions
- low wages
- local area may benefit but the country as a whole does not
- skilled jobs are not given to the local people
- processing of the raw materials is carried out abroad
- the TNC is not tied to the country so can move at any time.

5.10 Development projects in LEDCs

Many LEDCs are former European colonies which have gained their independence; they are trying to develop their economies to the level where they can achieve international status and trade on a par with other countries. As we have seen in earlier sections the LEDCs are sometimes disadvantaged by the actions of MEDCs and are forced to build up large international debts in an effort to break out of their circle of poverty (see Unit 5.7).

Money is often borrowed from the former colonial power, which leads the former colony into a new situation of dependence called neo-colonialism.

Money may also be borrowed from the World Bank or the International Monetary Fund (IMF). Both these organisations impose strict guidelines as to how borrowed money may be spent—profits must be made so that the loan will ultimately be repaid. The types of project funded in this way are not always the most appropriate means of assisting the development of an LEDC.

Whenever money is borrowed it has to be paid back with interest and it is often the huge interest debt which LEDCs find so difficult to repay.

The borrowed money is usually referred to as **aid**. Aid can be given in a number of different ways and for a number of different reasons.

Types of aid

There are two main sources of aid:

1. **Voluntary aid** comes from the money raised by charities and organisations such as Oxfam, Save the Children, Christian Aid, Action Aid and CAFOD.
2. **Official aid** is given by countries and banks and comes in two forms:
   - **bi-lateral aid** is given by the government of one country directly to another
   - **multi-lateral aid** comes from funds given by countries to an international organisation such as the IMF, the United Nations (UN) or the World Bank. These organisations distribute funds to LEDCs who apply for help, once approval is given as to how the money will be spent. Since this money is a loan and not a gift, the banks want to be sure that the development proposed will create sufficient wealth to enable the country to repay the debt.

Aid may be given as emergency aid following a disaster, to alleviate immediate problems. This is sometimes referred to as short-term aid.

Aid may be given for defence, which would be termed **military aid**.

Aid may be given for **development** to improve the economy and the quality of life for the people. This type of aid may be called **long-term aid**.

At one time aid money was ploughed into huge projects costing millions of dollars. Such large prestigious projects were seen as 'flagship' developments which would encourage growth in other sectors of the country, e.g. the Volta Dam project in Ghana and the Aswan Dam development in Egypt.

More recently these large scale projects have been criticised for benefiting TNCs operating in the country more than the people of the country itself. In Ghana 80 000 people had to be resettled when the Volta was flooded; and the Narmada Valley project in India displaced 1.5 million people. In addition, in both projects much farmland was lost and traditional ways of life lost, as well as loss of habitat and wildlife.

Smaller scale development projects are now more usual to help small communities improve the quality of their lives. The provision of clean, piped water, local medical centres, self-build housing projects, and the construction of primary and secondary schools, are the sorts of development which charities like Comic Relief, OXFAM, Christian Aid, CAFOD and Intermediate Technology are involved with.

The Rio Summit

There is an increasing awareness that economic development is compromising the natural resources of the earth which everyone relies on so heavily. The MEDCs seem to accept that their methods of production have been responsible for this current situation. The LEDCs, striving to develop their industrial base, frequently perpetuate the problems initiated by the MEDCs. Global interdependence is so clearly evident now that something had to be done to address the problems of development to everyone's advantage.

The Earth Summit held in Rio de Janeiro in 1992 brought together 118 countries, with the specific aim of developing strategies to overcome the environmental degradation which has been brought about by economic development. An Agenda 21 was devised to take the world into the 21st century in a sustainable manner, in other words adapting to methods which will not compromise the use of resources for future generations. Agenda 21 was to be put into operation at a local level so that the overall outcome would improve the situation at a global level; 'think globally, act locally', being the underlying philosophy.

Areas of international co-operation were identified, some are listed below:

- development programmes to alleviate poverty, meet basic human needs and address environmental health
- encouragement for the use of environmentally sensitive agricultural practices
- family planning projects to reduce population growth and to help the employment of women
- modification of projects detrimental to the environment that are already under way
- funding for the protection of habitats and the promotion of biodiversity (variety of plants and animal species)
- investment in projects to find alternative energy sources to reduce harmful emissions.

The United Nations Earth Summit Conference in June 1997 showed that the strategies agreed at Rio in 1992 had a very limited success. This is because some major industrial countries, such as the USA and Japan, have failed to reduce atmospheric pollution and conserve energy. Foreign aid has also been cut.

Summary

1 Industrial location is affected by a number of different considerations including access to raw materials, efficiency of transport networks, availability and quality of labour force and the amount of capital available.

2 Heavy industrial growth first occurred on coalfields and many industries remain in their original locations although the original reasons why they first grew there have disappeared. Footloose industries have been attracted to check unemployment.

3 Industries operate in continuously changing conditions which lead to the decline of older industries and the growth of service and high-tech industries.

4 The largest number of jobs in MEDCs is found in the tertiary or service sector, providing work in areas such as retailing, banking, teaching, construction, leisure and tourism.

5 Major changes in port handling techniques have led to the decline of many old ports and the emergence of new container ports, some of which are freeports.

6 Regions within a country respond and develop according to a number of different circumstances which may change over a period of time.

7 Since resources and wealth are unevenly distributed, some areas are more economically developed than others; the differences are described as the development gap.

8 Industrialisation is perceived to be the way to economic growth. This leads to the establishment of new industries in previously underdeveloped areas and also in the declining areas of MEDCs.

9 Some companies are so large that they operate across international boundaries and are able to influence patterns of international trade.

10 Aid is money which is given, or more usually loaned, to finance particular development projects in some LEDCs. Aid is also available in MEDCs, for example EU funds can be granted to areas where development is needed, e.g. the Scottish Highlands.

Quick test

5.1 Location of industry

1 The basic inputs used in the manufacturing process are called ....

2 What are the main advantages of a market location for manufacturing industry?

3 The investment needed to buy goods, and to run and promote an industry is called ....

4 What sort of items might be described as consumer goods?

5 In what way does the EU help areas of industrial decline within the member states?

5.2 An old-established industrial region

6 What is the 'heavy industrial triangle'?

7 Why has coal production declined?

8 What is industrial inertia?

9 What are 'footloose industries'?

10 Why have footloose industries been attracted to the heavy industrial triangle?

5.3 Industrial growth and decline

11 What are (i) primary industries (ii) secondary industries?

12 Why is the chemical industry important on Teesside?

13 Give two reasons for the decline of such regions?

14 What has been done to revitalise such regions?

15 Name one other former heavy industrial region in which traditional industries have declined in the UK.

5.4 Service industries

16 How would you describe the types of employment which are classified as service industries?

17 By what other name are service industries sometimes known?

18 Why are service industries prone to cluster together?

19 In what ways does the location of a new development such as the NEC in Birmingham, stimulate economic growth in the surrounding area?

20 Why have the recent changes in retailing been called the 'retailing revolution?

5.5 Ports
21 Why is rapid turnover an important consideration for shipping companies?
22 Why is a port area an attractive location for new industries?
23 Give two reasons for the success of Felixstowe as a container port.
24 What is an entrepôt?
25 What advantages has Singapore gained by being a freeport?

5.6 Regional contrasts
26 In what ways has the infrastructure of South Wales been improved to attract new industrial investment in the area?
27 Why do the Scottish Highlands lack industrial development?
28 What is Randstad's 'green heart'?
29 Where is Guangdon Province; how could you describe the area?
30 What two factors are responsible for attracting industries to locate in SEZs; what does SEZ stand for?

5.7 The development gap
31 What is the basic reason for the existence of the development gap?
32 List three general characteristics of LEDCs.
33 Measures of development are called ....
34 Which three needs have been identified as a basis for development?
35 What different approaches have been adopted to achieve more rapid development?

5.8 Establishing new industries
36 Why is industrialisation seen as the key to economic growth?
37 List three obstacles which may have to be overcome to achieve economic growth.
38 Making goods which a country has previously imported is called ....
39 Name some of the newly industrialised countries of the world.
40 Why do MEDCs also need to attract new industrial developments?

5.9 Trans-national corporations and international trade
41 How have the 'tiger economies' of south-east Asia influenced the pattern of international trade?
42 Why do some LEDCs feel they are caught in a 'trade trap'?
43 How did India's efforts to break out of the trade trap affect workers in Britain?
44 What is the major criticism levelled against the TNCs?
45 In what ways do TNCs bring advantages to the areas in which they locate?

5.10 Development projects in LEDCs
46 Many former colonies find themselves in a new situation of dependence when they borrow money for development projects; this is called ....-...........
47 What are the two types of official aid called?
48 Name types of small-scale development projects which the voluntary aid organisations help to fund.
49 Why are the large-scale development projects less acceptable to people than they used to be?
50 What is the underlying purpose of Agenda 21?

Chapter 6

Resources and their management

6.1 Exhaustion of natural resources

Renewable and non-renewable resources

Natural resources are the materials that nature provides under, on or above the earth's surface, and which humans use in order to live on and to create wealth. They are the minerals, rocks, soil, water, vegetation, living creatures and air which constitute our planet. These resources are not limitless and as the earth's population increases, some resources are becoming more scarce. Some resources, such as trees and living creatures are **renewable**, while others, such as minerals and fossil fuels (oil, natural gas, coal), are limited in their supply and are **non-renewable** resources.

Diminishing resources—trees

Figure 6.1 shows the variety of resources which are available from the tropical rain forests (see Unit 4.6). As these forests are destroyed, some of these resources will become in short supply and may disappear altogether. Some resources, such as medicines, which still await discovery in the rain forests may never be discovered if these forests disappear.

Timber is the greatest resource of the rain forests. There is an increasing demand for hardwoods such as mahogany, teak, iroko and sapele, and costs are rising. Hardwood trees need over 100 years to reach maturity. They are a diminishing resource because they are being felled faster than they can be replaced.

Softwoods supply about 70% of the world's timber needs. They come from the coniferous and mixed forest regions of the northern hemisphere. Some conifers mature in 30 to 50 years and there is extensive replanting in Scandinavia, Canada and the Russian Federation. In Britain the Forestry Commission owns about 1 million hectares of woodland, some of which has been planted in areas which were not previously forested. Provided softwood forests are replanted and waste paper is recycled, this renewable source of timber can continue to be used indefinitely.

Energy

There is worldwide recognition that fossil fuels must be conserved, although opinions vary as to how long existing resources will last. Many countries have regarded nuclear

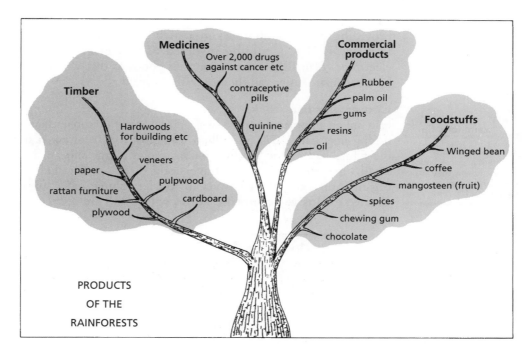

Fig. 6.1 Products of the rainforests

power as the energy source of the future, but the disaster at the Chernobyl nuclear power station in the Russian Federation in 1986 is likely to make many people oppose the further development of nuclear power stations (see Unit 6.3).

Alternative sources of energy which are being developed in relatively small-scale projects include:

1. Solar radiation—Negev desert, Israel
2. The wind—various sites in Britain
3. Tidal power—Rance estuary, Brittany
4. Geothermal energy—North Island, New Zealand
5. Wave energy—experimental stage only.

Resource conservation

As the world's population increases and standards of living rise, increasing demands are made on the world's natural resources. Both renewable and non-renewable resources are being depleted and **conservation**—the careful use and protection of resources—is more widespread, especially in MEDCs. Efforts are being made to conserve the rain forests, but there is limited enthusiasm from LEDCs, which can benefit in the short term from the wealth of these forests. The recycling of metal containers, car tyres, and bottles are practical attempts at conservation.

Figure. 6.2 shows that only small amounts of some commonly used natural resources are being recycled in the UK. The heaviest users of these resources are the MEDCs, led by the USA. Governments are increasing their recycling programmes, spurred on by

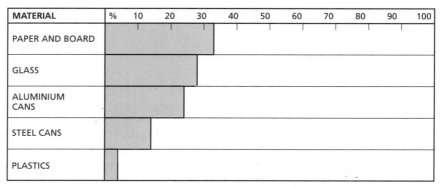

Fig. 6.2 Recycling of materials in the UK, 1994

environmental groups. More recycling centres are being opened, some local councils are providing plastic containers in which householders can put recyclable materials. Industry is also becoming involved. The German makers of Audi cars and the electronics firm IBM are making their goods so that when no longer required they can be taken apart easily and the materials recycled.

Conserving fish stocks

Fish are an important source of food and many countries have expanded their deep sea fishing fleets. In 1972, 56 million tonnes of fish were taken from the oceans, by 1992 the figure had jumped to 90 million tonnes. Large ships can fish more efficiently than small ones and are able to travel long distances for their catch. No international organisation exists with powers to restrict fishing and countries with coastlines have claimed **exclusive economic zones** within 320 km of their coastlines.

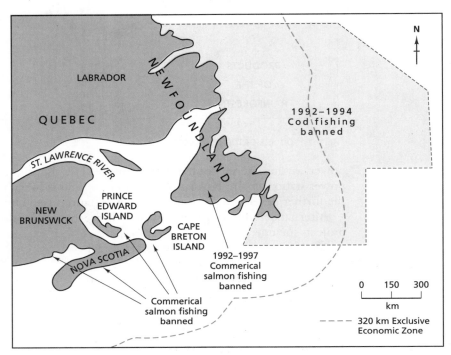

Fig. 6.3 Fish conservation in eastern Canada

Overfishing by Canadian fishermen in their exclusive economic zone resulted in cod catches dropping. To preserve stocks the Canadian government banned cod fishing off the coast of Labrador for two years (1992 to 1994). This cost 26 000 cod fishermen and other workers their jobs. The North Sea is heavily fished by the countries which border it and measures have had to be taken to conserve stocks. Herring fishing was banned by the UK between 1978 and 1982 and the EU has introduced fish quotas as a conservation measure. These quotas are causing hardship to fishing communities and many fishermen have left the industry to seek other types of work.

6.2 Water

Water supply in the UK

We take clean water for granted until a drought occurs and reservoirs begin to dry up. The heaviest rainfall in Britain falls on the north and west, whereas the greatest demand is from the cities on the east side of the hills and in the south.

In England and Wales the supply of water is the responsibility of the water companies. In Scotland services are provided by the local authorities and in Northern

Ireland by the Water Executive. These organisations obtain water from rivers and underground sources. In parts of the country with **permeable** rocks like chalk underlain by an impermeable rock such as clay, the chalk holds rainwater. A rock that will retain water is called an **aquifer**. Figure 6.4 shows the sources of water in England and Wales with the aquifers of the south supplying a great deal of the water needed.

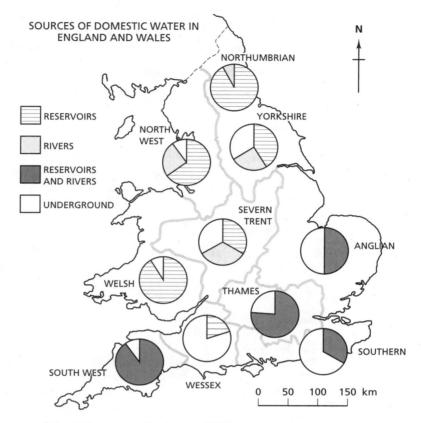

Fig 6.4 Sources of domestic water in England and Wales

E xaminer's tip

Find out from your local water company where supplies come from and what measures are being taken to: (a) improve purity, (b) conserve supplies.

Water supply in LEDCs

LEDCs are unable to afford the dams, purification works and network of underground pipes that are needed to supply fresh water to the people. Even in countries where water is plentiful, like Nepal, less than half the population has access to safe water.

With the help of charities such as WaterAid, **intermediate technology** (the use of simple technical methods and local materials and skills, see Unit 6.8) is improving water supplies and sanitation. The main methods used are:

- Protecting springs with fencing to keep animals away
- Providing pipes and drains to keep area clean
- Piping water downhill by gravity, keeping flow from springs clean
- Digging wells and capping them with concrete
- Improving sanitation with better designed latrines.

The advantages of clean water and sanitation are:

- The people are healthier
- Children are less likely to get diarrhoea and diseases
- Women who carry the water have shorter distances to walk.

Irrigation

Because of the high rainfall, only small amounts of water in Britain are used for irrigation. However, one third of the world's food is grown by irrigation and the demand for more water is increasing rapidly as the world's population continues to rise.

Some of the world's irrigation schemes are on a very large scale and are evidence of human interference in the water cycle. The largest schemes involve ponding back water behind a dam and controlling its flow downstream from that point. Many schemes are

Child mortality:

Mortality rates 1994

Under 1: 84 per 1,000 (*UK = 6 per 1,000*)

Under 5: 118 per 1,000 (*UK = 7 per 1,000*)

Access to safe water 1990–95

Total population	46%
Urban	90%
Rural	43%

Access to sanitation 1990–95

Total population	21%
Urban	70%
Rural	16%

Fig 6.5 Water supply in Nepal

multipurpose, involving the generation of energy and sometimes recreational facilities.

Irrigation can also produce problems, and large-scale developments, such as the construction of the High Dam at Aswan in Upper Egypt have far-reaching effects.

The Aswan High Dam

The Aswan High Dam, which was completed in 1971, was built to:
1. prevent flooding of the Nile in August and September
2. provide a regular flow of water for irrigation, eliminating drought which used to occur when the Nile did not flood
3. enable crops to be grown throughout the year, instead of during the six months following the summer floods
4. increase the amount of irrigated land
5. provide large amounts of electricity for both Upper and Lower Egypt.

All these objectives have been achieved.

Lake Nasser was formed behind the High Dam, with 80% of its water going to Egypt and the other 20% to the Sudan. The irrigated area of Egypt has been increased by one-fifth and farmers can now grow three crops in a year. Nevertheless, control of the River Nile has also brought its problems.
1. Fertile silt, which used to cover the ground when the river flooded, is now held back in Lake Nasser. As a result, the lake is slowly silting up.
2. Because there is no more silt to cover the fields, Egyptian farmers must buy expensive fertilisers for their crops.
3. In the past, salt in the soil was leached out by the floods. Today it rises to the surface, where it forms a crust, making the fields less fertile (Fig. 6.6).

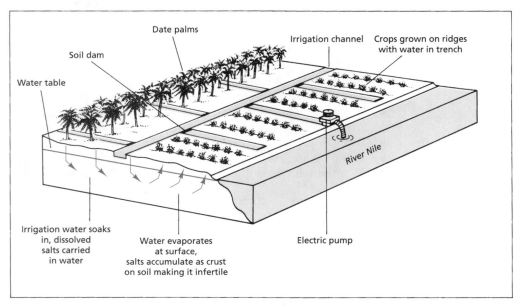

Fig. 6.6 How salts accumulate on irrigated land

④ The modern irrigation channels are breeding grounds for mosquitoes and parasites which transmit diseases and can cause death.

⑤ Some 60 000 Nubians were displaced when Lake Nasser was formed. Housing and new land has had to be provided, and it has not always been suitable.

⑥ Fishermen in the Nile delta region have had reduced catches, partly because the Nile silt which used to provide food for the fish is no longer present, and partly because the increased use of fertilisers, herbicides and pesticides pollutes the water.

⑦ Annual deposits of silt along the shoreline used to build up the Nile delta, extending it slowly outwards. This no longer occurs and for the first time erosion has become a problem. Summer resort villages built on the coast have begun to disappear.

The High Dam has been a significant factor in social changes which are taking place in Egypt. These include:

① A rapid increase in the population, which has risen from 19 million in 1950 to 62 million in 1995. The rate of population increase is 2.0% per year (100 000 each month), which is very high (the UK is 0.3%).

② Farm machinery and irrigation pumps driven by electricity or diesel oil have reduced the need for farm workers. Industries have flourished using cheap electricity, but there is unemployment, especially in rural areas, and many men seek work overseas, particularly in the oil states of the Arabian Gulf.

③ Although electricity and higher crop yields have brought prosperity to the villages, people are moving to the towns, especially Cairo. This has resulted in congestion, overcrowding and inadequate facilities. By the early years of the 21st century, Cairo may have doubled its current estimated population of 7 million.

6.3 Energy

British fossil fuel resources and the environment

Coal

In recent years coal mining has dropped sharply because other sources of energy, petroleum, natural gas and nuclear energy have been developed. In 1986, 108 m tonnes of coal were mined, the output dropped to 48 m tonnes in 1994, of which 16.6 m tonnes were obtained from open-cast pits. Underground mining scars the surface with waste rock which is heaped up into spoil tips. Open-cast mining (see Unit 6.5) can scar the landscape permanently if the pits are not refilled after the coal has been removed and the area carefully landscaped.

Oil

Nearly all British oil comes from the North Sea (Fig. 6.7). The oil is pumped in pipes along the sea bed and then distributed by pipeline to oil refineries. Oil is also transported in tankers. If the tanker is damaged or sunk the oil leaks out and becomes a marine hazard, polluting the sea and beaches, see Unit 1.10. The small onshore oilfield in Dorset is in an area of woodland, heath and marshland. Environmental groups are opposed to a request from the mining company for permission to increase the number of wells and storage tanks.

Natural gas

The large gas fields are under the North Sea and off the coast of Lancashire. Gas is brought ashore at a number of points and treated before entering the inland pipelines. Gas is much cleaner and more efficient than coal and is replacing coal in some power stations.

Changes in the demand for fossil fuels

Coal mining communities grew up in the 19th century and social life as well as work centred around the pit. Pit closures have left many communities with no local

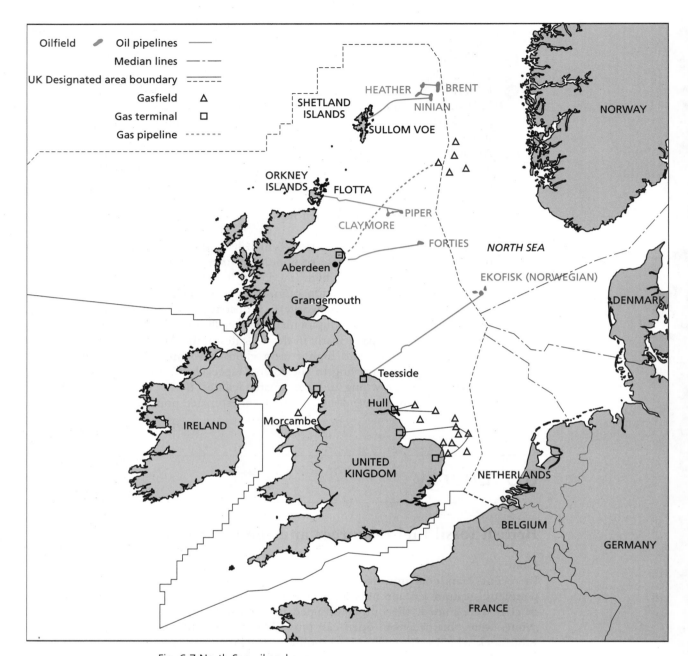

Fig. 6.7 North Sea oil and gas

employment opportunities and work has had to be sought elsewhere. By contrast the oil and natural gas developments have provided new employment opportunities to some coastal towns such as Aberdeen.

Power generation and the environment

Power stations

Power stations are found near the coalfields, near oil refineries and near large cities such as London, where the demand for power is very high (Fig. 6.8).

These power stations use fossil fuels (coal, oil and natural gas) to produce electricity. Large quantities of water are used which is obtained from local rivers or the sea and can be recycled after cooling. Coal-fired power stations are responsible for polluting the atmosphere with sulphur and nitrogen gases which cause acid rain to form (see Unit 1.10). Filters are being fitted to some of the largest power stations and natural gas or oil is replacing coal. These plants produce less than half the carbon dioxide produced by coal-burning power stations and they are more efficient so the environment benefits. The huge cooling towers of coal-fired power stations dominate the skyline and are an eyesore.

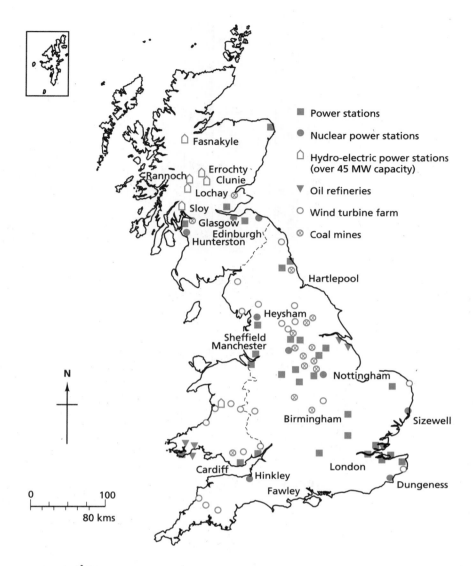

Fig. 6.8 Power stations, coal mines, wind farms and oil refineries

Nuclear power stations

Nuclear power stations are located on the coast and in remote areas such as Dungeness, away from large towns or cities. Although stringent safety precautions are taken, nuclear power is regarded with suspicion by many people, partly because of the Chernobyl disaster in the Russian Federation in 1986. One problem is that these power stations cannot be demolished at the end of their working life because of the presence of radioactivity.

Hydro-electric power stations

These are found in the highland regions of Wales and Scotland. Output is small and the schemes do little damage to the local environment.

Wind power

Wind farms are being developed in upland regions, encouraged by subsidies from the government. The amount of electricity produced is very small, the largest wind farm in the UK opened in mid-Wales in 1996 and generates enough electricity for 25 000 homes. Local people and environmental groups object to wind farms because they are considered an eyesore. They are built on high ground with turbines nearly 50 metres tall. The largest wind farm contains 56 turbines. National Power, the company promoting wind farms emphasises that wind power is clean, safe and natural. It is also cheaper than electricity from nuclear sources.

Energy production in the EU

Figure 6.9 shows primary energy production in the EU. Primary energy is the energy obtained from natural resources such as coal, oil, natural gas, water and the wind.

E **xaminer's tip**

Questions appear frequently on the environmental effects of the different types of energy production methods.

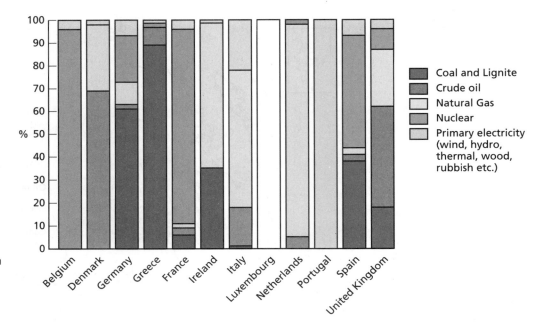

Fig. 6.9 EU production of primary energy, by source, 1994 (before Austria, Finland and Sweden joined)

Countries produce energy from their own resources or alternative sources. For example, France has very little coal or natural gas but extensive hydroelectric power resources which it has developed. In addition it has increased its dependency on nuclear power. A network of pipelines transport gas and oil to EU countries where more energy is used than produced. Italy, for example, imports liquified gas from Algeria and Libya, while gas pipelines cross the Alps bringing further amounts from the Netherlands and the Russian Federation.

Energy production in LEDCs

Figure 6.10 compares energy production for each member of the population (per capita) in five MEDCs and five LEDCs . The contrast is striking and shows the wide gap between more and less developed economies. Large amounts of capital are required to develop power resources, technological skills are also needed as well as an infrastructure (roads, pipelines, overhead electrical cables and so on)

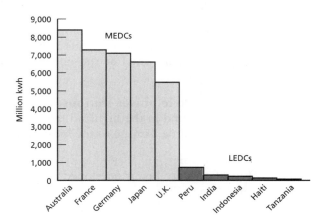

Fig. 6.10 Energy production per capita

which is only gradually being built up in LEDCs . In countries such as Tanzania, wood is used in the home to heat water and cook the food (see Unit 6.8). As the population increases, forest resources decrease and **deforestation** takes place. In some LEDCs loans and aid from MEDCs are helping to improve energy supplies. In Paraguay, for example, a hundred million dollar loan from the Inter-American Development Bank is helping to take electricity to the rural eastern areas.

6.4 Soil erosion and conservation

Much soil erosion is the result of bad farming methods, due to ignorance, neglect or greed. Mistakes were made in the past by European settlers who tried to use similar methods in new lands to those they had used at home. Immigrants to such regions as the USA, tropical Africa, Australia and New Zealand found that the farming methods they were used to could lead to soil erosion in regions with different climatic conditions. In recent years, speculators have bought land in the High Plains ranges of the USA, planted crops such as soy beans when prices were high, and then left the land fallow. Erosion can quickly occur in these circumstances once the soil is left exposed.

Water erosion

Erosion by rainwater occurs when soil is bare and has no vegetation or other form of cover to protect it. It is most common in the following conditions:

1. Where rain falls as large droplets which have enough power to blast soil particles apart.
2. Where the rainfall comes in very heavy storms and falls more quickly than it can be absorbed by the soil. This happens in hot countries, where much rain falls during heavy convectional thunderstorms.
3. Where slopes are sufficiently steep for the water to collect in small streamlets and run downhill.

Water erosion has become an increasing problem in the Sahel, where surface vegetation has died during the droughts, been removed as firewood or eaten by hungry herds of cattle. Large gullies have formed, making arable farming difficult in some areas.

Soil conservation measures to prevent water erosion include:

1. Leaving corn stalks and stubble on the fields after harvesting, and planting crops between the rows
2. Contour ploughing—ploughing round slopes instead of up and down
3. Alternating crops in strips, with a cover crop such as clover next to a crop growing in bare soil, such as corn. This is called strip-cropping. Fallow land is often left with a cover crop
4. Building terraces, so that the fields are nearly flat and water sinks into the soil instead of running off.

Fig. 6.11 Contour strip-cropping in America

Wind erosion

Like water erosion, this occurs when soil is left bare. It is most common in the following conditions:

1. Areas of low rainfall, or long periods of drought which allow the soil to become very dusty.
2. Where there are strong winds over large stretches of open countryside such as plains.
3. Where soils are loose and not bound together with organic material such as manure.

In the 1930s, the mid-west of the USA suffered severely from wind erosion. Top soil was blown as far as Boston, over 2000 km away on the Atlantic coast. The area of erosion is still known as the 'Dust Bowl'. Soil conservation methods to prevent wind erosion include:

1. Growing lines of trees, called shelter belts, across the path of the wind. This is a useful method close to crops but loses its effect at a distance
2. Leaving straw and other dead vegetation on the soil
3. Leaving stubble and plant stumps in the ground and planting crops between the rows (as for water erosion)
4. Alternating fields of grain with fallow fields, at right angles to the prevailing winds.

Government aid

In the USA, the Soil Conservation Service carries out research on soil and soil erosion, and advises farmers on conservation techniques. As a result of their efforts, roughly one-third of American cropland uses conservation methods. The Federal Government provides subsidies for farmers who practise erosion control, but soil erosion remains a problem in many areas.

Soil erosion in Europe

The Mediterranean regions of Europe are also being eroded, partly because increasing amounts of water are being taken from underground to irrigate fruit and vegetable crops and supply the expanding coastal resorts. This change in the demand for water is the result of the expansion of tourism (see Unit 6.10) and the increase in demand for Mediterranean crops in other parts of Europe. The lowering of the water table leaves hillsides short of moisture and liable to erosion during autumn storms. Gullies form, with rock and soil being washed down hillsides and causing extensive damage (see Fig. 6.12).

The Mediterranean regions most affected are Crete, Sardinia, Sicily, Spain and southern Portugal.

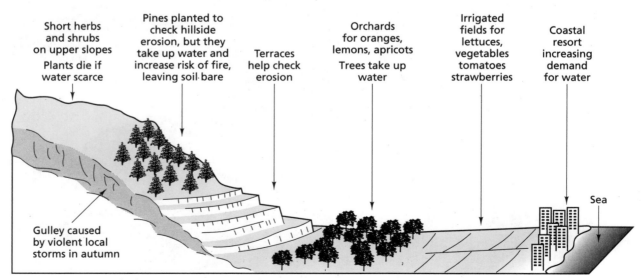

Fig. 6.12 Mediterranean hill slopes liable to soil erosion

Soil erosion in LEDCs

The poverty of many LEDCs is partly caused by mismanagement of the land. One of the worst affected areas is the **loess** (fine ground soil, deposited by wind) region of the Yellow River in North China. The soil is yellow and the river's name should give you a clue as to where much of the soil ends up. Every year enough soil is washed away to cover Greater London knee deep in mud. Erosion followed the removal of the trees and the growing of crops. During the rule of Chairman Mao Tse-tung more grain had to be grown and more soil erosion followed. Today the farmers can use the land as they think best and fuel can be bought from other regions. Gullies have been dammed and terraces built to check erosion. As yet the problems of the Yellow River basin have not been solved and during the summer rains extensive flooding occurs. This is mainly because the river bed is above the level of the surrounding land as a result of sediment deposits. Crops are ruined and people are drowned. Not surprisingly, the Yellow River is sometimes called 'China's Sorrow'.

6.5 Land reclamation

As population in a country increases there is a demand for more land which can be used for agriculture, housing and other purposes. **Land reclamation** is making flooded, derelict or waste land suitable for farming and other uses. Because reclamation is expensive, most schemes are found in MEDCs.

Reclaiming land from the sea

The Fens

Land close to the Wash in Eastern England has been steadily reclaimed for centuries as Fig. 6.13 shows. This part of the Fens, drained by pumps and waterways, has a deep fertile soil suitable for **intensive farming** (see Unit 4.2), growing fruit, vegetables and flowers. The land reclamation schemes in the Netherlands are on a much larger scale.

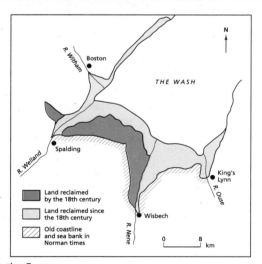

Fig. 6.13 Reclaimed land in the Fens

The Netherlands

Much of the Netherlands consists of either sandy heathland deposited as part of the outwash of an ice sheet, or clay formed as part of the river deltas of the Rhine, Maas and Scheldt. A belt of sand dunes edges the North Sea coast. Without land reclamation, the Netherlands would be under water, or marshland.

As a result of drainage, however, fertile land has been made available and supports one of the densest populations in the world, as well as providing valuable farm and horticultural products.

Small areas were drained in earlier centuries by building a series of dykes and using windmills to pump the water from the land. In the 19th century steam power made it possible to drain inland lakes and water meadows. There still remained two gaps in the Dutch coastline, that leading to the Zuider Zee, and the delta area of the south-west.

Twentieth-century schemes

1. **The reclamation of the Zuider Zee**—First a large dyke, 31 km long, was built with a road along the top linking the northern and southern halves of the country. Four polders (units of reclaimed land) have been formed, each surrounded by a dyke; streams draining into the new lake (the Ijsselmeer) have converted it into fresh water. A canal links the Ijsselmeer with Amsterdam. The drained land, which is below sea level, has had the salt removed. It is divided into rectangular fields with well-planned villages and farms spaced along the straight roads.

2. **The Delta Plan**—Catastrophic flooding in the south-west in 1953 revealed the weak link in the country's sea-defences. The Delta Plan was started with the following objectives:
   - Strengthen sea defences and shorten the coastline by building four main dams, and several subsidiary ones.
   - Provide access to Antwerp and Rotterdam but seal off the other delta inlets to form inland lakes.
   - Limit salt penetration of the land by converting some of the lakes to fresh water.
   - Make this water available for irrigation and town supplies.
   - Develop a major recreational area with yachting and bathing facilities.
   - Reduce the isolation of the south-west by building new roads, settlements and light industries.
   - Reclaim small amounts of land.

Land reclamation and the environment

In the past the Dutch were very proud of their land reclamation programme, draining wetlands and making new farmland from areas that were once part of the sea-bed. In recent years ecologists, fishermen and recreation groups have been speaking out against reclamation schemes, however, and as a result some schemes have been changed while others have been abandoned.

The first Ijsselmeer polders to be drained were used almost entirely for farming. Few trees were planted and the landscape still looks uninteresting and windswept. As the Dutch have become more urbanised, there has been a shift away from agriculture, with the result that the more recently drained polders contain urban centres. Land has been allocated for recreation and forests as well as for farming.

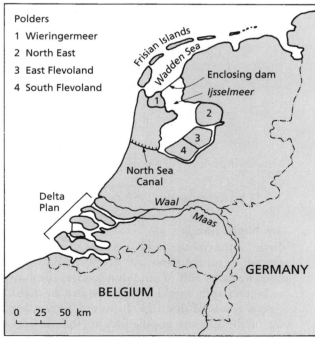

Fig. 6.14 Main reclamation areas in the Netherlands

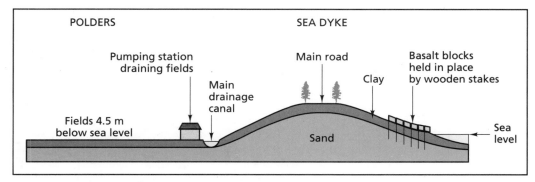

Fig. 6.15 Cross-section of polders and a sea dyke in the Netherlands

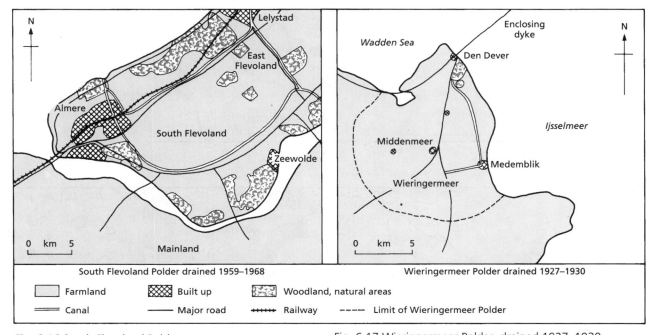

Fig. 6.16 South Flevoland Polder   Fig. 6.17 Wieringermeer Polder, drained 1927–1930

. Changes have been made to the Delta Plan, which was originally designed to have a series of freshwater lakes behind the coastal barrages. Opposition from fishermen and environmental groups resulted in retaining salt water in the southern section of the scheme and limiting fresh water to the northern inlets. The plan to reclaim a fifth polder in the Zuider Zee and the whole of the Wadden Sea by linking the Frisian Islands by barrages has been abandoned. Instead, the mudflats will be left as a nature reserve for birds, seals and marsh plants.

Table 6.1 Different land-use patterns on polders (%)

Land use	Wieringermeer (drained 1930)	South Flevoland (drained 1968)
Agriculture	87	50
Woods, natural areas	3	25
Settlement/Industry	1	18
Dykes, roads, water	9	7

Expanding cities

Some coastal cities in the more developed world are reclaiming land from the sea and coastal marshland to provide additional recreational facilities and more land for housing, commerce and industry. New York, London, Singapore, Tokyo and Hong Kong are examples where the high cost of existing land has made it economically worthwhile to spend large sums reclaiming land from the seabed.

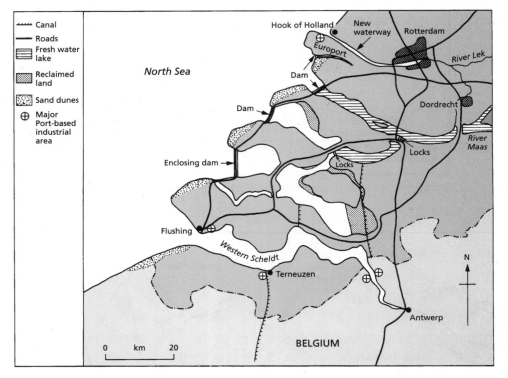

Fig. 6.18 The Delta Plan

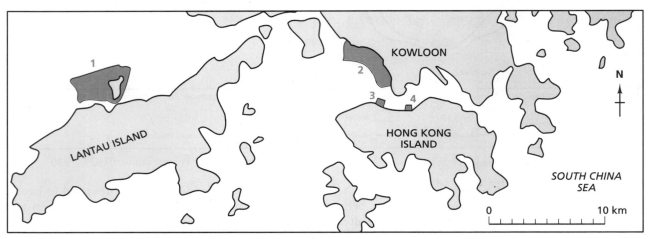

HONG KONG – LAND RECLAMATION PROJECTS 1997

1. New airport

2. Extensions to container port

3. Rail terminal for new airport

4. Extension to convention and exhibition centre

Fig. 6.19 Hong Kong— Land reclamation projects, 1997

Reclaiming derelict and contaminated land

In Britain and other EU countries such as Germany, mining for coal and other minerals has left scars on the landscape. **Open cast** mines in Britain supply over one third of the country's coal (see Fig. 6.20), and the government has made strict regulations requiring the mining companies to replace the subsoil and topsoil; they are then to plant grass so that in a year or two the land is back to normal.

In 1996 the government set up English Partnerships, a state-owned body to regenerate 56 disused coalfield sites. Money is provided from taxes, and from British Coal, to remove contamination by chemicals, landscape the sites and make them green again. Roads and other services are then added so that new houses, shops, workplaces, fields and forests can be developed. About half the area will be used for tree planting, public open space or agriculture. Local communities are being consulted and employment on the regeneration projects is available.

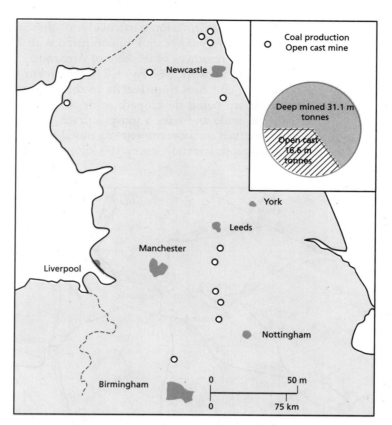

Fig. 6.20 Open cast mines in northern England

6.6 Opening up empty regions

Opportunities for economic expansion

About one-fifth of the world's land surface remains to be brought under cultivation. The rest is too cold, too arid, too mountainous or already cultivated.

The areas of the less developed world which offer opportunities for agricultural and other forms of economic expansion are:

- the tropical rain forests, e.g. Amazonia
- the savanna regions, e.g. the Llanos of Venezuela
- the arid lands, e.g. the area of Upper Egypt near the Aswan Dam.

In all these regions, however, agricultural development may also cause serious problems.

Amazonia

The rain forest of Amazonia has a low density of population caused by:

- the 'robber economy' of the early European settlers
- the decline in the number of indigenous Indians because of European brutality and diseases.

Efforts to encourage settlement and cultivation in the past were unsuccessful, mainly because of the system of land ownership. European landowners own the river banks and inland areas, leaving the peasants with no land and no access to the rivers, which have been the only means of transport.

Small-scale experiments have shown that food and tree crops can be grown in this region. Away from the alluvial flood plain, cocoa, coffee and rubber grow well, while closer to the rivers rice, maize and beans can be grown.

Developments by Brazil

With a population of 161 million, Brazil is the fifth largest country in the world. The very high population densities in cities like São Paolo and Rio de Janeiro contrast with the emptiness of the interior, particularly in the Amazon Basin. The overall density of population is only 19.0 per sq. km; compared with 234 in the UK.

To utilise the resources of its share of Amazonia, Brazil has embarked on the building of a major road network (see Fig. 6.21). The main highway, the Trans-Amazon, is over 5500 km long and runs from Recife to the border with Peru. It was finished in 1975. Other roads are being developed; some, like the Trans-Amazon with two lanes, are seven metres wide and have a gravel surface. Land on each side of the Trans-Amazon has been reserved for government-organised settlements. A commercial centre is being established at approximately every 100 kilometres.

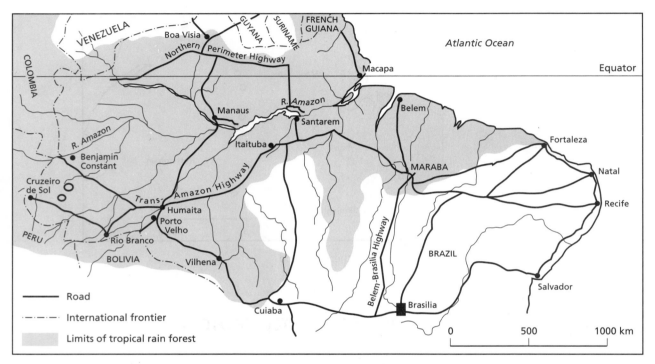

Fig. 6.21 Road network in Amazonia

Landless families, mainly farm labourers from north-east Brazil, are given 100 hectares, of which two hectares are cleared. The government helps the pioneers to build their houses and to obtain credit for the purchase of food, seeds and equipment. The majority of settlers are not, however, supported by the government. They have been attracted to the new roads by the prospect of free land. Conditions for the new settlers are harsh. Despite the lush appearance of the forests, the nutrients in the soil are rapidly leached out by the heavy rainfall, and soil erosion is an ever present danger.

Large clearings for pasture have also been supported by government funds. The government hopes that cattle rearing will produce meat that can be sold overseas as well as in Brazil. Brahman cattle, which can withstand the high temperatures, have been introduced. In many areas, however, pastures have deteriorated and the government programme has been abandoned.

The opening up of the forest lands of Amazonia has not, as yet, resulted in the large-scale inward migration for which the region was planned. Some of the largest settlements are the mining towns where iron ore, bauxite, manganese, tin and gold are extracted.

All the new developments seem designed to take what is valuable from the region as quickly as possible. This is a typical 'robber economy'.

Problems associated with the development

Ecologists are concerned at the widespread destruction of the tropical rain forest ecosystem, and the possible disappearance of the Amazonian forests because it could cause climatic changes and seriously affect the world's atmosphere balance.

- The land-hungry poor of Brazil are unlikely to support any moves to conserve the rain forest. They need to use the land to produce food and earn money. They will therefore exploit the initial fertility of the soil, with little regard for the problems which may occur in the future.

- The large landowners in other parts of the country see the opening up of Amazonia as a means of avoiding land reform nearer home, so they exert political pressure on the government for development to proceed as fast as possible.
- When the forest cover is removed, the topsoil is washed away by the heavy rains and soil erosion becomes a serious problem.
- Traditional ways of life are threatened and are already disappearing (see Unit 4.6).
- The Indian population has been reduced by 90%. Many have been killed, others have died of disease or starvation as their land has been confiscated or polluted by mining.

In the 1980s international concern at the destruction of the rain forest ecosystem forced the Brazilian government to introduce a programme for the Amazon region. The National Foundation for the Indian, FUNAI, was set up and the road programme slowed down. In 1994, however, the President signed an Amazon Charter speeding up construction of four rain forest roads. This has encouraged new settlers and threatens the survival of more Indian tribes.

Indonesia

Indonesia has a population of 203 million and is the largest country in South East Asia.

The population is not spread evenly over the many islands. Java has a population density of 580 per sq. km, whereas on Sulawesi it is less than 50 per sq. km. Java has over 60% of the total population but only 8% of the land area.

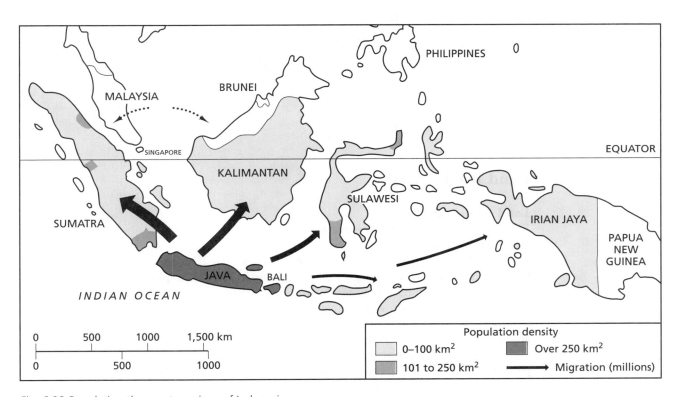

Fig. 6.22 Populating the empty regions of Indonesia

The Indonesian government encourages people to move from Java to less populated areas. This policy is called **transmigration**, moving across from one part of the country to another. Some 3 million poor and landless people have accepted free land, housing and supplies and in addition at least 2 million have moved without government assistance (Fig. 6.22). The scheme has brought conflicts with local people, particularly the tribes of the rain forest of Irian Jaya.

6.7 Land use and ownership conflicts

Figure 6.23 shows the different pressures on land, which result in conflicts of interest. Land is a scarce resource, particularly in the urbanised regions of the more developed world where there is sufficient wealth to exploit its potential in a variety of ways. People who have an interest in one particular form of development, or in preserving the existing land use, form pressure groups. These attempt to influence the final decision on how the land is used. Conflicting demands for land can become national or international issues. One example is the problem of nomadic people in regions as varied as the Arctic wastes of North America and the Australian outback.

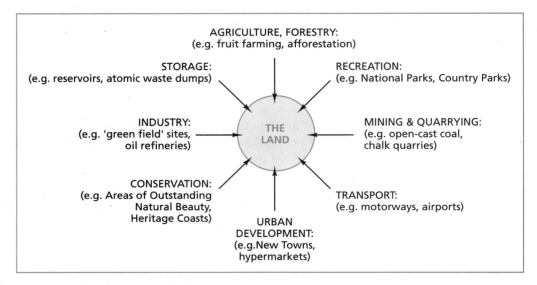

Fig. 6.23 Conflicting demands for land

Land use in Alaska

Land ownership
For many years, the native people of Alaska, consisting mainly of nomadic groups such as the Inupiat and Kutchin, regarded themselves as second-class citizens of the USA with no legal rights to the land, which technically belonged to the Federal Government. They became poorer as their territory was exploited by US companies anxious to profit from the minerals, timber and fish of this under-developed American state. The discovery of vast quantities of oil in the 1960s on the North Slope, near Prudhoe Bay, brought further protests, because land was needed for a pipeline right across Alaska to the ice-free port of Valdez on the south coast.

In 1971 the US government passed the Alaska Native Claims Settlement Act. This gave the 85 000 native people of Alaska nearly 18 million hectares of land and 1 billion dollars compensation. The people became shareholders in 13 regional and some 200 village profit-making corporations which were set up to administer the land and money. In return for this land and money, the other native claims were dropped and the land needed for the pipeline was granted.

The profit-making corporations which were set up invested money in timber, fisheries, reindeer herds, mining, hotels and other ventures. Many of these have prospered and paid dividends to their shareholders. Millions of dollars have also been used to provide electricity, schools, water, satellite telephones and other amenities to remote settlements. This increase in material comforts has also brought with it boredom, alcoholism and the breakdown of some families as people have abandoned their traditional customs and way of life. For those who still hunt whales, a quota system has been introduced; conservation groups protest at the continuation of this aspect of the traditional nomadic way of life.

The cost of living and unemployment are higher in Alaska than anywhere else in the USA, and although schools teach the traditional customs, many children finish their education in colleges in other American states and do not want to return to Alaska. Many people complain that they once collectively owned the whole of the state, whereas now they only own small pieces of it.

Recreation areas

A further complication relating to land use in Alaska has been the decision by the Federal Government in Washington, DC to designate 41 million hectares (an area larger than California) as ten national preserves and eight national parks (Fig. 6.24). The government believes that conservation of these areas now will check exploitation and will give the state valuable recreation potential. It should also prevent having to buy land in the future, when prices are higher, to protect it for conservation; this has happened in other American states. Alaskans who live off the land will be able to continue hunting, fishing and gathering.

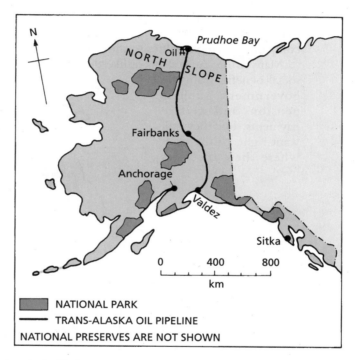

Fig. 6.24 National parks in Alaska

The Alaskans are unhappy at these developments, because they believe that important exploitable natural resources in the national preserves and parks will be locked away for ever. They also consider that they have not been given enough say as to how the land should be used. They say that they are also concerned about the environment and want to see their land wisely managed. They distrust the Federal Government, which has not had a good record in the past for looking after their rights.

Aboriginal land in the Northern Territory

The Aboriginal Land Rights Act

The Australian aborigines are one of the native groups in the world whose land and way of life are threatened by white settlers and miners. Australia was the home of the aborigines thousands of years before the first British settlers arrived in 1788. They were skilled hunters and knew how to make the best of their difficult environment, protecting the ecosystems for future generations. To the white settlers the aborigines, like the kangaroos, were a nuisance. Many were killed and their land taken away. The aboriginal communities have deep spiritual links with their land which they believe their spirit ancestors created and protected in the 'Dreamtime'.

In recent years some white Australians have begun to realise that they have a debt to pay to the aborigines. In 1976 the government passed the Aboriginal Land Rights Act enabling aboriginal groups to reclaim portions of their land. The government still claims ownership of minerals in Australia, wherever they are found, but development of minerals on aboriginal land is not permitted without the consent of the aboriginal owners. This has resulted in conflict with the owners who have found that they often lose out when mining companies want to move in.

The Northern Territory

The Northern Territory has an area five times that of the UK, but the total population is only 170 000, of whom 40 000 are aborigines. The aboriginal groups now own more than a third of the Territory (Fig. 6.25), including the three largest national parks— Kakadu, Nitmiluk and Uluru, where Ayers Rock is located. These parks are leased to the government for use as jointly managed national parks. Some sacred sites within the parks, near Ayers Rock for example, are closed to visitors. The other aboriginal lands, such as Arnhem Land can only be visited with a permit from the Northern Land Council, based on permission from the aborigine owners who have made these permits difficult to get.

Mineral exploitation on aboriginal land still takes place. There is a large uranium mine in Kakadu National Park and mining also takes place elsewhere with the mining companies paying royalties to the Aboriginal Councils concerned.

Many white Australians dislike the aborigines because they are able to claim the same social benefits from the government, such as pensions and welfare payments, but they still want rights to the lands where their ancestors lived.

Examiner's tip

Make two lists. The first putting the views about land ownership made by the aborigine groups. The second putting the views of white Australians.

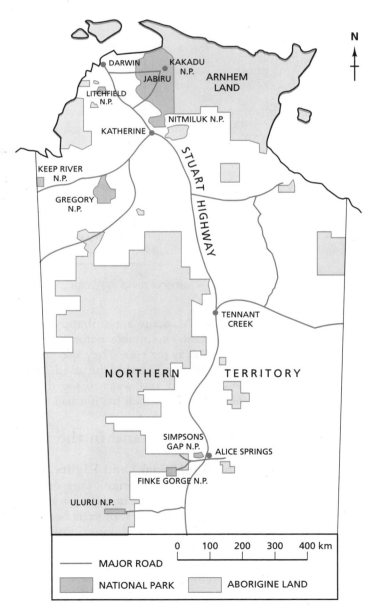

Fig. 6.25 Aborigine land in the Northern Territory of Australia

6.8 Large and small development projects

Large-scale schemes

LEDCs must decide the best ways to develop with the limited capital they possess and with what they can borrow from more developed countries and international agencies such as the World Bank. Technical assistance is also required from MEDCs.

Some development schemes are on a very large scale and aim to provide energy, irrigation and flood control as well as a regular supply of water. These are called **multi-purpose projects** and they are intended to provide a resource-base for agriculture and industry and improve the standard of living of the people. Multi-purpose schemes include the Volta River project in Ghana, the Damodar Valley scheme north-west of Calcutta in India and the Aswan High Dam in Egypt (see Unit 6.2). Other large projects in areas with adequate rainfall for agriculture aim to provide electrical energy for industries and urban areas. The largest scheme of this type in the world is on the River Parana in South America (Fig. 6.26).

The Itaipu HEP Project

The Itaipu hydro-electrical power station in southern Brazil was completed in 1990. It harnesses the power of the River Parana which forms the boundary between Paraguay and Brazil. It can generate 12.6 million kilowatts of electricity, enough to supply all the needs of Paraguay and the industrial regions and cities of southern Brazil. The reservoir created stretches for 160 km upstream and the cement used in building the power station and dams could pave a dual carriageway from Calais to Istanbul. Brazil paid for the dam with loans from a number of international banking organisations. Paraguay uses less than 5% of the energy and sells the rest of its 50% share at cheap rates to Brazil. Paraguay is, therefore, a large exporter of electricity even though a third of its people have no electricity in their homes. Brazil has the largest foreign debt in the world and people have made the following objections to the scheme.

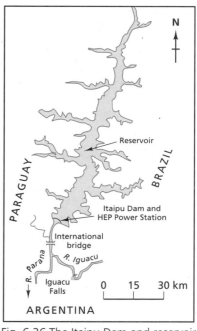

Fig. 6.26 The Itaipu Dam and reservoir

- Brazil neither needs nor can afford such a massive scheme.
- The dam was built to give the government more prestige.
- 40 000 families in the flooded area had to move out. They were given some assistance to live elsewhere.
- The micro-climate and ecosystem of the region have been changed, causing problems in the future.
- The country would be better served by smaller schemes nearer to centres where they are needed.

Small-scale schemes

Intermediate Technology (IT)

Intermediate technology is the use of technical skills that are suitable for the conditions found in LEDCs. The technology uses local resources, builds on local skills and the product is owned and maintained by the people who will benefit from it. Production using IT methods is small-scale. This makes sense in countries where capital is scarce, roads and other forms of communications are poor and where people are an abundant resource. Production is, therefore, close to the market.

Micro-hydro schemes in Nepal

In contrast with the colossal Itaipu Dam in Brazil, villages in Nepal are using the power of small streams to generate electricity. Until IT was introduced the main source of fuel was wood, leading to **deforestation** of the hillsides and **soil erosion**. By improving simple wooden water wheels sufficient power can be generated for a village. This power is used to grind corn, dehusk rice and light the houses. The simple generator is housed in a wooden hut and the machinery can be made by local manufacturers using materials available in the country.

IT for cooking

Over half the world's population relies on wood, other plant materials or animal dung as sources of fuel. Collection of the materials is done by women and children and is time consuming and tiring. As local timber resources are used up journeys have to be made further afield. The fuel is used in an open fire surrounded by three large stones which support a cooking pot. The method is inefficient, unsafe and unhealthy because there is a great deal of smoke.

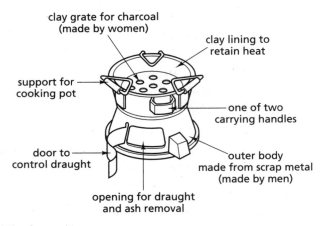

Fig. 6.27 Improved jiko for cooking

The IT solution is a simple **ceramic stove** called a *jiko* in Kenya. Women's groups, using local clay, have set up businesses to make and sell the stoves which cost about £1 in the market. The stove produces less smoke, less charcoal is needed and the kitchen is a cleaner and healthier place.

Building with soil

Soil can be **stabilised**, that is made firm, using lime, natural fibres or a small amount of cement. The soil blocks can be dried in the sun and used to replace expensive concrete blocks in house building. In a similar manner **fibre-concrete roofing (FCR) tiles** can be made using a mixture of soil, sand, cement and fibres. The tiles can be dried in the sun, saving fuel. They make better insulation for roofs than corrugated iron sheets.

IT has also been used very successfully to improve the water supply and sanitation of villages (see Unit 6.2).

6.9 National Parks

The enormous growth of towns and cities has underlined the need to preserve country areas which are especially attractive. Tourism and leisure activities in these areas need to be planned so that people can enjoy but not spoil them. As ownership of cars has increased and the motorway system developed, more and more people are able to travel easily to distant parts of the country and all parts of Britain have become threatened by over-use and unplanned development.

The National Parks and Access to the Countryside Act was passed in 1949 to preserve the beauty of the countryside and to help people enjoy it. As a result of the Act the first National Park was set up—the Peak District National Park at the southern

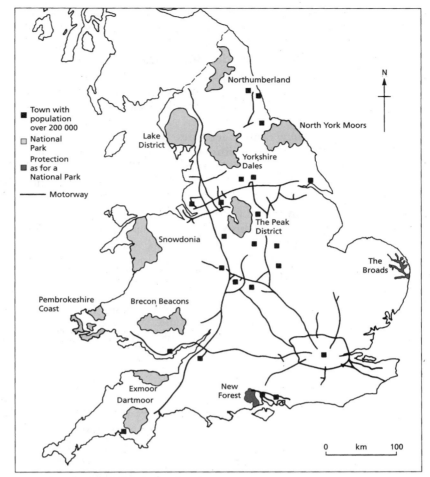

Fig. 6.28 England and Wales: the National Parks

end of the Pennines. Today there are ten Parks (shown in Fig. 6.28). In addition, the Broads and the New Forest are protected like a National Park.

Each park is run by a National Parks Authority. From 1 April 1996 in Wales and 1 April 1997 in England the national authorities assumed new responsibilities for funding. They were empowered to levy part of their income from local Parks, the rest being paid by the Department of the Environment, Transport and the Regions.

Purposes of the National Parks

1. Preserving the natural beauty of the landscape
2. Providing access to these areas and facilities for the enjoyment of the general public
3. Maintaining traditional farming practices in the park areas
4. Placing planning controls on buildings.

Problems of the National Parks

1. **Land ownership**—Only 2% of the land in national parks is owned by the National Parks Authorities. Landowners own or manage the largest amount, 43%, while the Ministry of Defence, the Forestry Commission and mining companies own or manage the rest. The interests of these owners do not always match with the preservation of the land for the public to enjoy—there are many conflicting demands which are decided by the Secretary of State for the Environment, Transport and the Regions. A recent attempt to control boat speeds on Lake Windermere in the Lake District National Park was turned down by the Secretary of State.

2. **Traffic**—Millions of cars visit the most popular parks each year. Traffic jams can be almost as bad as in the centre of cities on weekends in summer. If new roads

Examiner's tip

National Parks and their problems are popular with examiners. Give this unit high priority in your revision schedule.

were built they would alter the character of the land and encourage even more cars into the areas. Experiments are now being made to control the use of cars in the parks.

③ **Industrial development**—Although the parks were created to preserve the countryside, permission has been given for large-scale industrial development in some. For example, there are limestone quarries in the Peak and oil refineries in the Pembroke Coast Park. They were allowed to meet 'national needs'. The parks have also been surveyed for valuable mineral deposits, which could lead to new mining activities.

④ **Overcrowding**—More than 100 million visits are made to the National Parks each year. The most popular parts of the parks become severely overcrowded during holiday seasons and at weekends. The situation is made worse because most people stay in or near their cars. Favourite walks may be heavily over-used and roads become jammed.

⑤ **Second homes**—Since these areas are so beautiful, many visitors would like to live in the parks or have a weekend cottage. Some city dwellers can pay higher prices for cottages than locals can afford, and gradually artificial villages are being created in which only a few people live permanently and only a tiny minority work locally.

⑥ **Pollution**—Overcrowding of the parks can cause pollution: by exhaust fumes from many cars in traffic jams and motor boats on the lakes, and through litter left by careless visitors. The constant use of footpaths can destroy ground vegetation.

Forest Parks

Forest Parks have been created by the Forestry Commission. There are four parks in Scotland and one in Wales. A National Forest is being developed in the Midlands. It has a £2 million annual budget from the Department of the Environment, Transport and the Regions. It is planned to have 60% deciduous woodland and 40% of faster growing softwood. The creation of a forest park involves:

① opening up forests to the public;
② laying nature trails and walks of graded lengths and degrees of diffculty;
③ supplying sites for camping and caravanning
④ providing car parks for visitors
⑤ providing information services.

The most famous Forest Park in Britain is the Queen Elizabeth Park in Scotland, which stretches from the Trossachs to Loch Lomond.

Fig. 6.29 Different attitudes to providing leisure facilities in the countryside

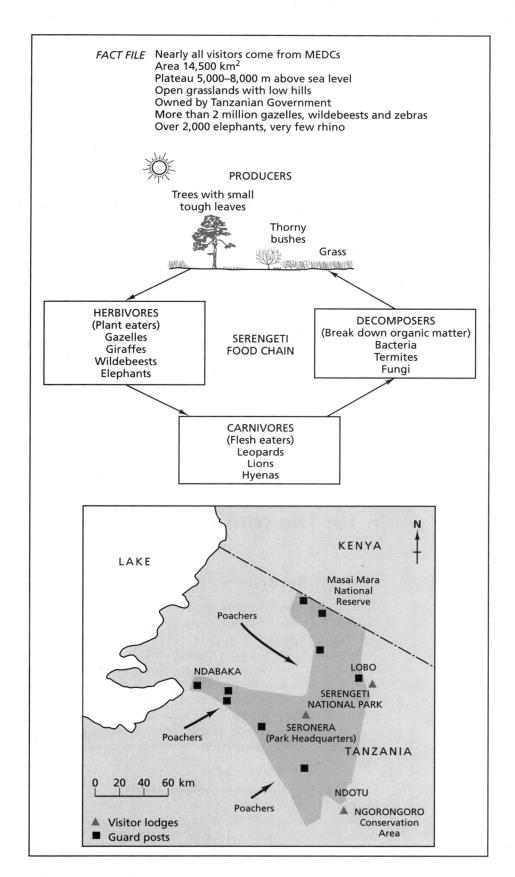

FACT FILE Nearly all visitors come from MEDCs
Area 14,500 km²
Plateau 5,000–8,000 m above sea level
Open grasslands with low hills
Owned by Tanzanian Government
More than 2 million gazelles, wildebeests and zebras
Over 2,000 elephants, very few rhino

PRODUCERS
Trees with small tough leaves
Thorny bushes
Grass

SERENGETI FOOD CHAIN

HERBIVORES
(Plant eaters)
Gazelles
Giraffes
Wildebeests
Elephants

DECOMPOSERS
(Break down organic matter)
Bacteria
Termites
Fungi

CARNIVORES
(Flesh eaters)
Leopards
Lions
Hyenas

KENYA

LAKE

Masai Mara National Reserve

Poachers

NDABAKA

LOBO

SERENGETI NATIONAL PARK

Poachers

SERONERA
(Park Headquarters)

TANZANIA

0 20 40 60 km

Poachers

NDOTU

NGORONGORO Conservation Area

▲ Visitor lodges
■ Guard posts

Fig. 6.30 Serengeti National Park

Country Parks

Country Parks are much smaller than National Parks and are set up by local authorities with the help of the Government. By setting up many local parks, it is hoped that they will attract visitors who would otherwise have travelled further or crowded into other rural areas.

The Serengeti National Park, Tanzania

The Serengeti National Park was set up in 1951, the same year that Dartmoor became a National Park. The two parks have little else in common. Serengeti is as large as Wales and contains the largest herds of grazing mammals in the world. The park is in the **savanna** grasslands (see Unit 4.5) and was the home of the cattle-rearing **Masai** tribes. The word Serengeti in Masai means 'open space'. These tribes are no longer allowed to graze their animals in the park which is a wild life sanctuary. The park attracts tourists who come on **safari** holidays and stay at lodges in the park, Fig. 6.30. There are no large hotels and hunting is forbidden. The income from tourism is very important to Tanzania where income per head is only US$90 (UK is US$ 18 410).

Poaching

Thousands of animals are killed each year by poachers. Most poaching is done by tribesmen living outside the park using bows and poisoned arrows or wire snares. The animals are killed for their meat which is dried and sold, and for their hides. More organised poachers with automatic rifles, two-way radios and trucks kill elephants for their tusks and rhinos for their horns. Many countries have banned the sale of ivory and rhino horns, but they are still valued highly in the black markets of South East Asia. Other trophies are smuggled overseas to be made into handbags, shoes, ivory ornaments and medicines. As a LEDC Tanzania cannot afford the aircraft, vehicles and patrols needed to stop the poachers.

6.10 The tourist industry

Tourism in Britain

Tourism has now become a major service industry in Britain, and the provision of holidays for foreign visitors has become an important source of foreign currency for the country. The main centre of the overseas tourist trade is London, although efforts are being made to encourage foreign tourists to stay in other parts of the country.

Each year, Britain attracts millions of visitors from all over the world. Over 20 per cent of overseas tourists come from North America, an important element of this trade.

The total income from overseas tourists in 1995 was £11.9 billion, which was a large proportion of the income of the entire holiday industry.

The attractions which Britain offers overseas tourists include historic sites, castles, cathedrals, the countryside, traditional events, royal pageantry, shopping and entertainment.

Effects of the changes in holiday patterns

Increased mobility of the people of Britain, increased leisure time and greater interest in outdoor activities have encouraged the setting up of National, Country and Forest Parks (Unit 6.9). The increased use of these amenities, however, has created pressure on the land and caused environmental problems which threaten the quality of the landscape. This is the result of overuse and over-development.

Changing holiday patterns have made it necessary for traditional holiday areas and resorts to adapt to new demands. Some have failed to do this and older seaside resorts such as Hastings have suffered.

The expansion of holiday activities and tourism has become an important source of

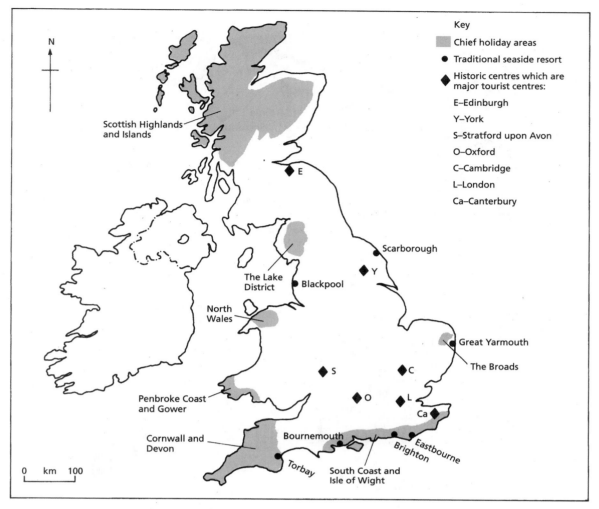

Fig. 6.31 Main holiday areas and tourist centres in the UK

income and provided many new jobs. To some extent, this growth has compensated for the national loss of jobs and wealth which has resulted from the decline of manufacturing industry.

Effects of the expansion of tourism

1. The development of the foreign tourist trade and the subsequent boom in hotel building have increased competition for attractive sites in our cities, especially in London (Unit 4.12). Some residents complain that hotels have taken up the land needed for more houses.

2. The over-concentration of the foreign tourist trade in London has increased traffic and pedestrian congestion and strained the transport system.

3. The most popular tourist centres outside London have also become congested and overcrowded in the peak tourist season. This destroys the atmosphere and character of ancient cities such as York—the very qualities the tourists want to experience.

4. Tourism has grown rapidly but is a risky business. Tourists are kept away from Britain by publicity on violence, terrorism, etc., and are also put off by changes in the value of the pound which may make holidays more expensive. As a result the hotel industry has to face years of slump and boom in rapid succession.

5. Tourist coaches and cars add to the traffic density and congestion on our busiest motorways such as the M1 and the M25.

Mediterranean tourism

Over 100 million people take a Mediterranean holiday each year, with the majority of the tourists coming from the cooler and less sunny regions of the UK, Scandinavia,

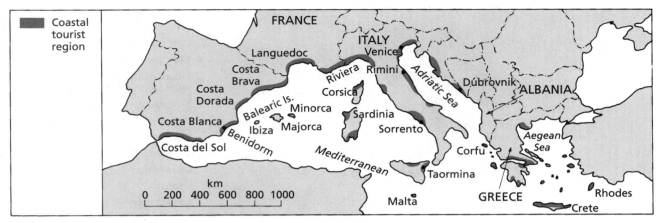

Fig. 6.32 Main resort regions around the Mediterranean coast of Europe

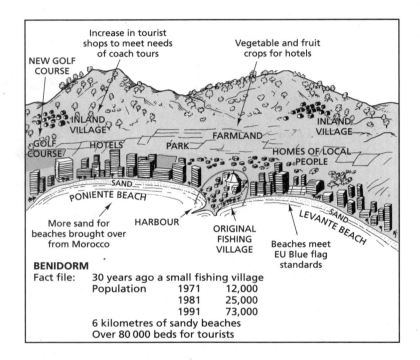

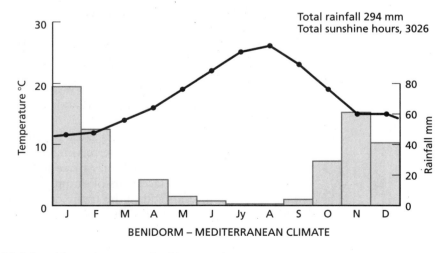

Fig. 6.33 A Spanish tourist resort—Benidorm

Benelux and Germany. The most popular stretches of Mediterranean coastline are those of Spain, which are visited by over 50 million holidaymakers a year. During the main holiday season, from April to October, the resident coastal population of many resorts is doubled. This inevitably puts pressure on the resources, while boosting employment in the hotel trade and other service industries concerned with tourism. The Spanish resorts, like those elsewhere, have grown at a very rapid rate since large-scale package tours became more popular in the early 1970s.

The Mediterranean tourist regions are some distance from the core industrial areas of western Europe (Fig. 6.33). They form the periphery and are often regions with lower living standards where, in the past, farming and fishing were the main occupations. For the EU countries of Greece, Italy, Spain and Portugal, tourism is an essential part of the economy, providing much-needed foreign currency. There are disadvantages and advantages in tourism for the people who live near the coast, as well as for the local environment. These can be listed as costs and benefits.

Costs

Examiner's tip

Case studies of tourist resorts and their problems are frequently asked for in questions on tourism.

1. **Pollution**—About 85% of the sewage from 120 coastal sites around the Mediterranean is discharged into the sea, with inadequate or no treatment at all. Industrial waste also enters the Mediterranean from oil refineries, chemical plants and other factories. Because the Mediterranean is almost landlocked and tideless, the pollution tends to accumulate, making bathing in some areas unhealthy. Some improvements are being made at considerable expense to the areas concerned.

2. **Haphazard building**—Hotels, shops and apartments have been built in large numbers, often with little thought for planning. As a result, scenery has been spoiled by tall hotel blocks and traditional building styles have been ignored.

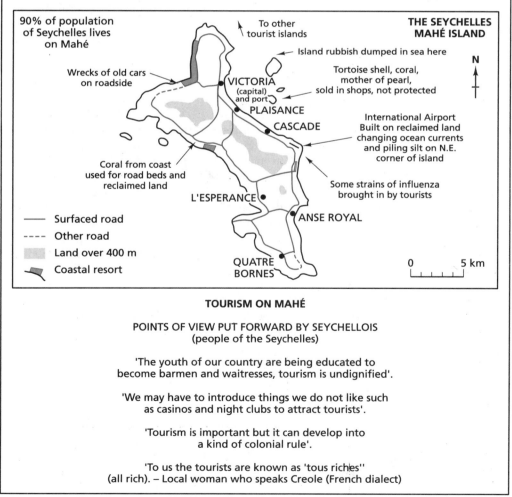

Fig. 6.34 Tourism and the environment on Mahé

③ **Changes in land use**—Because land prices have soared, good farmland has been built-over and countryside with scenic beauty has disappeared.

④ **Congestion**—The increase in the number of vehicles has resulted in some new roads being built, but many streets are congested and rural roads damaged by heavy traffic.

⑤ **Noise**—There is an increase in noise, with clubs and discotheques operating late at night and charter flights arriving and taking-off from local airports.

⑥ **Souvenir shops**—There is a spread of souvenir shops, take-away restaurants and similar facilities needed by visitors but of less interest to local people.

⑦ **Breakdown of traditions**—Local customs and traditions may disappear or be altered to meet the needs of the tourists: for example, the so-called 'flamenco' dancing put on in some tourist hotels in Spain.

Benefits

① **Employment**—There is much more employment in regions where previously there were few opportunities for work other than farming or fishing.

② **Standard of living**—Local people are likely to experience a higher standard of living as tourist money flows into the coastal regions. Farmers benefit by growing crops such as vegetables and fruit needed by the hotels.

③ **Infrastructure**—The infrastructure is improved to provide roads, promenades, hospitals and other facilities needed by the visitors.

④ **Entertainment**—Theatres, night clubs, casinos, cinemas and many other forms of entertainment are developed and are of benefit to local people as well as visitors.

⑤ **New interests**—New ideas and interests are introduced such as local radio, clubs and amateur dramatic groups.

⑥ **Conservation**—Funds are found to restore old buildings, local craft workers find new markets for their products and traditional customs may be revived to interest the tourists.

Tourism is a growth industry in countries bordering the Mediterranean, but it has been received with mixed feelings by many of the people whose homes are on its shores.

The Seychelles

The Seychelles is a group of islands in the Indian Ocean just south of the Equator. 72 000 people live on the islands, the largest of which is Mahé. The Seychelles is an LEDC with an average income per head of US$6210 (UK is US$ 18 410). Tourism is the most important source of wealth with most tourists flying in from France, Italy, UK, Germany and Switzerland. The monthly average temperatures average between 24°C and 31°C, with the heaviest rainfall between October and February.

With no major industries the Seychelles must import nearly all the goods and materials needed for the tourist industry. These include furniture, hotel fittings, some food and drink, clothing, electrical equipment and machinery. Hotel profits for the foreign-owned hotels and facilities go overseas. The main advantage to the islands is employment, but only 45% of the people have regular or seasonal jobs. The Seychelles, like other LEDCs, is encouraging **ecotourism**, that is tourism aimed at protecting the environment by not damaging the ecological balance. For example, fishing with spears and harpoons is forbidden around the islands.

Summary

1 Some renewable resources are being used up faster than they can be replaced.

2 In LEDCs clean water is a luxury which few can afford.

3 Changes in the demand for fossil fuels have brought hardship to coalminers, but opportunities to industries supplying the oil companies.

4 In LEDCs soil erosion often follows a pattern. An increase in population leads to forest clearance to grow more food and the exposure of the hillsides to soil erosion.

5 The urbanisation of the Netherlands has resulted in changes in land–use policies for new polderlands, with a greater concern for protection of the environment.

6 Economic exploitation has seriously depleted the rain forests of Brazil and resulted in the decline of the Indian population.

7 Native groups throughout the world have lost their land and way of life when overseas settlers move into their territory.

8 Intermediate technology may be a better way forward for LEDCs than large-scale projects.

9 Land ownership and tourist pressures have created problems and conflicting interests within national parks.

10 Tourism has advantages (benefits) and disadvantages (costs).

Quick test

6.1 Exhaustion of natural resources
1 Fossil fuels are examples of a ....resource.
2 The greatest resource of the rain forests is ....
3 To control fish catches, countries with coastlines have claimed
   ....
4 Which common material has the highest recycling percentage in the UK?
5 What has the EU imposed to conserve fish stocks?

6.2 Water
6 What is an aquifer?
7 How many months of the year could crops be grown in Egypt before the Aswan High Dam was built?
8 Why did fishermen in the Nile Delta have reduced catches after the High Dam was built?
9 What benefit does improved water supply give to women in LEDCs?
10 What fraction of the world's food is grown by irrigation?

6.3 Energy
11 What is open-cast coal mining?
12 Apart from the North Sea, where else is there an offshore gas field in the UK?
13 Why are nuclear power stations built in remote areas?
14 What is a wind farm?
15 What is the main source of energy in many LEDCs ?

6.4 Soil erosion and conservation
16 Soil erosion can be caused by .... and ....
17 What is contour ploughing?
18 What is a shelter belt?
19 A fine soil deposited by wind is called ....
20 Why is the Yellow River called 'China's Sorrow'?

6.5 Land reclamation
21 What is a polder?
22 Why was the Delta Plan necessary?

23 What region of the UK has been partly reclaimed from the sea?

24 Why do some coastal cities reclaim land from the sea bed?

25 A state-owned body called .... has been set up to regenerate disused coalfield sites.

6.6 Opening up empty regions

26 What is meant by a 'robber economy'?

27 What is the road called that crosses the rain forest in Brazil?

28 Why do the native Indians dislike new roads being cut through the rain forest?

29 What is transmigration?

30 What is the name of the most heavily populated island in Indonesia?

6.7 Land use and ownership conflicts

31 List three conflicting demands for land.

32 Name one native group living in Alaska.

33 Why do the native Alaskans dislike the quota system for killing whales?

34 Who owns the mineral rights in Australia?

35 What has the Australian government done to solve the problem of the claims by aboriginal groups for land?

6.8 Large and small development projects

36 On which river is the Itaipu HEP Project?

37 Which country shares the energy with Brazil?

38 What do the letters IT stand for?

39 What can happen on hillsides after deforestation?

40 Give two benefits for a rural village if water supplies are improved and the water made safe to drink.

6.9 National Parks

41 What percentage of the National Parks in England and Wales are owned by the National Parks Authorities?

42 Name the two areas that are protected like National Parks.

43 What is a honeypot?

44 In which part of England is the National Forest being developed?

45 Which of the following animals are herbivores? Giraffe, leopard, elephant, gazelle, hyena.

6.10 The tourist industry

46 What is the main centre of the overseas tourist trade in the UK?

47 Why do many people from northern Europe choose to go to Mediterranean resorts for their holidays?

48 Which are the peak months for tourists visiting the Mediterranean?

49 Why is pollution a special problem for countries around the Mediterranean?

50 Roads, water supplies and parks are all part of the................ of a town.

Chapter 7
Skills

7.1 Interpreting and representing data

Interpretation of the OS 1:50 000 map

All the Exam Boards include mapwork questions in the GCSE exam. The maps used are usually on the 1:50 000 or 1:25 000 scales, but maps of other scales are sometimes used. Overseas maps are also occasionally set. Some candidates find that the time allowed for the map question is barely sufficient, so be prepared to work fast and accurately. Do not be put off because the map is on a large sheet of paper. You should be given a large desk so that the map can remain flat.

When answering a map question follow the three stages below before you start writing your answer.

- Think of the map as a large picture and try to relate it to its region. The map of Southampton Water at the back of this book should remind you that Southampton is on the south coast and is a major port. You probably also know that there is a large oil refinery at Fawley.
- Do not look at the details on the map, instead try to find patterns in such things as land use, routeways and settlement. Often these patterns emerge more clearly if you half close your eyes. On the Southampton Water map the woodland of the New Forest shows up clearly as does the settlement around the oil refinery.
- Finally, before you start to write answers to the questions spend a minute or so looking at some of the detailed information which the map extract provides. Note the scale, the contour intervals and the symbols that recur frequently. The low tide symbols around the waterway are common on the Southampton Water map.

Types of questions asked

Map references and symbols
For example:
- Name the features at 491046 and 399078.
- Give map references for Beaulieu Abbey and Southampton Royal Pier.
- Remember that the eastings (top and bottom) numbers precede the northings (sides) numbers.

Compass direction
- In which direction is Netley (4508) from Beaulieu (3802)?
- In which direction is Calshot Castle (4802) from Marchwood (3910)?
You must know the 16 compass points (e.g. N, NNE, ENE, E etc.) to give an accurate answer.

Distances

To measure distances it is best to use either the straight edge of a piece of paper or a length of thick cotton. The length measured should be placed against the scale at the bottom of the map.

- What is the shortest distance in kilometres from Lower Exbury Fort (420988) to Bucklers Hard (409001)?
- What is the shortest distance by road?
- Why is one distance greater than the other?

Cross-sections

You may be given a cross-section to annotate, so find out how to make a cross-section and understand what it shows.

- Draw a cross-section from the triangulation pillar at 404046 to the spot height at 371009.
- Mark on it the Beaulieu River, a lake that has been dammed, and the B3054 road.

Communications

Questions about communications usually relate to the ways road or rail routes are influenced by physical features.

- Southampton Water breaks the east–west communications and road communications must avoid the lower Beaulieu River because there is no bridge until Beaulieu is reached. What other river prevents road or rail crossings near its mouth?

Settlement

Questions may be asked about the **distribution** of settlement. There is a marked difference in the distribution on the Southampton Water map between the west and the waterway margins. The **site** and **position** of the settlement is also important. Beaulieu is at a river crossing whereas Fawley is above the marsh level of the waterway. The map may provide evidence as to why the settlement grew where it did. This concerns the **function** of the settlement. Hythe, Holbury and Blackfield have grown up close to the Fawley oil refinery. A further significant factor is the shape of the settlement. It may be **nucleated**, **linear** in **bead-like clusters** or have some other distinctive shape for which a reason may be apparent. Fawley is nucleated, whereas East Boldre (3700) is linear in shape.

Descriptions of physical features and land use

You may be asked to describe and explain physical features on the map. For example, the differences between the east and west banks of Southampton Water. It may also be necessary to describe how a physical feature was formed. An example is the spit at Calshot (4802). Land use descriptions based on the Ordnance Survey conventional signs are also frequently set. Compare the land use in 4403 with that in 3999.

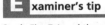

E xaminer's tip

Study Fig. 7.1 and the map extract to identify and name features A, B and C in the photograph.

Fig. 7.1 Oblique aerial photograph, Southampton Water

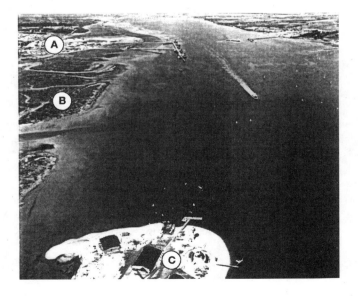

Interpretation of an aerial photograph

An oblique or vertical aerial photo may be used to test your skills in relating places and objects in the photograph with their counterparts on the map. Start off by orientating the photo with the map. A photo looking down Southampton Water should not be confused with one looking up. Be prepared to answer such questions as :

- In which direction was the camera pointing when the photo was taken?
- List three features to be seen on the photo and not on the map (or vice-versa).
- What does the photo tell you about the area which the map does not? On the Southampton Water map a photo might show up rows of yachts and other leisure craft. These would not appear on a map (see Fig. 7.1).

Examples in this book

Many of the skills needed for the GCSE exam are related to interpreting visual material, such as maps, diagrams and statistics. Section 2 of this book contains a wide variety of examples. To help you revise the different forms, examples have been listed below, together with their figure references. Check each carefully and make certain you understand what the illustration shows. Many exam questions will test your knowledge of, and ability to use, these techniques. You will also need to use them in your own coursework.

Maps	Figure numbers
OS map extract	Inside back cover
Settlement maps	3.2, 3.12, 3.13, 3.15, 5.3, 5.4,
Weather maps	1.1, 1.4
Sketch maps	1.16, 1.17, 1.21, 4.17, 5.10,
Distribution maps	1.6, 1.11, 1.22, 1.28, 2.7, 2.8, 3.4, 3.16, 4.3, 4.4, 4.5, 4.7, 4.11, 4.16, 4.17, 4.18, 4.19, 4.22, 5.1, 5.2, 5.6, 5.13, 5.14, 5.15, 5.18, 5.19, 5.21, 5.23, 6.3, 6.7, 6.8, 6.13, 6.14, 6.16, 6.17, 6.18, 6.19, 6.20, 6.21, 6.24, 6.25, 6.26, 6.28, 6.30, 6.31, 6.32, 6.34
Choropleth maps	2.2, 2.9
Flow maps	2.10, 2.12, 3.5, 6.22, 6.30

Diagrams	
Pie charts	5.16, 6.4
Line graphs	1.12, 1.30, 2.1, 2.3, 2.4, 2.6, 6.33
Bar charts	2.11, 4.12, 4.13, 5.12, 5.16, 5.20, 6.5, 6.9, 6.10, 6.20, 6.33
Population pyramids	2.5
Diagrams	1.5, 3.1, 3.19, 4.6, 4.8, 4.14, 4.21, 5.11, 5.17, 6.1, 6.23, 6.27
Block diagrams	1.7, 1.8, 1.9, 1.10, 1.14, 1.23, 1.25, 6.6, 6.12
Flow diagrams	1.31, 1.33, 2.10, 2.12, 3.3, 4.8, 5.17, 6.22
Cross-sections	1.2, 1.3, 1.18, 1.19, 1.20, 1.24, 1.27, 1.29, 6.15
Models	1.3, 1.32, 2.3, 3.4, 3.6, 3.7, 3.9, 3.10, 3.11, 3.14, 4.1, 4.2, 4.10, 4,15, 5.8

Photographs	
Ground photographs	1.26, 3.8, 3.18, 5.5, 5.7, 5.9
Oblique aerial photographs	1.13, 1.15, 5.22, 6.11, 7.1

Other material	
Cartoons, sketches	1.21, 1.29, 4.21, 6.29, 6.33

Statistical data	
Statistical tables	3.17, 4.9, 4.20

Summary

1 Interpreting visual material is an important feature of the GCSE exam questions.

2 The questions also test the candidates ability to use techniques.

3 Nearly all examinations include an OS map of 1:50 000 or 1:25 000 scales although other scales and maps of areas outside the UK are sometimes used.

4 Map questions are often linked with the interpretation of aerial photographs.

Quick test

7.1 Interpreting and representing data

1 A map that uses colours or shading to show area density patterns is called a ....
2 What does a population pyramid show?
3 On a pie graph of different ethnic groups, Muslims must be shown as 25% of the population. What angle would you draw for Muslims?
4 On an Ordnance Survey map, using the six- or four-figure map reference, which is read first, northings or eastings?
5 Which would you use on a map to show the routes used by immigrants to reach another country? Bar chart, line graph, flow diagram, model.

Chapter 8
Types of exam questions

Structured questions

The most common type of questions set for the GCSE exam are **structured** questions. This means that you are given information in a visual form such as a map, diagram, photo or chart and a number of questions follow. Some of the questions are directly based on the information, some may be indirectly connected with it. In addition there may be further visual material and questions. This is called a **multi-part** question and normally each part requires only a short answer. For example, a question starts with a weather chart showing isobars, fronts and weather symbols over the British Isles. The first part of the question asks for the pressure at point A. Parts 2 and 3 ask questions about the fronts and symbols along them. In the last part of the question you are asked to describe the weather at a certain place and how local outdoor activities might be affected by it.

Usually you will put your answers in a question book with lines drawn in it. Make certain you answer each part of the question as fully as possible. A six-line space for a part answer with four marks allocated to it requires more than a one-line answer. You will find examples of multi-part structured questions in the exam paper on pages 191–202.

Objective tests

One of the syllabuses, the Northern Examinations and Assessment Board, Syllabus A, includes an objective test as part of the examination. Objective tests are made up of questions for which there are precise answers and for which the marking can therefore be objective, that is, not influenced in any way by the personal opinions of the examiner. The questions are called multiple choice questions because you are asked to selected an answer from a number of possible alternatives. There are two types of multiple choice questions.

1 Simple multiple choice

Which one of the following activities is an example of a tertiary industry?
A fishing
B dentistry
C forestry
D building
E tin mining

2 Matching pairs

For each question, choose the letter representing the feature which most appropriately answers it. Each feature may be used once only.
(i)   Which tree is coniferous?
(ii)   Which tree stores water in its bark?
(iii)   Which tree is tapped for its sugary syrup?
(iv)   Which tree grows in tropical swamps?
        (a) kapok (b) maple (c) mahogany (d) larch (e) baobab (f) oak (g) mangrove

Answering multiple choice questions

• Read the question carefully and then look at the alternative answers you are given.
• If you are not sure of the answer, eliminate the alternatives you are certain are wrong. If this leaves you with two possible answers then take a guess as to which one is correct. Never leave a question unanswered and when you have finished check that each question has been answered.
• Multiple choice questions can slow you down if you cannot make up your mind quickly.

If there are more questions to be anwered on the exam paper make certain you move on to them after giving the multiple choice question its share of the total time available.

Short answer questions

These are especially common on Foundation Tier exam papers. Short answer questions can take different forms. Sometimes you may be asked to interpret an item on a map, graph or diagram. For example, using the OS extract provided, give the grid reference for an industrial estate. Sometimes the question requires a single-word or short-sentence answer. As each part of the question is likely to be worth only a few marks (perhaps only one), do not worry if you cannot answer one part, especially if you know the correct answers to all the other parts.

Longer answers

These are most likely to come towards the end of a multi-part structured question on a Higher Tier paper. You are expected to write a short essay-type answer and are given a dozen or more lines to write on. For example, 'Using one or more named examples, describe how governments have tried to attract industry to areas of high unemployment.' Always write your answer in sentences and not as a series of rough notes.

Mark allocations

Whatever form the question may take, keep a careful eye on the mark allocated to each part. The mark is a guide as to how important the examiner considers that part of the question. For example, when 2 marks are allocated for the question, 'Explain why most of Japan's industry is located along the coastline', you are likely to get only 1 mark if you give only one reason.

Typical exam questions

Question 1

(Time allowed: 30 minutes)

(a) Look at Fig. 1.1. It is a diagram which shows what a soil is made of.

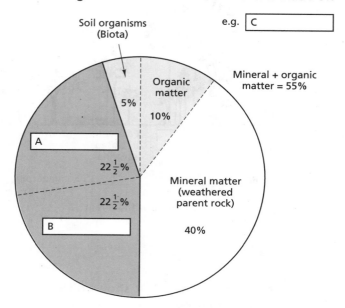

Fig 1.1

Fill in the boxes on Fig. 1.1. Choose your answers from the following list:

Sand   Water   Stones   Air   Earthworms   Humus

1   Name the two parts of the soil, A and B.
2   Name an example of a soil organism at C.

(3)

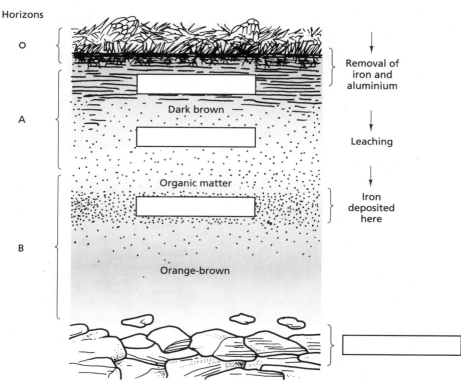

Fig 1.2

(b) Figure 1.2 is a diagram of one type of soil. It is a *podsol*. An *iron pan* has formed in this podsol.
(i) Write the following labels in the correct boxes on Fig. 1.2.

Horizon C   Iron pan   Ash-grey colour   Acid peaty layer   (4)

(ii) Complete the following by crossing out the wrong words.
In a podsol iron is washed out (leached) from the O horizon/B horizon. The iron is deposited in the O horizon/B horizon. These podsols may be found in the coniferous forests/tropical forests.   (2)
(iii) Describe the sort of climate that leads to the development of a podsol. (3)

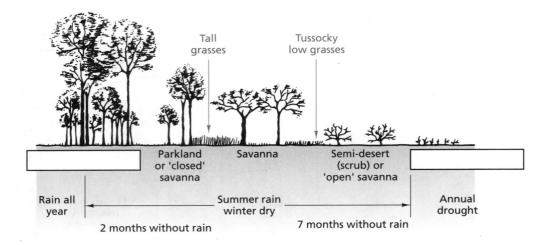

Fig 1.3

(c) Look at Fig. 1.3. It shows different types of vegetation in the Savanna. The Savanna grasslands are found between the tropical rain forests and the hot deserts.
(i)   Write the following labels in the correct boxes on Fig. 1.3.
Hot desert   Tropical rain forest   (2)
(i)   How do the grasses of the Savanna survive the long dry season?   (1)
(iii) Explain how the trees of the Savanna are adapted to their environment.   (4)

(d) Study Fig. 1.4, an incomplete diagram of an **ecosystem.**

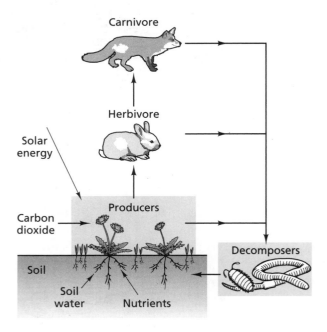

Fig 1.4

(i)   What is a carnivore? (1)

(ii) What part does the fox play in **this** ecosystem? (2)

(iii) Some ecosystems are very fragile. Choose an example where people have **damaged** an ecosystem. (Examples include deforestation, overgrazing, too much irrigation, acid deposition etc.)

Chosen example: ....

1. Describe the ecosystem **before** people damaged it.

2. Explain the problems which have arisen. (8)

(Total 30 marks)

London, Syllabus A, Specimen paper, Foundation Tier

Question 2

(Time allowed: 35 mins)

(a) (i) What is *rural–urban migration*? (2)

   (ii) Study Fig. 2.1.

Country	Urban population %	Agricultural workforce %
Bangladesh	14	44
Egypt	49	19
Greece	63	16
India	28	32
Peru	70	8
Malaysia	42	23
United Kingdom	93	2

Fig 2.1

Complete the scattergraph below by adding the information for Egypt and India. (2)

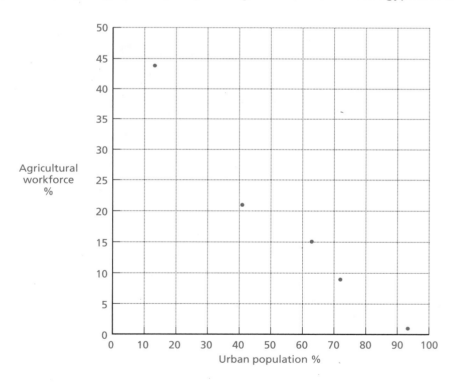

(iii) Describe the relationship the scattergraph shows. (1)

(iv) Explain the relationship you have just described. (3)

(b) Study Fig. 2.2

(i) Describe the trend the graph shows. (2)

(ii) The high rates of in-migration lead to the development of shanty towns near the large cities of Developing Countries. Give *two* reasons. (4)

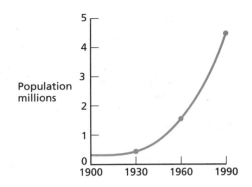

Fig 2.2
Population of
Lima, Peru

(c) Study Fig. 2.3
  (i)   What advantages does the position of shanty town **A** have over shanty town **B** for its inhabitants? Give *three* different advantages.   (6)
  (ii) Shanty town dwellers often have no legal right to the land on which they live. Give *one* reason why this is a disadvantage to them.   (2)
  (iii) Shanty towns often have appalling housing and living standards. Describe the attempts made by their inhabitants, government bodies or other groups of people to improve the quality of life of the shanty town dwellers. How successful have their attempts been? Use examples to support your answer.   (8)

(Total 30 marks)
WJEC May 1996, Higher Tier

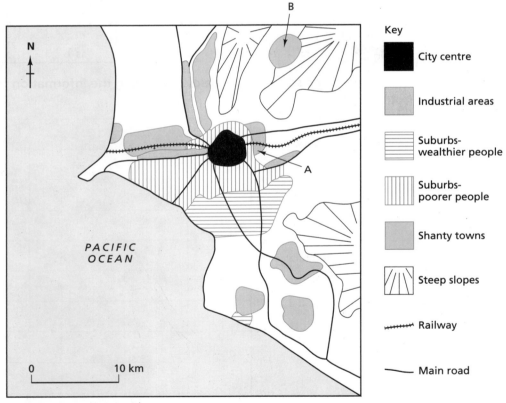

Fig 2.3 Urban zones of Lima, Peru

Question 3

(Time allowed: 15 mins)

(a) Study Fig. 3.1, which shows a cross-section of an urban area. Answer the questions which follow.

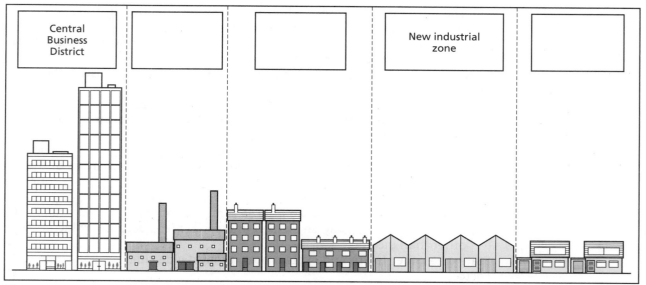

Fig 3.1

(i) Complete Fig. 3.1 by selecting the land use from the list below. Two zones have been completed for you.
Old industrial zone, Greenbelt, Newer house zone, Old housing zone (3)

(ii) Describe the Central Business District using the following headings.
Density of buildings. Use of land. Accessibility. (6)

(iii) Bid rent is high in the central business district. State the meaning of the term **bid rent**. (2)

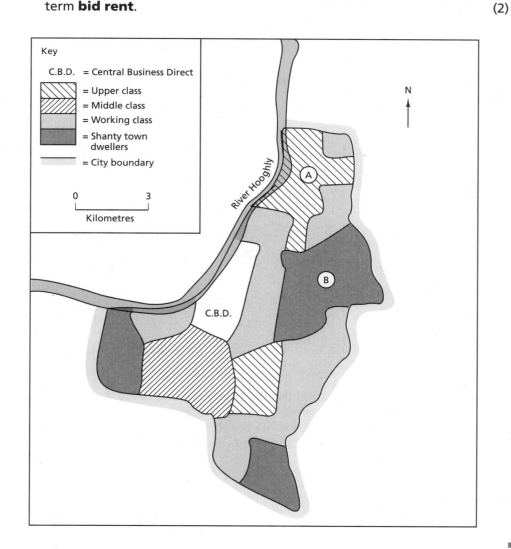

Fig 3.2

(iv) The newer housing zone is different from the old housing zone. State **two** ways, other than age, in which it is different. (2)

(v) Many modern factories are located in the new industrial zone. State fully **one advantage** of such a location. (3)

(b) Study Fig. 3.2, which shows social divisions in Calcutta, India. Answer the questions which follow.

(i) **Complet**e the paragraph by adding the missing words

upper class, middle class, shanty town dwellers, working class, migrant workers

There are four main social groups living in Calcutta. The _____ and _____ are the two groups living beside the C.B.D. Only two areas of the city are occupied by the _____. _____ are found in three areas near the city boundary. (4)

(ii) State one reason why people in Area A might not like to live in Area B. (2)

(iii) Cities like Calcutta may be divided into social areas because of factors other than income.

State **one** other factor and explain how it may divide cities

Factor (1)

Explanation (2)

(Total 25 marks)

NICCEA, May 1996, Foundation Tier

Question 4

(Time allowed: 34 minutes)

(a) Figure 4.1 shows the extent of the area in Africa north of the Equator at risk from desertification (the expansion of desert into other areas).

Fig 4.1 Risk of desertification in Africa north of the Equator

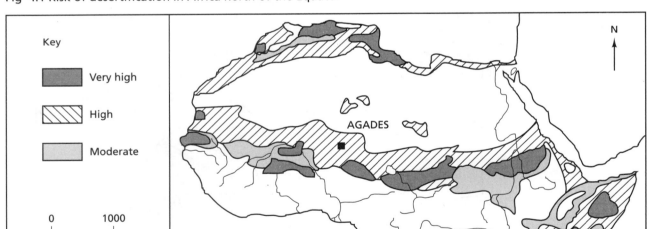

(i) Study the information given in Fig. 4.2 and explain why desertification develops in areas shaded in Fig. 4.1 (5)

(ii) Describe the main features of the rainfall distribution for Agades in Niger over the five years shown by the data in Table 4.1 (4)

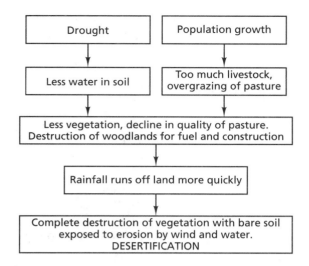

Fig 4.2

Table 4.1 Rainfall Distribution —Agades (Niger)

Month	Year 1	Year 2	Rainfall (mm) Year 3	Year 4	Year 5
January	–	–	–	–	–
February	–	–	–	–	–
March	–	2	–	–	–
April	–	–	50	–	–
May	22	–	1	18	–
June	7	2	20	1	–
July	11	58	61	9	22
August	36	67	26	51	14
September	21	26	8	3	4
October	–	–	–	–	–
November	–	–	–	–	–
December	–	–	–	–	–
Total	97	155	166	82	40

    (iii) Suggest how the information described in both (i) and (ii) may change the lives of pastoral nomads in areas shaded in Fig. 4.1   (4)

(b) Many of the areas shaded in Fig. 4.1 have suffered serious famines resulting from drought. Over 25 million people in the area are threatened with starvation. If you were an adviser to a world organisation offering help to this region, state the advice you would give to the organisation to reduce the threat of starvation.   (4)

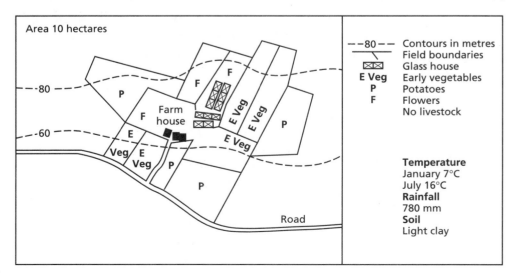

Fig 4.3
Farm A (near the south coast of SW England)

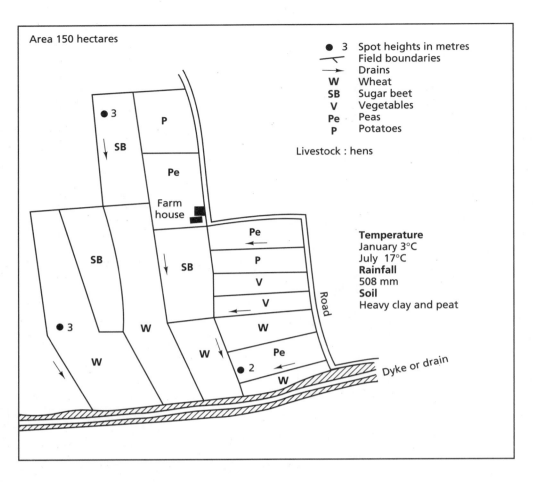

Fig 4.4
Farm B (in the Fens,
Eastern England)

(c) Study Figs 4.3 and 4.4, which show two farms in different parts of the United Kingdom.
  (i) State the contrasts shown between the two farms.
  (ii) Choose **either** Farm A **or** Farm B and suggest how physical factors (including climate) and human factors might have influenced the farmer to use the land as shown. (8)

(Total 25 marks)

MEG, Syllabus B, June 1995, Higher Tier

Question 5

(Time allowed: 35 minutes)

Study Fig. 5.1, which shows the percentage of people living in poverty in five areas of the LED (less economically developed) world, according to three indicators of development and welfare.

(a) (i) 'Many people in LEDCs (less economically developed countries) are illiterate, unwell and have to drink filthy water.'
    Do you agree with this statement? Use information from Fig. 5.1 to give reasons for your answer. (3)
  (ii) Give **one** reason why female illiteracy is generally higher than male illiteracy in LEDCs (less economically developed countries) (2)

(b) Read the headline from a recent newspaper, Fig. 5.2.
  (i) What does 'absolute poverty' mean? (2)
  (ii) Give **two** other ways (not shown in Fig. 5.1) which show that people are living in absolute poverty. (2)
  (iii) In some areas environmental conditions might help to explain the absolute poverty. Give an example of such an area and two reasons for these difficult conditions. (4)

(c) Large differences in the level of development and welfare can exist between

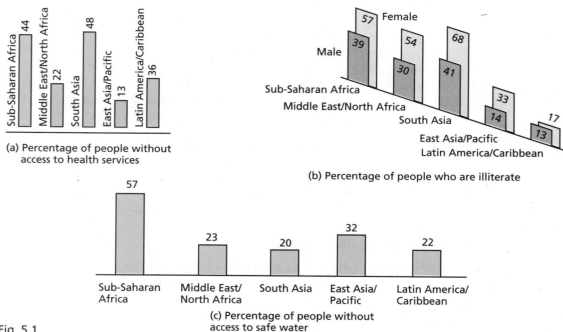

(a) Percentage of people without access to health services

(b) Percentage of people who are illiterate

(c) Percentage of people without access to safe water

Fig. 5.1

"A quarter of the world's population, living in LEDCs, are condemned to absolute poverty."

Fig. 5.2

areas close to each other. Give an example of two such areas and one consequence of their different levels of development. (3)

(d) Study Fig. 5.3.
What is the evidence that wealth and trade are not equally shared around the world? (3)

(e) Suggest why absolute poverty in LEDCs might be caused by this uneven sharing of wealth and trade. (4)

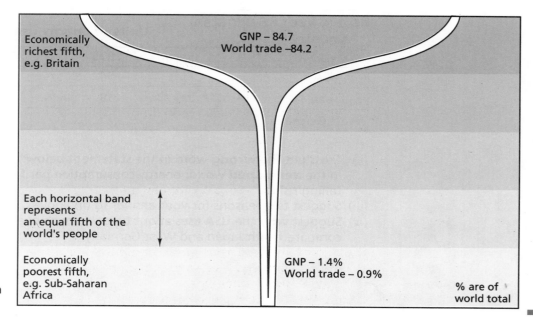

Economically richest fifth, e.g. Britain

GNP – 84.7
World trade –84.2

Each horizontal band represents an equal fifth of the world's people

Economically poorest fifth, e.g. Sub-Saharan Africa

GNP – 1.4%
World trade – 0.9%

% are of world total

Fig. 5.3 World distribution of wealth and trade, 1991

(f) Many LEDCs encourage either:
  the use of improved but appropriate technologies
  or the arrival of multi-national companies
  as ways of increasing their national wealth.
  (i) For a named country, describe the advantages of **one** of these
  approaches. (4)
  (ii) For the approach you have identified in (i) above, describe how the
  environment of an area of the country has been affected by it. (3)
  (Total 30 marks)
  NEAB Syllabus C, Specimen paper, Higher Tier

Question 6

(Time allowed: 36 minutes)

(a) Study Fig. 6.1, which gives information about the relationship between the
use of energy and Gross National Product (GNP).

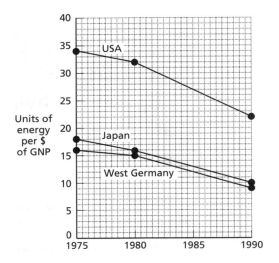

Fig. 6.1

(i) Complete the table below:

Country	Units of energy used per $ of GNP	
	1975	**1990**
USA	34	22
Japan	18	....
West Germany	....	....

(1 1/2)

(ii) Cross out the **wrong** word in the statement below:
  In the **developed** world, energy consumption per $ of GNP has been
  falling/rising. (1/2)
(iii) Suggest two reasons for your answer to (ii) above. (2)
(iv) Suggest **why** the USA uses about twice as much energy per $ of GNP
  compared with Japan and West Germany. (1)

(v) Draw a line on the graph below to show the **general** relationship between GNP per person and energy consumption per person.   (1)

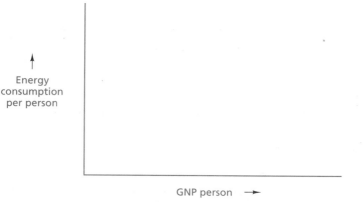

↑
Energy
consumption
per person

GNP person →

(b) Study the table below, which gives information about energy consumption in the United Kingdom.

Appliance	Electricity consumption per year in KW hours	
	Average household	**Household using latest energy efficient appliance**
Freezer	1 000	80–180
Washing Machine	400	40–210
Dishwasher	500	50–240
Colour Television	340	70

(i) What does the table tell you about energy efficiency in the United Kingdom? Use two items of data to illustrate your answer.   (2)

(ii) Study Fig. 6.2, which shows two ways of making a fire in Burkina (a **developing** country). What does it tell you about the efficiency of a traditional three-stone fire?

(iii) Why do people often resist suggestions which would reduce energy consumption? Answer from the point of view of each of the following:

1. Pupils in a school which is trying to lower its heating and lighting bills

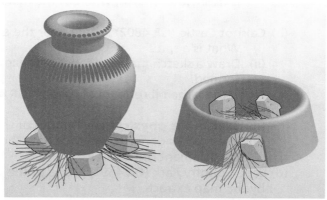

The traditional three stone fire (left) gains in efficiency when surrounded with a simple shield of clay (right). The clay is free and widely available.

Fig. 6.2

2. A poor family in Burkina asked to try the new fire shown in Fig. 6.2

3. A UK manufacturer who does not want to make freezers which use a small amount of electricity.   (6)

(c) Study the table below, which gives information about types of energy used in **developed** and **developing** countries.

Type of energy	% using energy type		
	Developed countries	Developing countries countries	World
Oil	37	23	32
Coal	25	27	26
Natural Gas	23	7	17
Biomass	3	35	14
Hydro-electricity	6	6	6
Nuclear	5	1	4
Others	1	1	1

(i) Write the words '**fossil fuels**' and '**renewable energy**' in the correct boxes above. (1)

(ii) State **two** differences in the types of energy used in **developed** and **developing** countries. Use data in both answers. (2)

(iii) Name **one** type of biomass energy. (1/2)

(iv) Name **one** type of energy which would be included under 'Others'. (1/2)

(v) Choose **one** of the following types of energy:

Biomass   Hydro-electricity   Nuclear

Discuss the advantages and disadvantages of developing and using your chosen type of energy. Use at least one example in your answer. (6)

(Total 25 marks)

London, Syllabus A, May 1996, Higher Tier

Question 7

(Time allowed: 30 minutes)

1 (a) Study the Ordnance Survey map extract inside the back cover of this book.

(i) Name **TWO** natural coastal features shown by the symbols in grid square 4703. (2)

(ii) Using evidence from the map, **explain why** the marsh in grid square 4104 is freshwater marsh, whereas the marsh in grid square 4398 is salt marsh. (2)

(b) Calshot Castle (GR 4802) is built near the end of a spit.

(i) What is a spit? (1)

(ii) Draw a sketch map and label it to explain how the spit at Calshot was formed. (3)

(c) Study the large oil refinery at Fawley (GR 4404) and neighbouring grid squares.

(i) Explain the **physical** advantages of this site for an oil refinery. (3)

(ii) Use map evidence to describe how the oil refinery has affected the environment of the area. (3)

(d) Lepe Country Park (GR 4598) is one of the Country Parks in the area covered by the map extract.

(i) What is a Country Park and how does it differ from a National Park? (2)

(ii) Why are Country Parks known as 'honeypots'? (2)

(e) Over 4 million people visit the New Forest National Park each year, part of which is shown on the map. Visitors to the New Forest and other National Parks may come into conflict with people who live and work there.

Give examples of problems that might arise between visitors and local people. Your examples need not come from the New Forest National Park. (7)

(Total 25 marks)

Higher Tier

Answers to exam questions

Question 1

(a)   (i) air, water   *(2)*

             earthworm *(1)*

(b)   (i) From top–acid peaty layer; ash-grey colour; iron-pan; horizon C *(4)*

    (ii) 'O' horizon; 'B' horizon *(2)*

   (iii) precipitation throughout the year; long cool/cold winters *(3)*

(c)   (i) tropical rainforest (left); desert (right) *(2)*

    (ii) die down; leaves are inward curving *(1)*

   (iii) deciduous; drought resistant; waxy leaves; thorn like; long roots; gnarled trunks; thick bark; baobab tree holds water in large trunk; flattened crowns of acacia giving shade to roots   *(1 for each good point)*   *(4)*

(d)   (i) flesh eating *(1)*

    (ii) eats herbivores; when it dies it provides decomposers with organic matter   *(2)*

   (iii) **1** Norfolk Broads. Originally this area was a series of lakes (Broads) connected by streams. Marshland surrounded some lakes and the edges were lined by sedges and reeds. The clean water was a fertile breeding ground for freshwater fish. Rare butterflies, insects and a variety of birds, including wildfowl, made the habitat their home. Badgers, foxes and rabbits were the main wild animals present.

         2 The problems result from two major changes in the region. The first is the development of tourism and the second is the increased use of chemicals by local farmers. The popularity of the Broads for boating has increased the number of propeller-driven boats, churning up the water and breaking down the banks with their wash. Pollution from litter and increased sewage has threatened the ecosystem. Runoff from farmland pollutes the waterways with chemicals, mainly phosphates and nitrates used as fertilisers. Other chemicals come from herbicides and pesticides. These chemicals speed up the growth of algae, the oxygen content of the water is reduced killing fish and plants. The food chain is destroyed and some Broads are now 'dead'. *(8)*

(Total 30 marks)

Examiner's tip

Describe an ecosystem you have studied with as much detail as possible

---

Question 2

(a)   (i) The movement of people from the countryside to cities. Do not repeat the 'rural to urban' in the question. Say 'countryside to town or city' so that the examiner knows that you understand the meanings of 'urban' and 'rural'.   *(2)*

    (ii) Locate Egypt (49 on horizontal axis, 19 on vertical axis) and India (28 and 32) as accurately as you possibly can. Carelessness can lose you these marks   *(2)*

   (iii) The agricultural workforce falls as the urban population increases   *(1)*

   (iv) You can refer to push–pull factors here. People are pulled (attracted) to the city; they are pushed by landlessness and poverty from the country; as workers leave the land for the city the percentage of urban workforce increases. Agricultural workers who reach the city have to try to find urban jobs.   *(3)*

(b)   (i) There has been an overall increase in population. The increase was slow at first but then accelerated. The very fast rate of growth signifies a population 'explosion'

    (ii) Two from ideas such as:

- so many people arrive so quickly the cities cannot provide permanent housing
- LEDC governments do not have the capital for major residential developments in the cities
- migrants cannot afford rents for decent houses
- planning is not as well developed as in MEDC
- empty land on the urban–rural fringe provides rent-free space for shelters. *(4)*

(c)   (i) Three from:

- A is nearer the city and near city transport systems.
- A is near a wealthy area which may provide low-paid jobs.

- Physically it is not on a hillside and is safe from landslides.
- It is near an industrial area which may provide jobs. *(6)*

(ii) One from:

- They can be removed at any times.
- No incentive to improve homes
- Little chance of getting official grants or subsidies for improvement projects *(2)*

(iii) Use examples you know. You might include:

   1 Provision of sewage systems and piped water to improve health standards

   2 Provision of sound concrete bases on which temporary houses can be built

   3 Grants and subsidies for self-help project.

The most successful appear to be those that involve self help. *(8)*

(Total: 30 marks)

Question 3

(a) (i) Left to right: old industrial zone; old housing zone; newer housing zone *(3)*

(ii) Density of buildings: try to use key phrases—tightly packed, often along obsolete historic road patterns. Where space is short, buildings have been built higher.

Use of land: commercial—shops, offices, administrative buildings. Higher-order services (department stores) are clustered here. Relatively few houses.

Accessibility: the heart or hub of the city with all roads leading to it. The centre of the city transportation networks and also the most congested because of the volume of traffic. *(6)*

(iii) The rent that a land user will pay to obtain the land for a particular land-use function—what people are prepared to pay for land in order to put it to a particular use. *(2)*

(iv) Two from:

- less cramped conditions
- houses may be bigger and of a better quality
- houses are less crowded together
- better facilities—parks, nearer the countryside
- less pollution.

You can also give negative differences:

- further from the facilities of the city centre
- further to travel to work for those that live in the CBD. *(2)*

(v) One from:

- Traffic is less congested and the factories are new ring roads and access to motorways.
- land is cheaper so production costs are less.
- much more pleasant environment.
- more room to expand.
- for those who live in the outer suburbs it is easier to travel to work than going into the city centre *(3)*

(b) (i) working class and middle class; upper class; shanty town dwellers *(4)*

(ii) one from:

- upper-class residents of A would not want to mix with poorer people
- they would not want the makeshift, poor-quality housing
- they would want to avoid the risk of disease and of contaminated water and food
- crime and violence might be a problem
- social life would be less rich *(2)*

(iii) one from:

- religion
- race
- language
- colour
- caste
- political factors *(1)*

People of the same religion, caste, race or colour prefer to live in the same areas because they share common values.

Ethnic minorities feel safer together.

Negative factor–they may not be accepted in areas where people of different religions, caste etc live.

(2)

(Total 25 marks)

Question 4

(a) (i) Physical and human factors bring about desertification in the shaded area. The physical factor is drought in an area of marginal rainfall. The human factor results from population growth and the need for more food. Drought results in less vegetation and poorer grazing land. People cut down the trees and bushes for fuel leaving less vegetation covering the soil. Rain is not held in the soil by roots and runs off, leaving the ground exposed to soil and wind erosion. The region is now suffering from desertification.

(5)

(ii) Agades receives virtually no rain for six months of the year from October to March. In April and May rainfall is erratic, falling in small amounts in some years and none in others. In the wettest months, June–September, rainfall totals vary considerably from year to year. For example, in Year 1 the July rainfall was 11 mm, in Year 2, 58 mm. There is also a downward trend in the annual rainfall totals over the five year period. Years 4 and 5 not reaching the totals for the other three years.

(4)

(iii) Pastoral nomads in the area where desertification develops will be faced with famine unless they move to another region. Their animals are their source of life, providing food, shelter, clothing, dung for fuel and access to grain and other needs through barter. Many nomads will move to a town where water is plentiful. Their herds will overgraze the surrounding area and desertification will follow. Some nomads will give up their way of life and become town dwellers.

(4)

(b) Immediate aid may have to provide basic food if the people are starving. The main task should be a search for underground water by digging wells. Organisations such as WaterAid have the expertise for this, using intermediate technology. People need access to land so that they can grow food crops to support the community. The trend towards growing cash crops has reduced the ability of the people to support themselves. Subsistance farmers and nomads have increasingly been forced on to marginal lands which are subject to degradation very quickly. The opportunity for better management techniques in farming, coupled with increased access to land, could help people restore their ability to feed themselves. More efficient stoves and cooking systems should also be introduced so that less wood is removed as fuel.

(4)

(c) (i) Size–A is one fifteenth the size of B.

Soils–At farm A the soils are light clays whereas as farm B they are heavy clays and peat.

Drainage–Farm A is on sloping ground and no drains are shown so drainage must be good. Farm B is on flat, low-lying land where drains are essential to remove surplus water to the nearby dyke.

Crops–Both farms grow vegetables and potatoes but at farm A the vegetables are an early crop. Farming at farm A is more intensive with glass house cultivation and flowers with no livestock. At farm B there are arable crops of wheat and sugar beet and hens are kept. Fields are larger on farm B.

Examiner's tip

The question asks you to show the contrasts between the farms *not* their climates

(ii) At farm B the land is flat with a rich soil of peat and heavy clay. This makes the land suitable for crops rather than livestock. It also means market garden crops such as peas and other vegetables will do well. There is a balance between the arable wheat and sugar beet and the market garden crops; if some crops do poorly, the others may make up for the loss of earnings. The climate with severe winters, and low rainfall will mean the market garden crops are not early but will be available in the summer months. The low rainfall will also give dry conditions for harvesting the wheat. With the drains taking away surplus water the soil will not become waterlogged. Hens may be kept to provide an additional source of income.

(8)

(Total 25 marks)

Question 5

(a) (i) Figure 5.1 clearly shows a high rate of illiteracy in Sub–Saharan Africa and south Asia, with a high proportion of female illiteracy in both areas. The Middle

East/North Africa also shows a similar pattern with, slightly less male illiteracy. All areas show that female illiteracy is higher than male illiteracy.

The percentage of people without access to health services is 48% and 44% in south Asia and Sub-Saharan Africa respectively. The Latin America/Caribbean figure at 36% is also high. These figures indicate that many people in the areas shown on the graph must suffer from ill health.

The graph shows that 57% of the population of Sub-Saharan Africa do not have access to safe water so have to drink filthy water. Although the figures are lower in the other areas shown, even in these areas 20–30% of the population are not supplied with clean water. *(3)*

(ii) In general the women look after the family, growing and preparing the food, which is essential work in terms of supporting family life. In many cultures it is not seen as necessary to educate the women because it is the men who will need to earn money away from the family home. *(2)*

(b) (i) complete poverty; without access to the basic necessities of human life such as those shown in Fig. 5.1, e.g. no access to clean water and no access to health care. *(2)*

(ii) two from: hunger; malnutrition; infant mortality rate; life expectancy. *(2)*

(iii) There are several areas you could use in answer to this question, two examples follow: Area 1. Some groups of people living in the Sahel region of Sub-Saharan Africa have been subjected to absolute poverty in recent decades. One reason for their poor living conditions is that they have suffered many years of drought. In times of drought the land cannot support grazing and crop cultivation so that land becomes degraded and desertification may result.

Area 2. In Bangladesh many people have lost their homes and their livelihoods as a result of flooding. The flooding is accentuated by deforestation taking place higher up the river valleys. The lack of vegetation cover means that run-off is greater so the water surges into the lower reaches of the valley. Fertile soil has accumulated on the delta lands of Bangladesh supporting intensive agriculture. However, the flooding takes away the fertile top soil, leaving degraded land behind. *(4)*

(c) In this question there are, again, several areas you could select. One suitable example is North Korea and South Korea. The countries are split by political differences. South Korea is one of the newly industrialised countries and a 'tiger' economy, making rapid progress in manufacturing and international trade. North Korea remains politically isolated and has not received capital investment to promote economic growth. *(3)*

(d) Figure 5.3 clearly shows that one-fifth of the world accounts for 84.2% of the total world trade. This means that four-fifths of the world must share the remaining 15.8% of the world trade. The figure for world GNP at 84.7% for the economically richest fifth of the world also indicates the wide gap that exists between the rich and poor worlds. It is evident from these figures that wealth and trade are very unevenly distributed across the countries of the world. *(3)*

(e) Without financial support a country cannot help its people to improve upon their quality of life. A basic human need such as food is considered a commodity to be bought and sold on international markets. The possibility of gain in wealth by growing cash crops sometimes overrides the use of land for basic food crops. Grain is overproduced on the world market so international trade is not worth while and the country does not earn money from the crop to improve the welfare of its people. The people have less access to land for food crops; the whole process becomes a downward spiral; poverty is increased. *(4)*

(f) (i) Again, there are lots of examples you could use to answer this question. The worked example is for Taiwan, where the arrival of multinational companies (MNCs) has increased the national wealth. During the 1960s and 1970s the people of Taiwan were willing to work for very low wages. The cheap labour attracted many Japanese MNCs to move production to Taiwan. As a result of industrial growth, the country's GDP per capita has risen from $120 in 1960 to $14 000 in 1996. Labour is no longer cheap and Taiwan is now a country which seeks out production sites where labour costs are lower. Taiwanese people have benefited from the improved standard of living now enjoyed by a large proportion of the population of the country. *(4)*

(ii) Taiwan's development has been at the expense of the environment. Clean air is a problem since sulphur emissions are high, as is the pollution from cars and other vehicles. The waste products from the manufacturing processes have also polluted the soils and the water supplies. Water supplies also become contaminates as sewage treatment is not a high priority. *(3)*

(Total 30 marks)

Question 6

(a) (i) 10; 16; 9 *(1 1/2)*

(ii) falling *(1/2)*

(iii) 1. energy conservation has been encouraged by governments *(1)*

2. people are more conservation-conscious; energy is expensive. *(1)*

(iv) Energy is cheap in the USA because there is lots of it. *(1)*

(b) (i) A colour TV uses 340kwh/year, whereas one that is energy-efficient uses only 70 kwh/year. An energy-efficient dishwasher can use as little as one-tenth the amount of electricity used by a conventional dishwasher. *(2)*

(ii) Traditional methods are often very inefficient. *(1)*

(iii) 1. If heating and lighting are cut to lower bills, we will be cold and our eyesight may suffer.

2. The new fire is likely to be more expensive than the three stones.

3. My costs as a manufacturer will be raised and sales may not increase. *(3 × 2)* *(6)*

(c) (i) fossil fuels; renewable energy *(1)*

Examiner's tip

The question only says *describe*, not explain.

(ii) Largest energy source in developing countries is the biomass. 23% of the developed world's energy comes from natural gas, compared with only 7% in the developing world. *(2× 1) (2)*

(iii) dung; wood; sugar cane; brushwood. *(1/2)*

(iv) wind; wave; solar; geothermal; tidal *(1/2)*

Examiner's tip

Not biomass.

(v) Nuclear—The advantages are that it does not pollute the air with smoke from the power station; it does not depend on large quantities of fossil fuels; it does not have to be made in a particular location because of dependence on local raw materials. The disadvantages are that it uses radioactive materials, which are highly dangerous. Any mistake in the production process, as at Chernobyl, can release radioactivity into the atmosphere, causing death or illness. Atomic power stations have a limited life and cannot be dismantled for very many years after they have been closed down. *(6)*

(Total 25 marks)

Examiner's tip

Be sure to include at least one example and see your answer is balanced, giving both advantages and disadvantages.

Question 7

1 (a) (i) salt marsh; mud and sand at low tide; creeks *(2)*

(ii) The marsh in 4104 is drained by a stream and is 3 km from the coast at a height of approximately 30 m above sea level. At 4398 the marshland is between the high and low water marks with a coastal location. *(2)*

(b) (i) A long deposit of sand and shingle extending out into the sea. . *(1)*

(ii) See Fig. 8.1. *(3)*

(c) (i) Level flat land for the refinery to be built on; close to Southampton Water and shipping lanes; wide waterway for tankers to berth at jetties *(3)*

(ii) marshland drained for oil storage tanks; network of railway lines to site; many rows of storage tanks; refinery buildings and flare towers; growth of built up area for workers' homes *(3)*

(d) (i) Country park—An area of countryside close to urban areas catering for large numbers of people taking part in recreational activities. It is smaller than a National Park and managed by the local authority not a national authority. *(2)*

(ii) They are designed to attract large numbers of people away from other rural areas not planned to cope with large numbers. *(2)*

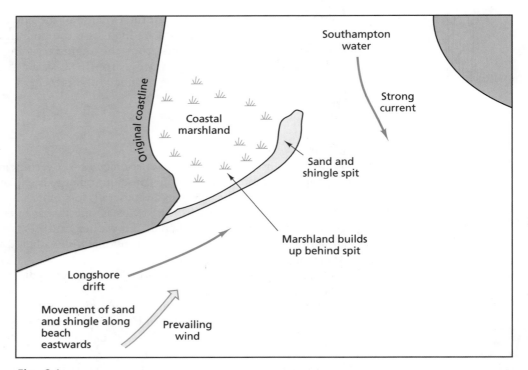

Fig. 8.1

(e) (i) Problems—Conflict with farmers by breaking down fences; walking dogs among farm animals; trespassing on sown fields. Conflict with conservationists by wearing away footpaths; picking wild flowers; disturbing natural habitats; removing fossils. Conflict with villagers by pollution caused by vehicle exhaust fumes; parking illegally; crowding on local buses; noise. Conflict with forestry officials by leaving litter; starting fires; breaking down young trees; disturbing woodland habitats

(7)

(Total 25 marks)

Chapter 9
Coursework and fieldwork

This chapter deals with:
- the part played by coursework in the GCSE exam
- questions that students ask about this part of the exam
- suggestions on how to organise your work and produce high-quality coursework.

Coursework

All the exam groups include coursework as part of the GCSE exam. The majority weight coursework as 25% of the total marks, but NICCEA and WJEC give coursework 20% of the total. Although the exam groups all use the term 'coursework', they have differing views as to the type of coursework they require. There are also different interpretations in the syllabuses offered by the same group, so be certain you know what syllabus you are studying and what coursework is involved. The Syllabus Checklists and Paper Analysis on pages 3–20 will help you. For example, MEG Syllabus C requires two pieces of coursework, a geographical investigation supported by fieldwork (15% of the total marks), and either a coursework unit or a portfolio of coursework pieces (10% of total marks). By contrast, London Syllabus A describes the coursework as 'A geographical investigation based on fieldwork.'

Fieldwork

The most important aspect of coursework is fieldwork. Fieldwork is very important because it consists of first-hand investigations on a local/small scale. It gives you the opportunity to collect primary (first-hand) data, such as a survey of stream flow rates or of local land use. This is followed up by recording what you have observed and analysing your findings. Fieldwork tests your ability to think and work as a geographer, using the knowledge, understanding and skills you have developed during the course.

Other forms of coursework

Those exam groups that require a second piece of coursework normally insist that it must be different from the fieldwork investigation. MEG Syllabus C requires a separate Decision-Making Enquiry. This enquiry should be built on secondary data (information from textbooks) provided by your teacher or obtained by you. The enquiry gives candidates the opportunity to:
- demonstrate their ability to appreciate values and attitudes
- explore contemporary issues
- make decisions.

For example, having been provided with background information and statistics, candidates might be required to investigate whether a new limestone quarry should be permitted in the Peak District National Park. Each candidate must submit a written report for the exam. WJEC requires the second piece of coursework to be a 'teacher-devised classroom investigation based on secondary data'.

Questions about coursework

Why is coursework so important?

There are number of reasons why coursework is a very important part of the exam.

- It enables you to show your ability to design, organise, carry out and display a geographical investigation.
- You are able to show that you understand what you have been taught and can apply your knowledge
- It gives you the chance to demonstrate a variety of geographical skills, including field sketching, see Fig. 9.1; careful observation and the recording of data. You may also be able to show your mastery of higher-order skills, such as the ability to analyse, synthesise and evaluate the information collected.

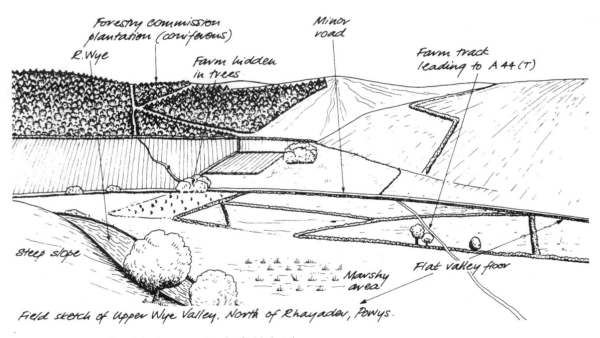

Fig. 9.1 An example of a field sketch

How much help can my teacher give me?

The exam groups recognise that you will need help from your teacher and that some students will need more help than others. To make sure everyone is marked fairly your teacher will fill in a form recording details of the way you have undertaken the work, including particular difficulties you experienced and assistance you were given. If you need extra help, this will also be noted on the form. In general you can expect your teacher to give you most help at the beginning of the coursework and to help you less as the work proceeds.

So what help can you expect?

- Your teacher must first make certain you know what coursework you are required to do for the exam and its maximum length.
- He or she will help you choose your topic by discussing ideas you put forward. Your teacher must ensure that you choose a topic covered by the syllabus which

will give you the chance to show the extent of your knowledge, understanding and skills.

- Your teacher will also advise you on where to look for information; how to design a questionnaire; what visits you should make; techniques you might use to display your data and so on.
- There should be progress checks when you can show your teacher the progress you have made and receive further advice.

You cannot expect help from your teacher beyond the recording stage when you are:

- analysing and interpreting the data you have collected
- formulating your conclusions
- writing up the work for presentation.

Do I have to work on my own?

You may be allowed to carry out the fieldwork on your own or you may work as a member of a group. Sometimes a whole class may be involved in the same piece of fieldwork. Whatever form the fieldwork takes you will have to submit an individual report. The finished piece of coursework '**must be the work of the individual candidate**, particularly in the analysis and conclusions. Each piece of coursework **must** show evidence of individual input.' (London Syllabus A)

Can I use books and other secondary sources?

In a fieldwork investigation secondary material, such as books, magazine articles, newspaper cuttings and duplicated notes from your teacher can only be used on a limited scale to substantiate your investigation or to compare with your own findings. Candidates who copy out pages of lesson notes or sections from books will not receive marks for their efforts. If you have to do a second piece of coursework for the exam it may well be based on secondary sources.

What happens if someone cheats?

No credit will be given for work known to have been copied directly from textbooks or from other candidates. Your teacher knows you well enough to spot work done by someone else and a serious case of cheating would mean that your teacher would not sign the authentication certificate and would report you to the Exam Group. This could result in your not being allowed to take the exam.

How will the coursework be marked?

Unlike the written exams, there are no entry 'tiers' for coursework. You will be assessed in the same way as all the other candidates. Your teacher should see that the tasks you are set make it possible for you to demonstrate your highest level of achievement, i.e. give it your best shot. Unlike the written exam papers, coursework will be marked by your teacher(s), following very precise rules set out by the Exam Group. A sample of your school's geography coursework will also be seen by an external moderator. This person can adjust marks if it is felt necessary, and will send a report to the school after the exams are over.

How to write a good piece of coursework

Choosing a topic

Choose a topic which involves:
considering an argument with points to be made for or against, e.g. the arguments for and against a local by-pass, or
investigating a problem, e.g. why a local shopping centre seems to be in decline, or
testing an assertion, e.g. that levels of air pollution are highest near major roads.

You must be quite clear about the purpose of your investigation, so you must define your objectives precisely. The following stages should help you to produce a well-structured investigation, whether it is based on fieldwork or secondary sources.

Stage 1 Identify a question to be considered, a problem to be solved or an issue to be investigated.

What topics particularly interest me? Shall I do it alone or as part of a group?

Stage 2 Define your objectives in carrying out this investigation.

What do I hope to have achieved by the end of the investigation? Does my teacher think this is a worthwhile investigation?

Stage 3 Collecting data.

What information do I need? How can I best collect it? What special arrangements do I need to make? For example, interviewing a farmer, visiting a factory. Does my teacher approve of my methods?

Stage 4 Collecting and recording data.

How shall I record the data—e.g. on tape, video, photographs, field sketches?

Have I used a variety of techniques? Are my maps, diagrams etc relevant to the study and not just decorative?

Stage 5 Describing and analysing data.

How shall I present my information? Have I used a variety of presentation techniques, e.g. maps, diagrams, sketches, charts? Have I achieved a good balance between writing and visual material in the presentation of my investigation?

Stage 6 Generalisations and conclusions.

Have I achieved my original objectives? Have I explored fully the questions, problems or issues I identified in Stage 1?

Stage 7 Evaluating the evidence and conclusions

Were the objectives suitable for this investigation? What were the limitations of the data collected? How valid was the evidence and the conclusion I drew based on that evidence? What suggestions can be made for improving or making any further investigations of this topic?

Presenting your investigation

Do not try to disguise a weak investigation with over-elaborate artwork and quantities of material which are not completely relevant. At the other extreme, do not hand in sets of loose pages of different sizes which can easily get out of order. Here are some points to help you present your work neatly and professionally.

- Maps should be clearly labelled with a title, compass, direction, key and scale.
- All sketches, diagrams, tables and other visual material should be numbered and referred to in the written text.
- Bulky items, including an original questionnaire with its summary, may be best included in an appendix.
- Your teacher will give you guidance on the size of the folder or file in which the work is presented; this information is sometimes provided by the Exam Group.
- Your presentation should include:
  - a title
  - a table of contents
  - a statement setting out the objectives of the study
  - methods used to collect data
  - the data and other fieldwork with precise acknowledgments, where necessary, e.g. the author, title, publisher and date of a book from which a quotation has been taken
  - analysis and interpretation of the data
  - evaluation and conclusions
  - a bibliography (if appropriate)
  - an appendix (if needed).

Finally, remember that your investigation is part of the GCSE exam and that marks will be awarded for good spelling, punctuation and using the rules of grammar accurately.

Answers to Quick Tests

1 Physical systems and environments

1 cyclonic, convectional, relief or orographic; **2** radiation; **3** windspeed; **4** over a warm sea; **5** insolation; **6** high; **7** sky obscured, mist, wind speed 3–7 knots, from SE, 7°C. **8** high; **9** drizzle; **10** falls; **11** carbon dioxide; **12** aerosols; **13** ice caps will melt; **14** global warming; **15** natural gas, oil, coal; **16** infiltration; **17** the loss of water vapour from plants; **18** corrasion; **19** alluvium; **20** water flow; **21** moraine; **22** esker; **23** cirque, cwm; **24** clay, sand, gravel and boulders deposited by meltwater; **25** Cairngorms; **26** waves carry material along beach; **27** swash; **28** Chesil Beach; **29** by two caves on either side of a headland joining; **30** The Ministry of Agriculture, Fisheries and Food; **31** pavement; **32** calcium deposits growing up from the floor of a cave; **33** water table; **34** scarp and dip slopes; **35** limestone; **36** a piece of the earth's crust; **37** shield; **38** epicentre; **39** Asia; **40** the quantity of energy released by an earthquake; **41** horizons; **42** temperate grassland; **43** a community of plants and animals sharing the same environment; **44** humus; **45** one where the resource removed is replaced, continuing the balance of the ecosystem; **46** sulphur and nitrogen; **47** inversion layer; **48** nitrates and phosphates; **49** catalytic converter; **50** sewage, oil, refuse.

2 Population

1 substantial decrease in death rates and an increase in both rates; **2** the difference between the birth and death rates; **3** average numbers; **4** better warnings and medical care; **5** one fifth; **6** migration; **7** stage 3; **8** number of deaths of infants under 1 year old per 1000 live births in any given year; **9** MEDCs; **10** the percentage of people that can read and write simple sentences; **11** unevenness; **12** LEDCs; **13** biological, social and demographic; **14** concentrated people on or near coalfields; **15** urbanisation; **16** migrants, source or origin, destination: **17** internal migration; **18** at times of recession migrants are perceived as taking jobs from local people and as being a burden on services; sometimes they are unwilling to be integrated into the society of the host country; **19** people who seek refuge in another country as they have been forced to leave their own country; **20** migrants supply the labour force for the rapidly developing industrial areas of China.

3 Settlement

1 dispersed and nucleated; **2** dispersed settlement; **3** the physical location—the land on which it is built; **4** some of the villages have become commuter villages; **5** traditional services such as the village store may be lost, but new services such as restaurants and riding stables may be developed; **6** central field or sphere of influence; **7** Increased use of cars and decline of bus services; **8** central place theory; **9** the organisation of central places into a series of orders or grades; **10** the maximum distance over which people will travel to purchase that good from a central place; **11** no; **12** it explains why people leave the countryside and the ways in which big cities act as magnets to migrants; **13** an unplanned squatter settlement; **14** three from: better housing would reduce overcrowding; a healthy water supply; provision of health centres; provision of proper sanitation; **15** the movement of people and employment to small towns and villages beyond the city limits; **16** part of urban area with a distinctive land use, e.g. industry; **17** downtown; **18** residential segregation; **19** inner zone; **20** replacing out of date buildings with new areas; **21** to manage the impact of growth upon the environment; **22** this is the oldest part of the city with the oldest buildings, deteriorating housing and obsolete industrial plant; the need for redevelopment is greatest here and so is the need for careful planning because of the attractiveness of the city centre sites; **23** (i) ease traffic congestion by building roads that can cope with modern traffic needs; (ii) separating people and traffic, e.g. by developing pedestrian precincts and walkways; **24** in many countries resources are not available to undertake major and expensive redevelopment; **25** one from: establishment of out-of-town shopping centre; over-spill estate; new or satellite town; ring road or ring motorway to by-pass the city (e.g. M25); **26** an excess of population that leaves the city because of overcrowding or as a result of urban renewal programmes; **27** three from: they would develop the character of country towns; people could live within walking or cycling distance of their work; everyone would live close to the countryside; a community spirit would develop quickly in a small town; small towns could be built quickly; **28** Milton Keynes; **29** *either* the move of industries out of old inner city areas to new industrial estates in new towns took jobs away from the city; *or* mass movement of young people away from the city centre to the new towns accelerated the decline of inner cities; **30** to relieve overcrowding and to cope with rapid urbanisation; **31** Cairo; **32** three from: high birth rates; decreasing death rates; in-migration; stimulus of independence; **33** three from: effective birth control; low birth rates; counter-urbanisation; strong planning policies—new towns etc have absorbed population increase; **34** In LEDCs large city population densities are much higher; **35** Industrialisation in Mexico was concentrated in Mexico City; it is now a huge industrial region with a permanent cloud of pollutant gases; roughly 30 000 children and 70 000 adults in the city die annually from pollution-caused diseases; **36** two from: homelessness; traffic congestion; decay of the inner city; employment opportunities for the most disadvantaged; **37** urban sprawl; **38** sheer size of the cities means that problems are large scale; rate of growth of population; speed at which changes have occurred; **39** LEDCs: water often polluted causing disease and death; many new squatter areas have no piped water; sanitation standards are very low and cause disease; MEDCs: wealthy nations use vast quantities of water per capita; technological advance and rising living standards have increased use of water but there is a finite limit on water supply; **40** lack investment and capital.

4 Agriculture

1 a system; **2** climate/relief/soil/geology; **3** profit; **4** camping /caravanning/bed and breakfast/pony trekking; **5** diversification; **6** intensive; **7** commercial crops are grown for sale; subsistence crops are grown for personal consumption; **8** glacial deposits; **9** competition from wheatlands of North America; there were local European markets for dairy produce; **10** monsoon; **11** uneven distribution; **12** circle or cycle of poverty; **13** two-thirds; **14** carbohydrates, proteins, fats, minerals and salts; **15** poor diet is linked with illness therefore people in LEDCs tend to die younger than those in MEDCs; **16** high- or heavy-yielding varieties; **17** it created an increase in plant growth; **18** fertiliser, pesticides, HYV seeds, irrigation; **19** too dry; limited availability of irrigation in areas where it is most needed; **20** gene revolution; **21** dry; **22** long branches give shade; store moisture in trunk; thick bark, narrow leaves and thorns all reduce transpiration;

23 South America and Queensland, Australia; 24 North Africa along the southern rim of the Sahara desert; 25 to create a desert from previously productive land; 26 every afternoon; 27 selva; 28 a community of plants and animals which share the same environment; 29 clearing and cultivating small plots of land then moving on; 30 timber and ranching projects; 31 tea, coffee, cocoa, bananas, rubber, palm oil, sugar cane; 32 in the wet zone or southwest of the island; 33 most of the tea industry is still British owned; 34 tin; 35 carefully managed to prevent soil erosion; also access difficult and labour in short supply; 36 common agricultural policy; 37 fragmentation; small size of farms; latifundia; 38 wine, milk, butter, grain, beef; 39 set-aside; 40 under threat from farming activities but also having historical and habitat importance.

5 Industry and development

1 raw materials; 2 lower transport costs, local labour supply, local customers aware of local products; 3 capital; 4 TV, hi-fi, dishwasher, washing machine etc.; 5 funds are available and can be applied for to revive the poorest areas, according to particular needs; 6 formerly the most important heavy industrial region in western Europe; 7 new sources of energy, especially oil and natural gas, have replaced coal, and cheaper supplies are available from abroad; 8 industries remain in their original location even when many of the reasons why they grew up there no longer apply; 9 industries which are not tied to a particular location; 10 ready supply of labour, good transport facilities, government grants and subsidies, long industrial tradition, environmental improvements carried out; 11 (i) primary industries make available natural resources for processing in other industries, e.g. coal and iron mining (ii) secondary industries process raw materials and produce goods, e.g. shipbuilding; 12 by-products from both the coal and oil industry are used as raw materials and the Tees salt field also provides chemicals; 13 two from: disappearance of markets, inability to compete with new industrial regions, failure to invest in modern technology, failure to attract new industries to the region; 14 new housing estates, new towns, new roads and motorways, grants and subsidies attract foreign investment; 15 Clydeside, South Wales, Belfast region; 16 facility or service provided, nothing is manufactured; 17 tertiary sector; 18 more efficient and more economic to be near competitors; 19 people drawn into the area so shops, banks, eating places and overnight accommodation are encouraged to open; 20 complete change in shopping habits from the high street to out-of-town retail parks and regional shopping centres; 21 cargo ships are expensive to run so need to be kept working and dock fees are high; 22 easy import of raw materials, manufactured goods easily exported, rapid transport systems to the port; 23 two from: faces Europe; early start as a container port; cost kept low; road improvements including M11/M25 links; 24 a port which receives goods from one part of the world for onward transmission to another part of the world; 25 it has become the second largest port in the world, high-tech industrial development has been encouraged in the free trade zones; 26 major road and motorway improvements to improve access; 27 landscape difficult to 'tame', lack of raw materials and generally isolated from other industrial developments; 28 protected area for farming and recreation which is surrounded by a huge urban 'ring'; 29 a rapidly developing industrial region in south-east China; 30 large subsidies and exemption from taxes draw industry to Special Economic Zones; 31 LEDCs have a limited industrial base; 32 from: little modern industry, high birth rate, farming main employment, few employed in services, low education and technology levels, poverty, poor diet, malnutrition, poor transport, lack of basic services; 33 indicators; 34 industrialisation, capital, trade agreements; 35 national plans, export stimulation/export substitution, intermediate technology, revolution, rapid development of industry; 36 it is believed that income and job opportunities will result; 37 from: limited capital, limited expertise, lack of skilled

labour, limited markets, trade barriers, poor infrastructure; **38** import substitution; **39** Singapore, South Korea, Taiwan, Hong Kong, Thailand, Malaysia, Indonesia, Mexico, Brazil; **40** to take the place of declining traditional industries and spread wealth to peripheral regions; **41** established a shift away from the old pattern of trade between North America and Europe towards the Pacific Rim; **42** MEDCs impose trade barriers or seek substitute products; **43** a decline in the demand for British manufactured cotton goods led to factory closures in Lancashire; **44** able to shift location at very short notice; **45** may provide housing, schools, medical centres, create employment to stimulate local economy etc; **46** neo-colonialism; **47** bilateral and multilateral; **48** clean piped water, medical centres, housing schemes, building schools etc.; **49** rarely seem to help the poorest members of society, often disadvantage them by displacing them from their land; **50** to take the world into the 21st century in a sustainable manner.

6 Resources and their management

1 non-renewable; **2** timber; **3** Exclusive Economic Zone; **4** paper and board; **5** quotas; **6** rock that retains water; **7** six; **8** less silt containing food for fish; increase in herbicides and pesticides; **9** less time and energy collecting water, improved health; **10** one third; **11** removing coal from just below the ground level by stripping off the soil and overburden; **12** Morecambe Bay or off coast of Lancashire; **13** as a safety precaution if radioactivity released; **14** place which generates electricity by using wind turbines; **15** wood; **16** water, wind; **17** ploughing round slopes instead of up and down; **18** line of trees checking wind; **19** loess; **20** it floods, causing damage and loss of life; **21** area of land in the Netherlands reclaimed from the sea bed; **22** serious flooding in 1953 and need for better coastal defences; **23** the Fens; **24** to provide additional land for recreation, housing, commerce and industry; **25** English Partnership; **26** an economy which takes resources and puts nothing in their place; **27** Trans-Amazon Highway; **28** the roads bring settlers who destroy food supplies and take their land; **29** people moving across a country, in Indonesia moving from one island to another; **30** Java; **31** agriculture, forestry, recreation, mining and quarrying, transport, urban development, conservation, industry, storage; **32** Inupiat, Kutchin; **33** hunting whales provides them with their traditional source of food; **34** the government; **35** passed the Aboriginal Land Rights Act allowing aboriginal groups to reclaim portions of land; **36** Parana; **37** Paraguay; **38** intermediate technology **39** soil erosion; **40** healthier, less carrying of water by women, less disease among young children; **41** 2%; **42** New Forest, Norfolk Broads; **43** a Country Park which will attract people away from other rural areas; **44** the Midlands; **45** giraffe, elephant, gazelle; **46** London; **47** warmer, more sunshine, different scenery; **48** April to October; **49** the Mediterranean sea is land-locked and tideless; **50** infrastructure.

7 Skills

1 choropleth; **2** the age-structure of the population; **3** 90°; **4** eastings; **5** flow diagram.

Glossary

Acid rain Rainfall with pH values of less than 5.6. The acidity is caused by sulphur and nitrogen gases combining with water vapour to form weak sulphuric and nitric acids.

Administrative centre A settlement that is responsible for the control of its region. It may be the capital city or an important local town.

Age/Sex pyramid A type of bar graph that illustrates the structure of a population. It is made up of horizontal bars representing different age categories, which are placed on either side of a central vertical axis.

Agribusiness Large-scale commercial farming often with business links with other parts of the food system such as supermarkets and fast-food outlets. The capital usually comes from a business group, which appoints a manager who is responsible for the day-to-day running of the farm.

Air mass A mass of air, with similar properties of temperature and moisture covering a large area of the earth's surface and bounded by fronts. (See *Front*.)

Alluvial plain Level land bordering a river on which alluvium (fine material carried by the river) is deposited, e.g. plain of the R. Ganges.

Altitude The vertical distance above mean sea level, usually measured in metres or feet. It can also mean the distance above the horizon of the sun or stars.

Anticline A fold of rock strata forming an arch. (See *Syncline*.)

Anticyclone A region of high atmospheric pressure. (See *Cyclone*.)

Aquifer A porous, tilted layer of rock between impermeable layers which allows water to travel distances underground, e.g. central Australia.

Arable land Land which is ploughed and used for growing crops.

Area of Outstanding Natural Beauty (AONB) In the UK an area of land that has special landscape value which is considered worthy of protection. AONBs are the responsibility of local planning authorities, who have powers to preserve and enhance the natural beauty of the area.

Arête A knife-edge mountain ridge, often formed by the erosion of two adjoining cirques, e.g. Striding Edge in the Lake District.

Arid region An area with low rainfall where the conditions are desert or semi-desert, e.g. Painted Desert of Arizona.

Asylum Refuge given by a country to a person whose well-being is in danger in the country in which they live, e.g. as a result of political or religious beliefs or because of ethnic origins.

Atmospheric pressure The weight of a column of air at a particular point. At sea level, pressure equals about 1000 millibars, which represents a force of 1000 dynes acting on one square centimetre. Above sea level, the column of air is shorter and the pressure is lower. Atmospheric pressure is increased when air is descending. (See *Anticyclone* and *Millibar*.)

Backwash The flow of sea water back down a beach towards the sea. (See *Swash* and *Longshore drift*.)

Barometer The instrument used for measuring atmospheric pressure. (See *Atmospheric pressure*.)

Basin irrigation A means of providing water for cultivation that involves the flooding of basin-like hollows surrounded by earth banks.

Bid rent theory This assumes that in a free market the rent for land will be that offered by the highest bidder. The highest bidder is likely to be the one who will make the maximum profits from the site and so can pay the highest rent. Rents are highest at the centre of a city, here competition for land is keenest because this is the most attractive commercial area.

Biome The largest of the ecosystem units. Each biome obtains its name from the dominant type of vegetation found in it, e.g. tropical grassland. (See *Ecosystem*.)

Boulder clay The rocks and finely-ground rock flour carried down by a glacier and left as a deposit when the ice melts, e.g. soils of East Anglia.

Built-up area That part of the landscape covered by houses and other buildings.

Calcareous Containing a considerable proportion of calcium carbonate, e.g. calcareous soils of the North Downs.

Campos The tropical grasslands or savanna of Brazil, south of the Amazon Basin.

Capital 1 A town or city that is the chief town of a country, province or state and which contains the seat of government. **2** In economics, the stock of money and goods used for promoting and conducting a business. Capital is one of the factors of production, together with land, labour and business expertise.

Cash crops Crops which are produced for sale and not for consumption locally, e.g. coffee.

Central Business District (CBD) The commercial, social and cultural core of a city, where the chief shops and offices are concentrated. It is also the focus of the urban transport network and is often the area of maximum traffic congestion. It is the area of higher land values, so buildings are concentrated and are built to maximum heights.

Central place An accessible location from which goods and services are provided for the surrounding area.

Central Place Theory The theory that there is a pattern in the number of towns, cities and villages (central places) and in the ways in which the central places provide goods and services for their surrounding areas (hinterlands.)

Chemical weathering (See *Weathering*.)

Cirque, corrie, cwm An armchair-like hollow with steep sides and rear walls formed through erosion by ice and snow and found in regions which are, or have been, glaciated. Sometimes the hollow is filled by a lake, e.g. corries in Snowdonia.

Climate The average weather conditions of a place or region throughout the seasons.

Cloud A mass of small water droplets or ice crystals formed by the condensation of water vapour in the atmosphere.

Cold front The boundary line between a mass of advancing cold air and a mass of warm air which the cold air pushes under. (See *Warm front*.)

Common Agricultural Policy (CAP) The policy drawn up among the member countries of the EU to ensure a fair standard of living for farmers and farm workers and the availability of farm products at reasonable prices.

Commuter A person who travels a considerable distance regularly (usually daily) to and from work.

Concentric model of urban land use A model describing the arrangement of functional zones within a city.

Condensation The conversion of a vapour into a liquid. Clouds are formed by the condensation of water vapour in cold air above the earth's surface.

Confluence The point at which two streams join together, e.g. confluence of the Red River and Mississippi.

Coniferous forest A forest of mainly cone-bearing trees which have needleshaped leaves. Such trees are usually evergreen, e.g. Sitka Spruce.

Conservation The protection of the natural environment and its resources for the future. It also includes the protection of some old buildings and historic sites.

Continental climate The climate experienced in the interiors of the large continents, especially in North America, Eastern Europe and Central Asia.

Continental shelf A gently-sloping shelf forming the sea bed bordering the continents. It is normally less than 100 fathoms in depth and eventually the sea bed drops steeply to the ocean depths.

Contour A line drawn on a map to join all places at the same height above sea level.

Conurbation An extensive area of streets, houses and other buildings formed by the joining up of several neighbouring and formerly separate towns, e.g. West Midland conurbation

Convectional rainfall Rain caused by the heating of surface layers of air which then rise and cool until condensation takes place and rain falls. Convectional rainfall frequently occurs over land on hot afternoons in the tropics. The rain takes the form of heavy thunderstorms which quickly disperse in the evening.

Co-operative farming Farmers share selling and distribution of produce, purchase of large machinery, equipment, feedstuffs, seed and fertiliser, but retain the management of their own holdings.

Core region The area where economic activity is at its greatest, for example the Glasgow–Edinburgh section of the central Lowlands of Scotland. (See *Peripheral region*.)

Corrasion The wearing away of rock by material being transported, e.g. by ice, rivers, wind or waves. The commonest form of corrasion is produced by a river and its load.

Correlation A statistical technique that determines the extent to which a relationship exists between two variables.

Corrosion The wearing away of rocks by chemical action, e.g. the solution of chalk in river water.

Counter urbanisation The movement of people and employment to locations outside the city. It is the result of improved transport facilities, the need by some factories for 'green field' sites and the availability of edge-of-city shops and services.

Country park An area of countryside close to an urban centre designed to cater for large numbers of people who use the park for recreational activities. Most country parks are run by local authorities.

Crater The funnel-shaped hollow in the cone of a volcano, through which molten rock and other materials find their way to the surface. Extinct volcanoes leave craters which may fill with water or which form large basins, e.g. Ngorongoro Crater in Tanzania.

Cyclone A region of low pressure, sometimes called a depression. It also means a violent storm which occurs in the tropics. (See *Anticyclone*.)

Deciduous forest A forest consisting mainly of trees which lose their leaves at some time of the year.

Deforestation The removal of the tree cover of an area by felling or burning.

Delta The area of alluvium formed at the mouth of a river where the material is not removed by tides or currents, e.g. Nile Delta.

Density of population The average number of people living in a particular area, e.g. 500 per sq. kilometre.

Denudation The wearing away of the land by various forms of erosion.

Depopulation The decline or reduction of population in a geographical area.

Depression (See *Cyclone*.)

Desert An almost barren area where the precipitation is so low that very little or no vegetation can grow, e.g. Kalahari desert.

Desertification The creation of desert-like conditions in an area which previously supported plant life.

Development area In the UK an area where economic growth is encouraged by grants and subsidies to industries which set up factories there.

Dry farming A method of farming in areas of limited rainfall where the land is treated in various ways to conserve the moisture it contains, so that crops can be grown. Dry farming does not involve the use of irrigation, e.g. western states of the USA.

Dry valley A valley in which there is normally no stream. Dry valleys occur in the chalk downlands of southern and eastern England.

Dune A mound or ridge of sand formed by the wind, either near the sea or in a desert, e.g. dunes of Death Valley, California (desert), coast south of Blackpool, Lancashire (onshore winds.)

Dust bowl An area of desert created by over-grazing, deforestation or the ploughing-up of unsuitable land. The term is usually applied to areas of central and western USA such as Oklahoma, where there was severe wind erosion in the 1930s and where strict conservation measures have been introduced in recent years.

Ecology The scientific study of the relationship of a plant or animal to its natural environment.

Ecosystem A community of plants and animals sharing a particular environment. Ecosystems can be at different scales, for example on a world scale the rainforest is an ecosystem. A pond is a small-scale ecosystem. Ecosystems have inputs of oxygen, nutrients, water, heat and carbon dioxide. The output is organic matter such as leaves.

Ecotourism Tourism designed to interest people in the environment and encourage them to protect it.

Effluent The waste products from a factory or industrial site. Effluent is often discharged into rivers or the sea.

Entrepôt A place which acts as an intermediary centre for trade between two or more foreign centres, receiving goods from one part of the world for onward transmission to another part of the world, e.g. Rotterdam, Hong Kong.

Epicentre The point on the earth's surface immediately above the origin of an earthquake. (See *Seismic focus*.)

Erosion The wearing away of the earth's surface by various natural agents, particularly wind, water and ice.

Estuary The mouth of a river, which is kept clear of alluvium by tides. It is usually funnel-shaped and suitable as a harbour, e.g. Mersey Estuary.

Evaporation The process whereby a liquid turns into a gas. Water vapour in the atmosphere is the result of evaporation from the earth's surface and transpiration the release of water vapour by plants.

Factory farming Intensive rearing of animals in small units using modern industrial methods.

Fahrenheit scale The temperature scale used in some parts of the world, e.g. the USA. The freezing point of water is set at 32° and its boiling point at 212°F.

Floodplain The plain bordering a river which has been formed from river deposits, e.g. flood plain of the River Thames. (See *Alluvial plain*.)

Fold mountains Mountains which have resulted from folding of the earth's crust, e.g. the Alps.

Food chain The links by which energy is passed from one form of living organism to another. For example, green plants provide food for herbivores which are eaten by carnivores. Different food chains are often linked to form a food web.

Footloose industry An industry which is not tied to a particular location by raw materials, energy or labour requirements. Hi-tech industries are footloose, since they use easily transported components and electricity as the form of power.

Fragmentation The process by which farmland is divided up into small scattered units, so that one owner may have several fields in small parcels in different parts of a locality.

Front The line separating cold and warm air masses. (See *Cold front* and *Warm front*.)

Functional zone An area that is dominated by a particular function in a town or city, e.g. a residential or industrial zone.

Gap town A town situated on a gap between hills, usually where a river has cut through the hills. Gap towns are often important route centres, e.g. Dorking, south of London.

Gene revolution Latest techniques of microbiology which alter gene structures in plants and animals to create 'more and better' products for human consumption.

Geyser A hot spring which at intervals throws a jet of hot water and steam into the air. Geysers occur in volcanic regions, e.g. Old Faithful in Yellowstone National Park, USA.

Glacier A mass of ice which moves slowly down a valley or across the earth's surface until it melts or breaks up in the sea as icebergs, e.g. Rhone Glacier in Switzerland.

Global warming The gradual increase in the earth's temperature.

Gorge A deep, steep-sided valley, e.g. Cheddar Gorge. The American word canyon. has a similar meaning, e.g. Grand Canyon.

Green Belt A belt of land around a town, city or conurbation where there are severe restrictions on new buildings. The restrictions are imposed to preserve the open character of the countryside, e.g. London's Green Belt.

'Greenfield' site An area of countryside away from towns used as the location for a factory or office.

'Green Heart' The name given to the rural area in the Netherlands, which is almost surrounded by the Randstad. The region consists of farmland and woodland.

Greenhouse effect The effect of certain gases in the atmosphere in trapping the sun's heat. Increases in the quantities of these gases result in higher temperatures on earth—global warming.

Green revolution A programme increasing the productivity of cereals mainly as the result of the introduction of high-yielding varieties of wheat and rice.

Gross Domestic Product (GDP) The total value of goods and services produced by a country over a period of time, usually a year.

Gross National Product (GNP) The gross domestic product plus the income obtained from investments abroad, less income earned in a country by foreigners.

Guest workers (*gastarbeiter*) Workers from other countries who are attracted to a country by higher employment and wages than they can obtain in their own country.

Gully A channel cut by rainwater. Gullies are usually long, narrow and not very deep. They are often formed on hillsides by water erosion.

Habitat The natural environment of a plant or animal, e.g. the natural habitat for orchids is the tropical rain forest.

Hanging valley A tributary valley which enters the main valley high above the valley floor. Streams flowing down the tributary valley form a waterfall or rapids at the point of entry, e.g. Bridal Falls in the Yosemite Valley, California. It is usually the result of glaciation.

Heavy industry The production of goods which are heavy and normally bulky when compared with other industries, e.g. iron and steel, shipbuilding and the manufacture of railway rolling stock.

Hectare (ha) A measurement of land area, 10 000 square metres, about the size of a soccer pitch or two hockey pitches.

Hinterland The land behind a seaport which provides most of the exports of the port and takes most of the imports, e.g. the hinterland of Rotterdam stretches to Switzerland.

Honeypot A recreational area such as a Country Park designed to attract large numbers of people who might otherwise visit other country areas not planned for recreation.

Humus The decaying or decayed remains of animal and vegetable matter in the soil.

Hydraulic action The process by which flowing water impounds and compresses air pockets. This pressure may break down the rock.

Hydrograph A graph showing the amount of flow of a body of water such as a river over a period of time.

Hydrological cycle (See *Water cycle*.)

Ice ages Periods in the past when the polar ice-sheets extended much further towards the Equator than at present. Ice-sheets and glaciers covered large areas of land and sea.

Igneous rock Rock that has been solidified from molten magma, e.g. basalt and granite.

Impervious rock Rock which does not allow water to pass through it easily, e.g. clay.

Industrial inertia The tendency for firms and industries to remain in a location after the causes which determined the original location have disappeared or are no longer significant, e.g. the manufacture of cutlery at Sheffield.

Infiltration The seepage of water into the soil.

Infrastructure The roads, piped water supply, communications and other services which are essential for the development of a complex society. Infrastructures reach their more advanced form in more developed countries such as the United States. They are less developed in LEDCs such as Bangladesh.

Intensive cultivation Methods of cultivation in which large amounts of capital and/or labour are applied per unit of land.

Intermediate technology (IT) The use of technical skills based on local resources and local skills to produce small-scale technical improvements, e.g. making simple cooking stoves which are more efficient than the normal open fire surrounded by three large stones which support a cooking pot.

Irrigation The artificial distribution of water on the land to allow crops to grow in areas where there is insufficient rainfall for cultivation, e.g. Central Valley of California.

Isobar A line on a map joining places with the same atmospheric pressure.

Isohyet A line on a map joining places having the same amount of rainfall over a certain period.

Isotherm A line on a map joining places having the same temperature, either at one time or over a certain period of time.

Karst A limestone region with most drainage underground, making the surface dry and barren, e.g. Dinaric alps of Bosnia-Herzogovina.

Lagoon A shallow stretch of water, either partly or completely separated from the sea by a narrow strip of land or coral reef.

Lava Molten rock, or **magma**, which flows from a volcano or zone of crustal weakness. When hardened, it forms a black rock, e.g. King Arthur's Seat, Edinburgh.

Levée The raised bank of a river formed during flooding, when alluvium is deposited.

Ley farming The planting of grass on arable land to form a pasture.

Llanos The tropical grasslands or savanna north of the Amazon Basin.

Loess A layer of fine silt or dust which has been deposited by the wind. It forms a very fertile soil in parts of central China and western Europe. In Benelux and France it is known as *limon*.

Longshore drift The movement of material such as sand and shingle along a beach as the result of waves breaking at an oblique angle upon the shore. The movement along the English Channel is from west to east, because the prevailing winds are from the southwest.

Mangrove swamps A swampy area on the coast or near a river mouth in tropical areas, covered by mangrove trees. Long roots hold the trees in the mud and also help to collect fresh deposits, which allow the mangrove swamp to enlarge itself, e.g. parts of the Nigerian coast.

Manufacturing industry Industry that processes materials or assembles components to produce finished goods or components, e.g. the car industry.

Maritime climate A climate influenced by the sea, giving a low range of temperatures between summer and winter. The sea cools the land in summer and warms it in winter, e.g. Devon and Cornwall.

Marginal land Land that is only sufficiently fertile to yield a return that just covers the costs of production.

Meander A bend or loop in the course of a river as it crosses flat land, e.g. lower Mississippi.

Mechanical weathering (See *Weathering*.)

Microclimate The climate of a small area, e.g. a hedgerow or a playground in a city.

Migration The movement of individuals or groups from one place of residence to another. The movement can be within a country (internal), or to another country (international).

Millibar A unit of pressure equal to one-thousandth of a bar. Isobars are usually drawn at intervals of four millibars, e.g. 1000,1004,1008, etc.

Mixed farming The combination in one farm or district of both pastoral and arable farming.

MNC See *TNC*.

Model 1. A scaled-down representation of an area or object. 2. An idealised representation of a specific situation, e.g. Von Thünen's model of agricultural land use.

Monsoon The type of wind system found mainly in the tropics, where there is a reversal of direction from season to season, e.g. the south-west monsoon which brings rain to India, Bangladesh and Pakistan in summer.

Moraine The rock material brought down by a glacier and deposited when the glacier melts providing morainic deposits such as terminal moraine, e.g. Cromer Ridge in Norfolk.

Multiple nuclei model A model of urban land use based upon the assumption that urban functional regions develop through the integration of a number of separate nuclei.

National Park A region preserved in a natural state, partly to provide recreational areas for people to enjoy and partly to conserve the area because of its scientific and historical importance, e.g. Peak District National Park.

Natural vegetation Vegetation that has developed in an environment untouched by human activity and which therefore closely corresponds to the prevailing conditions of climate and soil.

NIC Newly industrialised country, e.g. Malaysia.

Nomadism The practice of roving from place to place which is still carried on by some groups, such as the Bedouin, in search of pastures for their livestock and for trade. Nomadism is a declining way of life; many nomads now live in settlements.

Nucleated settlement A form of rural settlement in which farms and other buildings are clustered together, especially around a central feature such as a church.

Oasis A fertile area in a desert where water is found, e.g. Kharga Oasis in Egypt.

Occlusion The joining of a warm front and a cold front in a low pressure area to make an occluded front.

Organic farming Farming without the use of artificial fertilisers and pesticides. Instead, animal manure, compost and natural additives are used.

Outport A port which, because it is nearer the sea than its parent port, is more accessible to large vessels, e.g. Cuxhaven is the outport for Hamburg.

Overpopulation An excess of population in an area in relation to the available resources and skills needed for further development.

Pampas The grasslands lying inland around the River Plate estuary in South America.

Pastoral farming The practice of rearing and breeding animals which feed on grass, e.g. sheep and cattle.

Perennial irrigation Irrigation methods that provide water for agriculture all through the year.

Peripheral region A region which is remote from the centre of economic activity (the core.) Peripheral regions are on the edge of regions and some way from the main centre of activity, e.g. Brittany is a peripheral region within France. (See *Core region*.)

Permeable rock A rock which allows water to soak through it, e.g. sandstone.

pH scale A measure of the alkalinity or acidity in a soil or liquid. 0 is completely acid and 14 highly alkaline. pH 7 is neutral (the pH value of pure water.)

Plantation An estate, usually in tropical or subtropical regions, devoted to the large-scale production of one or more cash crops, such as bananas or sugar-cane.

Plateau An extensive, mainly level area of high land, e.g. the Deccan Plateau of India.

Plates The large rigid segments into which the earth's crust is divided. Six major plates are recognised which 'float'. Plates may collide by converging and form a destructive plate margin. Diverging plates form a constructive plate margin, with new material welling up from below.

Pollution The fouling of the environment by humans, making it harmful for living organisms. Pollution can also reduce the amenity value by creating eyesores, such as rusty vehicles abandoned in the Australian outback.

Prairies The gently undulating, generally treeless, plains of North America. Once grasslands, the Prairies are now the grain-growing areas of the continent.

Precipitation Water in any form which falls to earth. It therefore includes sleet, snow, hail and dew as well as rain.

Prevailing wind The most common wind experienced in a locality, e.g. south-westerly winds in Great Britain.

Primate city The largest city in a country or region. It is the centre of political affairs, trade, economic and social activity.

Push–pull factors A model of migration. The 'push' factors encourage people to leave a particular area; 'pull' factors are the economic and social attractions (real and imagined) offered by the location to which people move.

Rain shadow An area with a relatively light rainfall, when compared with neighbouring areas, because it is sheltered from the prevailing rain-bearing winds by high land, e.g. the Midlands are in the rain shadow of the Welsh Mountains.

Raised beach A former beach that has been raised above sea level as a result of the land rising relative to the sea.

Randstad Literally 'ring city', it is the urban region which forms a horseshoe shape in the Netherlands and includes Haarlem, Amsterdam and Utrecht in the north, with The Hague and Rotterdam in the south.

Range of a good The maximum distance people will travel to purchase a good or obtain a service offered by a central place.

Raw materials Materials used for manufacturing into saleable commodities, e.g. flour (already partially manufactured), iron, cotton.

Renewable resource A resource, such as timber which comes from trees, which can be replaced by replanting. Non-renewable resources include fossil fuels and minerals, of which there are limited supplies and which, in time, will become exhausted.

Richter Scale A scale that indicates the quantity of energy released by an earthquake. There is no upper limit to the scale. The largest observed magnitude is 8.6.

Ridge of high pressure A long and relatively narrow area of high pressure giving anticyclonic weather for a limited time before it moves away.

Rift valley A valley caused by the sinking of land between two roughly parallel faults, e.g. Great Rift Valley of East Africa.

Rotation of crops The planting of crops over a period of time on the same land in a particular order, e.g. wheat, potatoes, barley, grass.

Run-off The amount of rainfall which reaches the streams. Some flows over the surface and is known as surface run off. Some sinks into the ground and appears elsewhere as springs. This is called throughflow.

Scatter diagram A diagram using data plotted on a graph to show the amount of correlation between two sets of statistical data.

Scrub Low-growing shrubs and short trees found in areas of low rainfall or poor soils, e.g. some hill areas in Mediterranean countries where the scrub is known as *maquis*.

Sector model A model based on the principle that the structure of an urban area is determined by the location of routes radiating out from the city centre.

Sedimentary rock Rock formed in layers that have been deposited, in many cases as sediments under water, e.g. sandstone, limestone.

Seismic focus The place of origin of an earthquake in the earth's crust. (See *Epicentre*.)

Selva The equatorial rainforest of the Amazon Basin.

Service centre A place that provides goods and services for the surrounding area.

Service industry An industry that provides a facility or service instead of manufactured goods, e.g. banking and tourism.

Set aside Taking land out of cultivation for a specific purpose such as to follow EU farm policy.

Shanty town (squatter settlement) An unplanned settlement built illegally on land in or on the edge of a city. Shanty towns are found mainly in areas of the less developed world, in which city populations are growing rapidly.

Shifting cultivation (or 'bush fallowing' or 'slash and burn'). A form of primitive agriculture practised in the tropics (e.g. New Guinea). A piece of forest is cleared, the trees and shrubs burnt and crops planted in the ashes. After a few years the soil is exhausted, erosion may have stripped away the fertile soil and so the plot is abandoned, allowing poor secondary forest to develop. The farmer moves home and the procedure is repeated elsewhere.

Silt A deposit of fine material laid down in a river or lake.

Sink hole or swallow hole A saucer-shaped hollow in a limestone region, formed by water dissolving the rock, allowing water to flow down to underground streams.

Slum A deteriorating urban area, usually part of an inner city, characterised by poverty, overcrowding and dilapidated housing.

Smog A fog laden with smoke and other pollutants, usually found in industrial or densely populated urban areas, e.g. Los Angeles.

Snow line The lower limit of snow on a mountain. In summer the snow line will move up the mountain side, in winter it will be lower down.

Soil erosion The wearing away of top soil, mainly as a result of wind and rain action.

Sphere of influence The area surrounding a town, within which the town has major social and economic influence.

Steppes The level, generally treeless plains of Eurasia, used, like the Prairies, for grain production.

Subsistence farming The type of farming in which the produce is used mainly by the farmer and family and little is therefore sold, e.g. as practised by primitive groups in Malaysia.

Sustainable resource A resource that can be replaced so that there is no need for world supplies of the resource to run out, e.g. trees are a sustainable resource because others can be planted to replace those felled.

Swallow hole (See *Sink hole*.)

Swash The forward movement of sea water up a beach after a wave has broken. (See *Backwash* and *Longshore drift*.)

Syncline A trough or inverted arch in rock strata. (See *Anticline*.)

System A series of linked inputs and processes which result in a combination of outputs. The system is a method of analysing relationships between components, e.g. in the hydrological cycle.

Taiga The coniferous forest zone of the northern Russian Federation and Europe.

Tank irrigation Irrigating cropped land with water stored in small reservoirs or pools. It is commonly used in India and Sri Lanka.

Terrace cultivation Terraces are steps cut on the slopes of hills, edged by mud walls to make platforms of flat, cultivable land which can be irrigated if necessary, e.g. the island of Bali.

Third World Another name for the economically less developed countries of Africa, Asia and Central and South America .

TNC Trans-national company or corporation, also known as a multinational company or corporation (MNC.) The organisation has factories and other economic activities in a number of different countries.

Tor A body of rock standing up above a hill or undulating land surface. Granite tors are found on Dartmoor

Tourism The industry which provides accommodation and other facilities for people travelling for pleasure.

Toxic chemicals Chemicals that are poisonous, such as sulphates and the soluble salts of copper, zinc and lead.

Transhumance The practice of moving herds between different regions to benefit from the best grasslands at different times of the year, e.g. as practised in Spain with movement from the dry centre and Mediterranean to the mountains and wetter north in summer.

Transmigration The movement of people across from one part of a country to another, e.g. from Java to the other islands of Indonesia.

Transpiration The loss of water vapour from plants. Water drawn upwards from the roots passes out from minute pores (stomata) into the atmosphere.

Tsunami A sea wave generated by an underwater earthquake. The waves can travel across the oceans for considerable distances, reaching heights of tens of metres in shallow water. They can cause considerable danger to shipping and coastal regions.

Tundra The almost treeless plains of northern Canada, Alaska and Eurasia found mainly within the Arctic Circle and consisting of patches of lichens, bushes and some dwarf trees.

Urban field (See *Sphere of influence.*)

Urban renewal The regeneration of urban areas, especially inner city areas. It is designed to keep people and jobs in the inner city areas and to improve living conditions by replacing out-of-date housing.

Wadi A dry, usually steep-sided river valley in desert areas which can suddenly fill with water after a storm.

Warm front The boundary line between a mass of warm air and cooler air over which it rises. (See *Cold front.*)

Warm sector The region of warmer air lying between the cold and warm fronts of a low pressure system.

Water (or hydrological) cycle The circulation of water from the oceans, rivers and lakes by evaporation into the atmosphere where it condenses and falls as rain, so enabling the cycle to continue.

Water table The level under the ground which is saturated with water. This level will drop during dry weather and varies with the nature of the rocks.

Weathering The disintegration of rocks as a result of exposure to the atmosphere. Weathering is either mechanical (frost-thaw etc.) or chemical (by solution and chemical change.)

Wind farm A site, normally on high ground in the countryside, where propeller-driven turbines are erected to generate renewable electricity. The sites contain clusters of tall masts to which three-bladed propellers are attached.

Wind rose A diagram showing the proportion of winds blowing from different parts of the compass at a certain place over a period of time.

Zone in transition A zone on the edge of the CBD of mixed land use. Industry, commerce and poor housing are mixed together and are changing as business and other activities move outwards from the CBD.

Index